PRAISE FOR *FROM START-UP TO GROWN-UP*

As a former start-up founder, I know firsthand how difficult the journey is from founder to CEO. Luckily, entrepreneurs now have an indispensable guidebook. *From Start-Up to Grown-Up* is a great read filled with excellent insights.

Maxine Clark, Founder and former CEO of Build-a-Bear Workshop, and board director

This book is a breakthrough and should be essential reading for anyone who is ready to lead and to make a difference. Highly recommended.

Seth Godin, author of *This is Marketing*

Start-up founder to CEO is a big stretch along the entrepreneurial path. Read this useful, tough-love guidebook and you will understand why Alisa Cohn is such a sought-after start-up coach.

Eric Schurenberg, CEO of *Inc.* and *Fast Company*

Alisa Cohn is the number one start-up coach in the world and reading *From Start-Up to Grown-Up* feels like getting coached by her directly. It will help you build your start-up into a world-class company.

Marshall Goldsmith, World's #1 CEO Coach and Thinkers50 #1 Leadership Thinker in the World

Being a start-up CEO is lonely, and the more successfully you grow your company, the lonelier it gets. Alisa Cohn's *From Start-Up to Grown-Up* offers friendly frameworks that will help any start-up founders and all leaders navigate that path with grace.

Kim Scott, author of *Radical Candor*

D0022187

From Start-Up to Grown-Up is a treasure trove for company leaders of all stripes. It is rich with Alisa Cohn's years of battle-tested wisdom and sparkles with her warmth and humanity. Every start-up founder should invest in a copy.

Nir Eyal, bestselling author of *Hooked* and *Indistractable*

The Miami tech movement has been born and bred out of an innovative and collaborative spirit. *From Start-Up to Grown-Up* is an incredible resource to help the founders who are building our ecosystem grow as their companies scale.

Francis Suarez, Mayor of Miami

Finally, I have a comprehensive resource I can give to all aspiring entrepreneurs. Everything you need is in *From Start-Up to Grown-Up*, including the templates which are so valuable on their own!

Mo Bunnell, author of *The Snowball System*

Alisa Cohn's book provides a blueprint for becoming a better leader. It's not just about start-ups or CEOs—every leader will find bits of wisdom in here! I only wish I had the opportunity to read it sooner in my career.

Andrey Akselrod, Cofounder of Smartling and CTO of People.ai

Alisa Cohn wrote the guidebook for defining your own personal operating manual for CEOs. I wish I read this before starting my company. This is a gold mine of resources for every founder to win, and win the right way.

Mert Iseri, Founder and CEO of SwipeSence

From Start-Up to Grown-Up

Grow Your Leadership to Grow Your Business

Alisa Cohn

KoganPage

Publisher's note
Every possible effort has been made to ensure that the information contained in this book is accurate at the time of going to press, and the publishers and authors cannot accept responsibility for any errors or omissions, however caused. No responsibility for loss or damage occasioned to any person acting, or refraining from action, as a result of the material in this publication can be accepted by the editor, the publisher, or the author.

First published in Great Britain and the United States in 2022 by Kogan Page Limited

2nd Floor, 45 Gee Street	122 W 27th St, 10th Floor	4737/23 Ansari Road
London	New York, NY 10001	Daryaganj
EC1V 3RS	USA	New Delhi 110002
United Kingdom		India
ww.koganpage.com		

Kogan Page books are printed on paper from sustainable forests.

© Alisa Cohn, 2022

ISBNs
Hardback   978 1 3986 0140 6
Paperback   978 1 3986 0138 3
Ebook   978 1 3986 0139 0

British Library Cataloguing-in-Publication Data

A CIP record for this book is available from the British Library.

Library of Congress Cataloging-in-Publication Data

Names: Cohn, Alisa, author.
Title: From start-up to grown-up: grow your leadership to grow your
    business / Alisa Cohn.
Description: London; New York, NY: Kogan Page, 2022. | Includes
    bibliographical references and index.
Identifiers: LCCN 2021030845 (print) | LCCN 2021030846 (ebook) | ISBN
    9781398601383 (paperback) | ISBN 9781398601406 (hardback) | ISBN
    9781398601390 (ebook)
Subjects: LCSH: New business enterprises. | Leadership.
Classification: LCC HD62.5 .C6356 2022 (print) | LCC HD62.5 (ebook) | DDC
    658.1/1—dc23
LC record available at https://lccn.loc.gov/2021030845
LC ebook record available at https://lccn.loc.gov/2021030846

Typeset by Hong Kong FIVE Workshop, Hong Kong
Print production managed by Jellyfish
Printed and bound by CPI Group (UK) Ltd, Croydon CR0 4YY

To my parents—this would have made you proud.
To my brother, Dan—your steadfast support means
everything to me.

CONTENTS

FOREWORD

When Alisa asked me to add my two cents to her book, I can only assume it was with some trepidation. We had met at my local coffee house cum office a couple of years ago and had a delightful conversation. I was immediately drawn to her insights, honesty, warmth, and positive energy. We became friends and have discussed various issues about coaching and CEO development ever since. She knows that I am not convinced that every entrepreneur needs to or even should try to be a great CEO.

My opinion is based upon a simple observation. Managers and business leaders are trained by the dozen in business schools and large corporations. They are available for the picking. True entrepreneurs, on the other hand, are as rare as hen's teeth. If I had to choose between struggling to develop a CEO out of a brilliant entrepreneur or backing their next venture, I know where I come out. My mentor, friend, cofounder, and coach, the great Bill Campbell, used to say, "You can't coach height." Buddhists point out you can't create a mirror by polishing a stone.

Alisa says it well later in the book: your company needs a CEO, but you don't need to be that CEO. Regardless, the most dynamic, impactful ventures tend to have founder CEOs who continue to revitalize the business with their vision while also managing its performance. I always tell people that the biggest risks I take when investing in a new venture come on the day I write the check and the day I have to replace the founder with a CEO. I prefer that the second day never comes.

If you are a founder who wishes to grow with your company, let me share what I've learned from my own experience and what Alisa so wisely points out in this book. First and foremost, after being bashed over the head with the obvious, I learned that before you engage a coach you must be coachable. I am not questioning whether you are innately capable of being coached, but rather whether you are at that point in your career when you have to confront your limitations and enlist the ample benefits of a coach. You may have all the talent and natural gifts in the world, you may have a history of success that overshadows self-doubt, or you may just be stubborn—but if you aren't ready to commit to growth and improvement you will get tagged from behind. So the first thing is to fully prepare yourself to be coached.

Second, to be coached you need to make yourself vulnerable. Early in my career as a pretty aggressive lawyer at Apple and then a cofounder of Claris, Bill saw that I was emotionally guarded like Fort Knox. So he didn't try to tell me, he showed me. I remember clearly when our venture was struggling that Bill would put on a brave face and rally the troops at meetings. But when we retreated to his office, closed the door, put our feet up, and opened the beers, he would share his worries and fears. If Bill could do that, I damn well could too.

Third, you have to know yourself or at least be willing to be introduced. A good coach raises a mirror to your face, and you have to be ready to see what is really there. To get to that point requires a relationship of trust and confidence. One where you know no matter what your coach tells you, it is never meant to hurt, only to help. That it is not about them but rather about their commitment to you. Working with a coach is a special relationship, which is why, regardless of how skilled a coach is, if the chemistry isn't right, you won't improve.

And finally, being coached is not a one-time event. Frankly, once you see what a great coach can do to help you improve, you will wonder why you didn't find one earlier. There is always another challenge, always a new hill to climb. As Alisa says, "Problems, problems everywhere." After you do the work to become coachable, you will find yourself looking for coaching in all the right places. Professionally trained coaches, peer advisors, ethical mentors, even the newest member of your team asking the hard questions—these are just a few of the opportunities to find coaches in your life.

I have been searching a long time for a book on developing entrepreneurs into CEOs that I could share with my founders and mentees. One that provided a positive and insightful roadmap for how to navigate that difficult journey. A book that blends wisdom with heart and enthusiasm.

This book addresses all the essential elements that I have encountered in over thirty-five years of partnering with entrepreneurs to build successful businesses from their passions. These issues need to be addressed one by one to create the foundation for long-term success.

Leading is not just managing. While your title may make you the boss, your people make you a leader. Understanding how to subordinate your ego for the greater good is critical to becoming a great CEO. Governing your emotions with empathy in the best interests of whoever is across the table builds trust and confidence. It is easier to do when you feel genuine gratitude.

Striving for consensus is not leadership. Driving consensus around the best decision is. Holding yourself and others accountable in a fair and compassionate way is necessary for creating a culture of performance. And of course, that means being able to hire well and fire fairly.

Culture is not just a plaque on the wall. Culture is the living DNA of your organization. I am not one who believes you start a company with ten commandments etched in stone, but rather that you regularly take stock of the gap between the culture you have and the culture you want and articulate clearly where you are going. This clarity is particularly important as the start-up grows to a size where the founders can't directly model their culture to every person, every day.

Which is why communication is so important. When you start you can whisper your intentions and the room listens. As you grow you need to shout. At some point, you need a megaphone. There are many tools to choose from, but you have to be very deliberate about which you choose and then dedicate concerted effort to it. Otherwise your culture will wither.

The journey from entrepreneur to CEO is basically going from doing to telling to leading. For a great leader, it's the success of their people that defines their own success. If you can't take sincere joy and satisfaction in the success of those around you, you probably shouldn't be a CEO.

And let's not forget inclusion. It's not just a nice sentiment, it is an imperative. For the longest time the unspoken consensus was that to be a CEO you needed to be an extroverted, aggressive, self-confident, uhhhh, white male. I would like to say we are over that now, but we have lots of work to do. Style does not determine winners from losers. Cultures can be methodical or brash, CEOs can be soft-spoken or chest-thumping. The key is to find your style and to create your own culture with intentionality. Then you must walk the talk by recognizing and developing leaders in your organization who bring different experiences and points of view consistent with the values that unify the company. Monocultures ultimately collapse when they confront a singular adversary; diverse cultures simply reshuffle and fight on.

From Start-Up to Grown-Up is the book I was hoping for. It's a primer for the uninitiated and a refresher for those on the journey. And Alisa's luminous spirit shines through in the marvelous examples, insights, and accompanying warmth of this book. I know my founders will benefit greatly from reading and contemplating the important lessons in *From Start-Up to Grown-Up*. I expect anyone who is ready to declare themselves coachable will too.

Enjoy this wonderful book and grow in the process. And maybe, just maybe, you can coach height.

Randy Komisar
Author of *Straight Talk for Startups*
and Partner at Kleiner Perkins

INTRODUCTION

"Leadership is an unnatural act."

The person who said that to me was the exasperated founder of a five-year-old medical device start-up. Their products were gaining traction, and they were having trouble keeping up with demand—a good problem to have perhaps but a problem nonetheless.

His company was starting to see cracks, and that's why he had originally called me to coach him. In this particular coaching session we had just discussed that he needed to be more relationship-oriented with his cofounder and more task-oriented with his gifted but difficult chief marketing officer. We also changed the way he was going to approach his all-hands meeting by opening with a story rather than sticking with his natural swing of simply presenting data.

He was right: it is unnatural. It's also completely normal. In fact, it's the job.

I know this because I've been helping CEOs commit the unnatural act of leadership for twenty years. I focus on young, fast-growing companies, but I know that the external challenges and the internal emotions are the same for leaders of all kinds of companies. Believe me, I know how hard the path you've chosen is. Founders, CEOs, and other leaders open their hearts to me and share their real anxieties every day. Many shed tears.

This book will not sugarcoat the difficulty. I won't pretend that the work is quick or easy or that there is a single framework that covers every situation.

What I *can* offer are practical, clear-eyed approaches to the questions that I hear time and again from the leaders I work with. Every leader has questions. Every founder feels confused, overwhelmed, uncertain at various times. Whatever you're going through, I've seen it, and I promise you that many, many other people are going through exactly the same thing.

When I start with a new client, the first question I ask is simply, "What's going on?" The answer always boils down to some interpersonal problem they are having. Charlie, the CEO and cofounder of a fintech company, needs to convince his cofounder and CTO to build more process into engineering, a move his CTO is stubbornly resisting. Max, the CEO of a healthcare company, is furious that one of his board members told him—very directly—that he needed to meet his product release dates or they'd have a difficult conversation about finding a new CEO. Caroline, the CEO of an events company, is wondering why her team doesn't take projects and run with them.

I get it. Everyone needs help dealing with other people. But when we dig down deeper, the key always starts with what's going on with *you*. Charlie was so busy being indignant about his point of view that he wasn't putting himself into his cofounder's shoes to effectively influence him. Max was so defensive about what his board member had told him that he couldn't take in the feedback to learn what the concerns were. Caroline began to see both that she wasn't being clear enough with her people and also that she had the right people for her early-stage start-up but the wrong people for her current company. That's coaching. We start with "them" or with "the business." We dig into the underlying truth which is that it's *you*. And then we go back and apply that to them or to the business.

So that's why the book is organized this way. We start with managing you. We move on to managing them, so that together you and your team can manage it, the business.

Managing You

You don't have a boss anymore. You are certainly a boss to others, but this section is about how you need to be as the boss of you. And you can be pretty tough to manage (just ask your family).

For example, Charlie, the fintech CEO and cofounder, wanted— quite reasonably—to install some processes in engineering that his CTO and cofounder Jack had vetoed. In Charlie's world, Jack was the problem. As we talked it out, I saw that Charlie quickly turned defensive—almost belligerent—as soon as Jack brought up any of the concerns he had about how the team would react to these changes. It was no wonder that Jack didn't want to discuss it anymore.

As I coached Charlie, I helped him see that he was causing his own problem. I got him to see that he was so focused on being self-righteously right that he actually enjoyed antagonizing Jack. (It turns out he was doing that with his other executives too.) My coaching focused on getting Charlie to see his own role in this standoff and showing him how he could influence Jack rather than fight him.

Your blind spots will inevitably get in your way, as they did with Charlie. By definition, you can't see your own blind spots. But I can assure you, your employees and colleagues experience them all.

This section will help you improve your self-awareness. We'll clarify what the job of the CEO actually is. Then I'll help you get acquainted with your own natural style, your triggers, and some of your demons. We'll also talk about the need to get feedback from others and learn to see yourself clearly and adjust your style based on the people and the moment. This section will also cover some normal pitfalls that founders encounter, like imposter syndrome, mood swings, and—in some cases—depression and anxiety. I'll show you how to identify these problems, what to do about them, and how to develop some strategies that will help you take care of yourself and flourish amidst the up and down journey you will inevitably encounter as a start-up founder.

Managing Them

After you get a handle on some of your own issues, we turn attention to the others around you: your employees. Developing the perspective and skills to deal with them takes some time, and it's complicated by the confounding truth that there is no one-size-fits-all tool to deal with everyone. Far from it. People are different and managing them requires you to read the room and try the tool that seems to fit, not the tool that you used yesterday or just an hour before in a different meeting.

Caroline, the events company CEO, discovered this when we looked at her concern that executives weren't proactively figuring out the issues to work on and doing them without her guiding them. Even when she did guide them—painstakingly she thought—they still didn't get at the underlying problems.

As I coached Caroline, we uncovered two interlocking assumptions she was making in managing her team. First Caroline assumed her team should be operating at the same level that she was. And second, she had a dread of coming across as a micromanager. Her first boss had micromanaged her, and she had such a severe allergic reaction to it that she vowed never to even come close to that.

The result of these two assumptions was that she didn't have a strong sense of what her executives' skills and experiences were or how she could help them do their best work while supporting them in doing new things. In her fear of micromanaging, she tended to be vague about what she wanted them to accomplish and then swooped in at the last minute to overdirect or do it herself. (Her executives called it—you guessed it—micromanagement.)

Through our coaching, Caroline learned to assess the level of her executives and employees and give them the right amount of hands-on guidance and hands-off support to help them build their confidence so they could execute more independently. She also got much better at hiring, onboarding, and, inevitably, firing.

As you scale you'll need to build your skills quickly in these areas too. Hiring—something that most people do wrong—is a core skill, and I'll give you specific guidance about how to do it right. Firing, unsurprisingly, is even harder, but so is having difficult, sensitive conversations with your employees. The more people you hire the more you need a Head of People, someone to help with onboarding, training, and handling performance management for your employees. We'll talk about what to do about HR, what HR can do and can't do for you, and what managers need to do and to be.

And don't forget culture, the bedrock of the enterprise. We'll take a look at various cultures and why defining yours is so important. We'll discover how culture can be toxic even when everyone starts out with the best intentions and the most ethical standards. And then I'll show you how to structure your culture with your founder's story, creating purpose and meaning even in everyday work life, values, and rituals. I'll also answer the age-old question: Should you have a ping-pong table in your office?

Managing people takes practice, skill, and a little bit of magic. You develop it in part through trial and error. This section will give you a lot of things to trial and hopefully decrease your error.

Managing the Company

Of course, none of this matters without the business—you're running a company after all! When you're working on yourself and getting great at managing others, you certainly want to see it show up in your business results.

As a coach, I never want us to get too far from the question, "What does the business need from you right now?"

When Max, the CEO of the healthcare company, exploded in rage at the lack of support from his board member Peter, I absolutely understood his fury. After letting him vent, and even get a bit teary, I asked him to do a thought experiment with me. If he agreed with Peter's point of view for just twenty minutes, that the company needed a different CEO, what would he see?

After he had let off steam with me, he saw something that seemed rather obvious even to him. The product release dates were months late consistently, and the company was not making its numbers. Max had a lot of reasons why this was the case, but they all boiled down to Max's own inexperience. He didn't really know how to run a fore-casting process, and he wasn't holding a weekly executive team meeting to sync everyone up and get a handle on what was missing. He didn't have that much personal knowledge with the customers they sold to, and he hadn't hired an experienced enough head of sales, so it was taking much longer than it should to build the customer pipeline.

Once Max realized that, he relaxed completely. One thing Max—and most founders—are good at is solving problems. With my coaching, Max went back to Peter and had a different conversation. Peter was again bitingly honest (founders are not the only ones who need to shift their style), but Max and I had prepared and he didn't get defensive. Instead, he asked Peter to help him develop the tools, know-how, and maturity he needed to run the business.

You'll find as a founder growing into a CEO that having these tools is not optional, nor is running good meetings. This section covers the things you need to know about process, about metrics, and about decision-making to get you up to speed on running the business. We'll also cover managing your board as well as that special relationship with your cofounder. Finally, we'll take a look at the new workplace in which you're leading people remotely. Communication and systems are more important than ever. Pandemic or not, remote work, remote hiring, and remote meetings are going to be part of our lives.

Throughout this book I've added some thoughts about all of these topics from founders and CEOs who have learned all this from hard-won experiences. They are insightful, honest, and authentic observations of how they confronted the kinds of problems that you are very likely facing.

Finally, I've discovered that many founders really appreciate it when I role-play how they should say something that is delicate and difficult. They furiously take notes and ask me to repeat it, so I've collected some of the most common and most delicate ways to respond to these scenarios in scripts at the end of the book. You'll certainly have to put them in your own words, but these will give you a running start.

Just a note about identity: I promise everyone I work with privacy and confidentiality—that is a sacred trust. If you were my client you would have that same commitment from me. But I also know how important my clients' stories are to help you find your own way. So I have balanced the need to maintain privacy and make all the concepts relatable by making every effort to change their names, location, and the kind of business they are in. That's how you can get the value of their experiences while maintaining my commitment to their privacy.

I know you're busy, but a final word. If you come to this book worried about a particular aspect of running your company, you may want to skip to the chapter you're concerned about. That's great. Just be aware that everything about being a CEO is interconnected. The more you read, the more depth you'll have in understanding your own, your people's, and your company's operating system.

The bottom line is this: the journey of going from a founder to CEO requires you to stretch, to adapt, and to learn rapidly. Your job as a founder in the company's first few years is vastly different from what will be demanded of you as the company grows. The job will transform itself again when your company catches fire and begins to scale. And again when you hit an inevitable crisis.

This will be one of the toughest, most exuberant, heartbreaking, exciting, fun, miserable experiences of your life. But through it you will find growth, maybe even transformation. You will not be the same person at the end of this ride as you were at the beginning.

All of this will happen to you, but that's not my goal. My goal is to help you be successful—to help you be one of the very few founders who can build a company that scales and grows into something great. So let's go.

For more tools, worksheets and strategies to help implement
the practices provided throughout the book, go to
AlisaCohn.com/book

PART ONE

Managing You

01

Your Start-Up Self

Reflective Question: What three words would you want people to use to describe you?

Who Do You Think You Are?

In my initial meeting with Ronnie, the CEO of a customer data platform, she declared, "I'm extremely strategic. I'm always thinking strategically about where we are going, what paths we should pursue."

"Awesome," I said. "Is that how people see you? Would you say that's how you're known?"

"Definitely," she said.

That wasn't my sense, but what do I know? I like to get data. "Well, let's find out," I suggested. "How about if I do a mini-360 for you? I'll just ask one simple question: What are the three words that come to mind when they think about you?"

That's a quick and easy way for everyone to get a sense of how they're perceived by others, by the way. You can have someone coachy like me do that for you, or you can ask an executive you respect or the HR person to do it for you anonymously. Some CEOs I've worked with have done it themselves—if you think your people will be honest and not suck up to you, go for it!

In any case, I went out, asked Ronnie's people this question, and I got a set of words. They boiled down to "detailed, focused, critical."

That's honest feedback, and I reported all of it to her. "So," I said, "I'm interested that the word 'strategic' is not in there. Why not?"

She paused. "I don't know." That's also honest.

If the work is in you then the work starts with you, and that means it's a good moment to take a close look at yourself. In this book, I'll show you how to understand your changing role as you learn to manage you, manage them, and manage it—the business. But first you need to step back and reflect on your strengths, weaknesses, triggers, and dopamine hits. This process of radical self-examination will help you identify what leadership qualities you have, what qualities you need, and how you are going to make the most of your strengths, bridge the gaps in your skills, and strengthen some of your weaknesses.

The act of reflection needs to become reflex. Founders—all leaders—need to (1) learn to reflect, (2) get in the habit of reflecting, and (3) turn to reflection—rather than reaction—when bad things happen. Even when there's a crisis and the leader needs to act quickly, she still needs to take the time to stop, look, and listen: "What's going on here? What is getting to me? How did I cause this situation, either by what I did or what I didn't do? What should I do now?" Radical self-examination requires a sincere desire to see and own your own "stuff" so that you can grow.

One CEO I coached once told me, "It's eerie how the company looks more and more like me. Sometimes I can have trouble delivering difficult news and I'm often indecisive. Then I watch people have trouble delivering difficult news and being indecisive."

If you haven't done some self-reflection, you hire yourself over and over again without realizing it. Your company becomes a mirror of yourself, with all the good and all the bad. There won't be people who can cover for your weaknesses, fill in for your gaps, and bring skills to compensate for the ones you lack. Everybody thinks the same way, so there's no one to challenge established patterns or add new dimensions. That might be OK when you have ten people, but that gets very ineffective at thirty people. And once you reach north of one hundred and growing, forget it.

CHIP CONLEY

Founder of Joie de Vivre, strategic advisor to Airbnb, and author of
Peak: How Great Companies Get Their Mojo from Maslow[1]

I look at my triggers. I think a great leader understands their personality type. For example, I don't like the victim mentality because that is just taking you down a road where you're losing your motivation. I'm not saying that people don't have good justification to feel victimized, they do, there's lots of situations where that's true. But then the question is, how do you try to solve for that?

My triggers are people who are always saying that they're working hard but they're not getting much done. I tell people, "Don't mistake activity for achievement." I'm also a bit impatient, so I have to be careful of that. Over time it's gotten better. But I think a lot of entrepreneurs are impatient. I think that's almost a quality of being an entrepreneur.

There are many dimensions to building a healthy, thriving organization (I'll go into detail about culture in Chapter 4), but the end result is that people feel engaged and committed to a common goal. Healthy organizations are those in which people feel safe to talk things out, to exchange ideas. There's nothing to divert them from getting their work done, and even though things change all the time, they trust their leaders because they see rhyme and reason to what happens. To build that capability into your company, you have to put in the time, thought, and effort to get there. The CEO I mentioned who saw herself mirrored in her company learned to explain her thinking, to praise her people for being decisive, and when necessary, to deliver bad news "even when it makes me uncomfortable," she says.

When you're the founder, people watch you, mirror you, and follow your lead. As the CEO, your suggestions are interpreted as orders. You think you're just brainstorming, but they hear directives. You think you're whispering, but they hear shouting. When you say something it's like throwing a rock into a pond and watching the ripples. At Facebook, Mark Zuckerberg would say something and the next day it would be on the walls.

Anna was the founder of an agriculture supply company in a suburb of Dallas. After the Christmas party one year, held in a restaurant right down the street from their main office, she joked, "The only way for that to be more convenient is to hold it in our parking lot!" At some point in the summer of the following year, her assistant asked her if she wanted a tent for the Christmas party that year. She was confused—until she found out that word had gotten back to the organizers that "Anna wants the party in the parking lot this year." She said to me, "Can you imagine?" Actually, yes I can.

So looking in the mirror is essential as a starting point because you're going to see different versions of you all around your company.

Before we get into how to build yourself as a CEO, a foundational question you should ask yourself is whether you really want to *be* CEO. Many people think that founders make the best CEOs because they have the vision and the drive necessary to inspire employees and investors and keep them marching in the same direction. But you, you the founder, should reflect on whether you want to keep doing the job of CEO as your company grows. You'll be required to stretch yourself, to learn rapidly, and to recover from the many mistakes you'll inevitably make. All the while you'll be moving further away from your area of expertise (say, product, design, or engineering) and closer to the amorphous, frustrating role of leading people. It's not for everybody.

ALLI WEBB

Cofounder of Drybar

I never really wanted to be the CEO. It didn't appeal to me. At that time, I didn't want that kind of responsibility. I don't enjoy spreadsheets. It's like fitting a square peg into a round hole. I very much welcomed my brother being the CEO because I wanted to be more of the creative visionary. And it's also OK to want to partner with people and find those people who want to be a CEO. I'm sure I'd be a fine CEO, but I don't think I would have been serving the company as well. That's ultimately what my brother came to realize as well. Michael realized we were going to get ahead of our skis if we didn't bring in someone more experienced. I would say somewhere maybe around store twenty or so, we brought in John Heffner, who was a "professional" CEO, because Michael and the Board realized that he probably wasn't the best person to take the company to the next level. As for me, it was a great lesson in figuring out you don't have to be everything to be successful.

Michelle is a great example of this kind of honest reflection. She was a former teacher who had found herself unexpectedly cofounding a real estate company with her brother. After five years she left to cofound her second company, an education enterprise that had an innovative model to educate and connect K–12 students all around the world with a hybrid mix of live and prerecorded video training. Although she hadn't been the CEO of her first company, as a cofounder (and a sibling), she thought she knew what the job involved.

One day Michelle was talking to her product leader, Greg, who had been teaching a number of sessions because the company was short on teachers and speakers. He was happy to do it, he told Michelle, but it was taking him away from the part of the job that he loved: building and fine-tuning the overall platform. At one point, Greg said, "I joined this company because you told me we were going to reinvent education in a scalable way. And I wanted to do that. Not go back into the classroom myself."

Michelle told me about this later with some wistfulness. "That's what I want, too." She didn't want to raise money. She didn't want to go out and find a large anchor customer or agonize over whether she should fire or coach a difficult engineer. She wanted to build elegant products that would revolutionize education. That's wonderful, but building the product is not the job of the CEO fundamentally. Building a business is.

Before we worked on her skills, we had to work on her inner state. Before we could talk about her process for raising money or finding strategic customers, we had to ask if she wanted to be the CEO who would orchestrate all this, and did she want it enough that she was willing to look at her blind spots along with her superpowers and adapt herself to what was needed? Was she willing to go through the painful process of rapidly developing new skills, many of which made her uncomfortable? Michelle decided—after a lot of reflection—that yes, she was in. That helped her commit to the road ahead with determination—and the road ahead was rocky before the company got on stable footing. She needed to get to that clarity to be able to commit to the journey of building herself as not just the founder but the CEO.

When I begin working with people, I ask them to start by reflecting on a few things that are core to them. What are their values—the things they hold dear? What are their strengths and what are their weaknesses or areas for development? I ask them about the behaviors they want to subtract and behaviors they want to add and about some of the fears they have under the hood. I even ask them about their health and the practices they have in place already to maintain their physical, mental, and emotional health. Starting a company will involve and will test everything about you, so you need to know what triggers you and what drives you.

What Is Your Job Actually?

What's the CEO's job? It seems an innocent enough question, but it's not so straightforward and it changes. The CEO is in some ways the most abstract role of the company. You are the only one who doesn't have a specific group to run, a single role to play. So what's your job? Your job is to:

- Set the direction and culture of the company.
- Hire and manage the right people who want to follow you.
- Switch hats very quickly—zoom in and laser focus on detail when necessary and zoom out to let others handle things when you can.
- Deal with conflict, celebrate success, stay positive but also realistic to your team.
- Make sure people know what's going on and what they're supposed to do.
- Make sure that you don't run out of money.

While you might do all those things in the space of one day, how you do them might change from one day, one month, one year to the next. Basically, the CEO's role is to *adapt*—as circumstances change, your team changes, your company changes, and you change.

Easy to say. The trick is in the doing—in applying the right move at the right moment. How do you know when to zoom in on the details and when to zoom out to the big picture? How do you know the right person to hire to do the job you need done, especially when you've never done that job yourself? What if you're the kind of person who doesn't like conflict? The kind of person who is more attuned to what's gone wrong rather than helping people celebrate what's gone right? Maybe even the kind of person who gets irritated under pressure?

The problem is that when you don't go to the trouble of getting to know who you are, what your triggers are, what your blind spots are, and what motivates you, you'll unavoidably do things you'll regret. If you avoid addressing conflict, you'll explode in frustration at someone because you've let small issues build up. Do you keep your thoughts close to your chest? People will wonder what's going on in your head. Do you need to control everything? You'll be the bottleneck with everyone waiting for a decision from you, and you'll wonder why everything moves so slowly. Building a company is hard enough. If you can figure out some of this stuff now you'll save yourself a lot of headaches and heartache.

More urgently, time is not on your side. If your idea is any good you'll have companies chasing you, pushing to be the first, to be the best. And you also have a finite timeline—an end date of when you run out of money. Not only that, but if you're successful—and I hope you will be!—your company will start growing and then you'll have to adapt even faster! You'll have to change where and when you zoom in and out. You'll have to hire different kinds of people, and you'll definitely have to mediate interpersonal dynamics.

How Do You Show Up?

The net of this is that you have to develop your leadership style. That's kind of an abstract concept. When I first met Ivan, the founder/CEO of an enterprise data syncing tool, he started talking through some issues he was having with the many many many (already a red flag) executives on his leadership team. As he laid it all out, I asked, "What's your leadership style?" He laughed and replied, "I don't have a leadership style." I laughed too—Ivan is a very engaging, likable guy—but it turned out to be exactly true! When I talked to his executives, they said how much they liked Ivan, but they didn't count on him as a leader. They were left to figure things out on their own, they had to handle conflicts completely between themselves, and they did not feel like they were all going in the same direction. "It's a free-for-all," one of the executives told me. "It's not quite professional wrestling because we more or less like each other, but it's not the best idea that wins. The loudest voice wins. And nobody sees Ivan stepping in to shape things."

When I asked Ivan about this later, he thought about it, and said, "That's probably true. I don't want to hinder their creativity. I don't want to step on anyone. And I want them to think for themselves. So I really don't weigh in at all."

Ivan, it turned out, did have a leadership style. It's called "absent."

There have been multiple attempts to define different styles of leadership, and they are generally differentiated by how leaders influence people and communicate. (If you're interested, you can research leadership styles online. I personally have spent days and days getting to the bottom of this topic.) But no matter which style resonates most for you, your leadership involves guiding your people at your company. Choosing the right style for the right place and the right time with the right people requires situational sensitivity, and that's fundamental to effective leadership.

I've seen all the styles at play in different companies, and different styles at play within the same company. I've seen all of them be effective at certain times and places, and I've seen each of them sail the ship onto the rocks when used at the wrong time and in the wrong place. Highly directive leadership could be like a dictatorship and perhaps should not always be your first move, especially with more senior people. But if you're the one coordinating a response plan for a crisis at your company it may be the right tool. Supportive leadership—letting people do their own thing—sounds great, but then there's an Ivan, who takes it too far. If the leader doesn't step in to mediate conflict and take responsibility for defining direction, it's a food fight. Coaching is something every leader should do, but if you try to merely ask great questions to guide a junior employee to the answer, she simply won't have the experience to follow your lead. She'll get frustrated and so will you.

You'll probably lean toward one style or the other, but you also need to beware of using only your natural swing when another style would work better. Good leaders use a mix of these styles—at the right time and in the right place. Every founder/CEO needs to inspire her team with a vision of what the company can be—to make sure the music in her head plays the same as the music in their heads. But those people are all different from each other and that means they need something different from you, depending on who they are and depending on the situation. The work is in you—to get better and better at figuring that out on the fly.

Your Best Tool Is a Mirror

So start with some personal reflection. If you know who you are, you'll see where you need to get better and where you might even need to hire someone else who is better than you. Everyone has strengths and weaknesses. Everyone has inner demons and inner angels. Everyone has their own motivations. And everyone has a natural leadership style. Here are six questions I give to my clients to help them focus on key aspects of their leadership style. I'll show you a few quick examples of where founders demonstrate an extreme version of each aspect, and you can reflect on where you might show up on the spectrum.

1   How do you express yourself to people? Do you ask them questions, listen to the responses, and supportively explore solutions together? Or do you tell them what to do and hold them accountable for the result?

2   How do you deal with conflict? Do you lean into conflict to try to eliminate it, or do you avoid it and hope that people work it out for themselves?

3   What's your natural swing on giving feedback and having difficult conversations? Do you tend to wait to address issues or weigh in bluntly whenever you see a problem?

4   How much do you want to control the process? Do you watch over every step in the process or wait for the end result? Do you tend to assume you should handle most things or do you instinctively ask yourself who else could do a certain task? How much personal participation do you prefer and how much can you give up? Do you make decisions by yourself and let people know or do you gather opinions and get consensus from the team?

5   How do you respond to stress? Do you check out or shut down? Do you lash out? Do you work harder?

6   How do you make decisions?

Now consider your responses. Did any of your answers surprise you? Were you even maybe surprised that those were the right questions?

To help provide you with some perspective on your own responses, here are some examples from my work that I have found to represent the experiences of many founder/CEOs.

How Do You Express Yourself to People?

Your words have weight, much more than you realize. Scott Harrison, the founder/CEO of Charity: Water, recalls, "I had a business coach who had me stand on a conference table and lead a meeting with my company. He said, 'This is the CEO megaphone effect. Whenever you say something, it's taken in by others as if you are standing on the table, looking down at them from twelve feet. You need to have that

FIGURE 1.1   Assessing Leadership Styles

SOURCE Jon Hugo Ungar (2021)

awareness.'" Most CEOs have to learn this the hard way. A simple comment can kill debate.

Take Tony, who's the founder/CEO of a factory robotics company based in Miami. Tony is in his mid-forties. He comes across as fatherly—not hard for him since he actually has four kids. He's funny, smart, articulate, and he likes people. People like him too—in fact, in the 360-feedback I did for him almost half of the people I spoke to told me, "I came to this company because of Tony." He's got the makings of a great leader.

Despite his experience and his good intentions, he shuts down meetings with his six executives without meaning to. "We're in an executive meeting and I want buy-in—I don't want them just to fake it," he told me. "I want people to be involved. Their ideas together are better than my ideas alone. I want to have an open dialogue, a loose atmosphere. But somehow, I make a comment and everyone shuts down. There's this awkward silence. Why?"

We talked through what happened just the other day, in the executive team meeting that I observed. Holly, his COO, flagged some risks that the company was not prepared for: What if political pressure caused a backlash for robotics? What if their customers screwed up implementations and didn't achieve the right amount of work reduction? "We should take a look at scenarios that may impact our business and have a better contingency planning process," she said.

Tony thought that was a good idea, so much so that he jumped in with a lot of forceful energy and went through a fifteen-minute monologue on how they should orchestrate that planning, the things they should cover, and whom they should include. It ended with his specific directions on how to move this forward. (He told me all this, but I also heard all this detail from his team, who were a bit put off, shall we say, by his speech.)

He paused for breath. Silence.

"I was *agreeing* with her!" he told me, again forcefully. "What went wrong?"

Tony sees himself as a guy expressing his point of view with conviction—something he values—and he assumes that his team should feel comfortable fighting back if they disagree. Which they don't. Because he is the CEO.

When we debriefed this meeting, Tony was genuinely confused. "Should I let them guess what I'm thinking?"

No, he shouldn't, but he also should let them flesh out ideas in the meeting rather than immediately grab an idea—for all the right reasons—and therefore take ownership away from them. To become a great CEO, Tony has to learn how to encourage ideas to come to light by praising the team and drawing them out with questions rather than issuing directives.

How Do You Deal with Conflict?

Many people have only two speeds when it comes to conflict: silence or violence. Either they avoid it completely or they blow up, and sometimes one after the other. My client Mounir avoided it. He is the founder/CEO of a company which provides a platform for creators from developing countries to sell their goods.

Mounir is the textbook example of someone who loves people. He lights up any room he walks into and wants to create a workplace where people are happy, fulfilled, and know they are part of a big mission. Not surprisingly, his people love him. He is engaging and inclusive, and he makes you feel like you are part of his family.

Mounir's talented chief product officer, Dylan, had a habit of constantly nagging Mounir about his pet projects. If he didn't like someone, he wanted Mounir to fire him. If he read about a new business model, he'd push Mounir to adopt it. And he would disrupt executive meetings with his issues. You had to hand it to the guy—once he got his mind set on something he was unstoppable.

Rather than addressing this behavior with Dylan, Mounir simply quit having executive team meetings. I discovered this almost by accident. I asked him why he had stopped holding his meetings. "I don't have time," he answered. That made no sense. Then he stammered and said he wasn't good at running meetings. I waited to see if that was his final answer. Eventually he told me the truth. "I can't stand to be in the same room with Dylan anymore." Which is brutally honest and demonstrates how bad things can get when you don't want to address conflict. (There's a script for dealing with this kind of problem in the Sample Scripts at the end of the book.)

What's Your Natural Swing on Giving Feedback and Having Difficult Conversations?

This is separate from conflict, although obviously they are related. I like to call them cousins. Conflict is when people disagree or have a personal issue with each other. Feedback—and what I like to call straight talk—is just telling people something they may not want to hear. It may surprise you to know that some leaders are actually good at handling conflict but terrible at initiating a feedback conversation with someone. One founder once told me, "I just don't feel comfortable telling other adults what to do." I told you that leadership is an unnatural act, right? (I'll talk more about feedback and even give you a model to make it easier for you in Chapter 6.)

Back to Mounir and Dylan. Mounir saw his interactions with Dylan as conflict, but I asked him to think about them more simply as feedback he had to give Dylan. We talked about what he had to tell Dylan and how he should frame it. I asked him to think about what he could say that was fact-based and took out the emotion. "The behavior is disruptive," he said. True. "Dylan needs to control himself." Yes. "And if he doesn't I'm going to have to ask him not to come to the executive team meeting." Right. We did a role-play and a little pep talk, and he was able to discuss all of that with Dylan. Dylan got emotional, of course, but we had planned for that and Mounir stayed calm and didn't back off. The discussion reduced Dylan's disruptive behavior about 80% and Mounir got input from his team that the working environment was much improved, which was the most important thing to him. That gave Mounir the confidence to continue developing his ability to have straight talk with people even when it was uncomfortable.

How Much Do You Want to Control the Process?

Ivan, with his absent leadership style, had no need to control the process—quite the opposite. On the other end of the spectrum is Nora, the founder/CEO of an internet security start-up. The company was going through a big growth spurt when I started working with her. Nora was a former trader and was quite brilliant and articulate. You really couldn't argue with her because she truly was always right.

Nora was also a classic control freak. She had recently hired some pretty experienced people to her executive team, and she sincerely wanted to empower them. She knew they could do the job, but as she had grown the company, she had developed a habit of wanting to have the last word on major decisions. And medium decisions. And tiny little decisions.

When the company was thirty employees this didn't slow things down too much. Now that the workforce was close to 200, it was becoming a massive bottleneck. Not only that, but her capable employees and the more senior executives she had just hired ranged from annoyed to demoralized.

Nora was an analytical thinker, so I laid it out for her. Can you grow your company at the velocity you need to if you are going to be the final decision-maker on everything? Do you think your employees are going to give you their best or even stay with you if you don't give them more autonomy? Obviously the answer was no and no. Then, the acid test question: What's worse—the consequences of mistakes they make or the consequences of you slowing everything down? Nora couldn't argue with that logic. Yes, we did some inner work (I'll tell you more about that soon) to see why Nora's inclination was to control everything, but the most important thing we did was to identify the very small set of decisions that she needed to have final say on. She gave direction to the team on the rest and let them run. Things sped up and people were much happier.

How Do You Respond to Stress?

The thing about being a founder of a start-up is that it most often puts you under an extreme amount of stress. Start-ups are intense; as the founder you feel responsible for what happens to your investors' money and your employees' livelihoods. And, let's face it, your start-up is an extension of you in some ways. Many founders call their start-ups "my baby."

Pablo, the founder/CEO of a fast-growing biofuels company based on the outskirts of Madrid, was high-strung to begin with, but his company was causing him far greater stress than he had ever had before. That was turning him into a different—and scary—person. One time one of his employees asked him to weigh in on a process flow she was building for one of their top customers. It was the kind of thing he had always wanted to look at in the past, but this time he just got angry and roared at her, "I can't deal with this kind of thing right now! Anyway, isn't that your job? Just get it done."

Afterwards, Pablo calmed down and apologized to her, but that didn't mean the effects of his blow-up were erased. The whole staff saw what happened when she tried to talk to Pablo at the wrong time. Stories like that have legs—people talk about those moments with each other behind the scenes, so your reputation spreads. And then people will ask each other slightly sardonically, "How's the boss's mood today?" Yup, they're talking about you, and they feel they have to work around you because nobody wants to get yelled at, especially by the boss.

Pablo and I worked on this with some pretty low-tech stress management (more about these tools in Chapter 2). Pablo found that simply counting to five (I asked him to count to ten, but he told me five was all he could give me—I'll take it) gave him a brief pause to compose himself. He also took surprisingly well to a quick daily meditation practice in the afternoon when he was most likely to lose his temper. Oh, and I made him eat lunch. It's amazing how small things turn into big problems when we're just hangry (hungry + angry).

How Do You Make Decisions?

I worked with Alex, the CEO of an online learning platform. Very extroverted and naturally talkative, Alex liked to think of himself as a decisive leader. He was also a former fighter pilot, which is a profession where hesitation and consensus are not going to keep you alive when you have a split second to make a call.

Alex, being self-aware, knew what he was like, and he didn't want to overpower people in meetings. He mistakenly decided that all decisions should be made by consensus. He would sit in meetings without saying anything and nodding encouragingly at the team as they fought it out. Naturally it took a long time to decide really important topics and—ironically—he was accused of being indecisive. His people would get frustrated and at times disengage, so the decision might get made by the one who could outlast everyone else, not by collective intelligence.

I worked with Alex on learning how to adjust to the circumstances. Alex realized that consensus was only one tool to decide and that he needed to learn the nuances about when to speak up and when to be silent, when to direct people and when to let them work it out on their own.

What's your answer to these questions? How you respond to these questions will give you an overall sense of your style. Accept that you will skew toward one end or the other. There's nothing wrong with that, only in denying it. This is why self-awareness is so important. If you don't know what your normal state is and where your triggers are, you'll just react. Or you won't react when you need to. When you understand yourself you can correct for some of your natural tendencies, and you can choose a response rather than have a reaction.

A Leadership Style All Your Own

Now that you have a stronger sense of your starting point you can turn your attention to how you craft that into your leadership style. Everyone is different, so everyone has a different leadership style. Your job is to be aware of yours and develop it to work for you in your various circumstances. Get to know your natural style, your superpowers, and your kryptonite, and learn how to fill in your gaps. As a leader, you need to orchestrate your company in the right way— so that people *know* what they should be doing, *do* what they should be doing, and recalibrate when they get off track, so that you can all march toward the goals with less friction.

No matter where you are on a given spectrum, you'll have to tune yourself to the right or the left depending on the circumstance. In general, if you're at one of the extremes you'll have to do more inner work to be able to adjust. While extreme responses probably won't serve you all that well, that doesn't mean that the occasional off-the-charts reaction isn't a tool you can use. There are definitely times you'll be thankful for your instinct to wade directly into conflict, for example, or for your tendency to keep your thoughts firmly to yourself. But overall you'll want to have a set of tools to use in a variety of circumstances, and those have to be learned.

The right leadership style for you is composed of your core makeup, your values, your triggers—your insides—along with how you show up—your outside. I'll spend the rest of the book teasing out these building blocks and, I hope, making them available to you.

All You Have to Do Is Ask

Even if you've been scrupulously honest about your inner life and thoughtful about your natural style, you may come across to people quite differently than you think you do. A helpful tool for that is 360-feedback, finding out from the people around you how they view you. Although this process can be uncomfortable, it's always enlightening. You are the expert on your intentions. Everyone around you is the expert on your impact. To be an effective leader you have to get a handle on both of these.

I remember coaching Sunil, a founder of a technology consulting business in Bangalore. I spent about two days there meeting with his team and collecting 360-feedback about him from his executives, his board, and other employees. When I had all the data, we sat down at a sleek, modern conference table on the fifth floor of a brand-new building in a brand-new Bangalore technology park. The table was slate gray, and Sunil stared down at it and used his fingers as if to peel some paint off of the table while he listened to me read out what his people had said about him.

I always make sure that my clients are at the center of the process. That's important because it makes it more transparent—there's no awkward whispering about it. It also shows that the CEO is engaged in the process and wants input from them, the consumers of her leadership. That's why Sunil, in this case, is the one who asked his employees and others to give feedback, not me. We call the people who give feedback "stakeholders" because they have a stake in my client and a stake in the process of that person improving. We pick out some people we think will be balanced, thoughtful, and honest. Malcontents are not welcome, nor are sycophants. We choose the questions together, and then I go off and ask the stakeholders.

The questions I typically ask are simple. What are his strengths? What are her development opportunities, weaknesses, blind spots, or obstacles? When she is trying to influence you, how does she do it? How do you describe her leadership style? What environments bring out the best in him? What environments bring out the worst in her? What do her strongest allies say about her? What do her harshest critics say about her? The last question is always the same: What specific behavioral suggestions do you have for her that will help her be a better leader? You can frame these if you'd like as "What should she start doing, what should she stop doing, and what should she continue doing?".

As we talk, I probe to get specific examples. I think one of the problems with feedback is that people use generic words, the current buzzwords that actually mean quite different things to different people. Without specific meaningful suggestions, the person getting the feedback knows neither what's wrong nor how to fix it. That's so demotivating. There's nothing more frustrating than being told "she's not collaborative enough" or "he needs to be more strategic" with no sense of how to change that. I once told a senior executive that the feedback was he had to soften his style. He said, "Alisa, I've been told to soften my style for twenty years. Don't you think I would do that if I knew how?"

If someone tells me the CEO should be more collaborative, I'll ask, "What does it look like to be more collaborative?" Then I'll hear something like, "In meetings, he sort of declares, 'This is the answer' and wants to move on without checking in to see if anyone agrees. He's the CEO and he gets to decide, but why did he hire us if he doesn't want to know what we think?"

Or "He needs to give people more praise more regularly. Celebrate our wins."

Or "Have fewer one-on-one conversations. Bring everybody in so we all know what's going on all the time."

I put all the responses together into one document, sit down with the CEO, and we look at all of it together.

Now I just want to pause here. Sounds scary, right? Believe me, I am in constant admiration of all of my clients who put themselves through this process. It's really, really hard to receive this feedback. No matter how self-aware you are, you're going to hear things phrased in a way that surprises you and gives you pause. No matter how tough you seem on the outside, or how secure you actually are on the inside, when you hear bad news, no matter how mild, it stings. You may have thought all this, but when you see things in black and white, it's stark. And when you realize that people are watching your behavior, it's—at the least—kind of embarrassing. So I always admire the courage that founders and all leaders show when they undergo the 360-feedback process. Some founders get defensive. They want to explain, if not deny, every single item. Others just say, yes, that's right. Right. Right again. Even the defensive ones are actually pretty self-aware once they stop being so triggered.

Back to Bangalore. As I watched Sunil scratch the table, I couldn't read him. We looked at his strengths. His people said he was charming, optimistic, brilliant, commercially astute.

Barely a reaction. He looked up, nodded, and motioned for me to move on. I went to the development opportunities, which said things like: He was at times aggressive. He could be hot and cold on you. He was stubborn. And, worst of all, at times he was a bully.

Sunil's head came up. He looked at me. He grabbed the papers out of my hand and flipped through them. He looked at me again. "Bull," he said. "This is ridiculous. I'm going to get to the bottom of this." And he left the room.

That was a first. I sat there alone in the conference room. It was really quiet. I wasn't sure what was going to happen next, so I hung around. I wondered if he was going to go one by one to his team to confront them with the feedback. *That would not be good.*

Nothing surprised me more than to see him walk back into the room, smiling, forty-five minutes later. He sat down. Looked at me intensely. Tossed the papers back over to me. "I took a walk. Then I called my wife. She told me it was all true. Let's look at it again."

I mentioned getting feedback is hard, right?

But it's worth it. It's a moment of clarity when you can see yourself as others see you. Then you can course-correct enough to marry what you say to what you mean so that your people actually hear it. The goal of 360-feedback is not to make you feel bad, it's to help you align your behavior with your intention.

So Sunil and I worked through the responses together—specific themes with quotes. Then we talked about how to address each point. I don't tell CEOs what to do—I ask *them* what *they* want to do. Given all this input, what specifically is she going to do differently to be more collaborative or less emotional or more strategic? Then we make a coaching plan.

All that is very important, of course. But there's something else that is just as important. I send the CEO back to her stakeholders. They want to know they've been heard. Think about it—as an employee you spend your precious time with the coach reflecting on the strengths and weaknesses of the CEO. You take the emotional risk that maybe you said something that will get back to her from you and have bad consequences. Rather than worry about what you said you'd like to maybe hear back from the CEO what she heard.

I give the CEO a script for this too: "Thanks for spending time with Alisa. It was a very useful exercise. I found out some good things, and I found out some difficult things. I'd like to share them with you and then tell you what I'm going to do about it."

She names the good things and says that hearing them was valuable. Then she names the difficult things and tells them what she's going to do about it, again very specifically. "I'm going to stop doing this and start doing that. How does that sound to you? Do you have more suggestions right now? Can I come back to you from time to time and find out how I'm doing?" (There's a script for follow-up on 360-feedback in the Sample Scripts at the end of the book.)

What's important about going back to the team is that these follow-up meetings open up a space for the conversation around change. The discussions create the safety to talk openly about what's going on. What used to be taboo topics become things that the CEO and her people can talk about. When you tell people what's going on with you and what you need to change, they can open up and tell you what's happening inside of them too. Vulnerability yields vulnerability. You are working on yourself, and that gives everyone permission to work on themselves too.

What You Might Learn When You Ask

In my two decades of experience, I've talked to hundreds of people about their leaders. You'd think the areas I hear about would be different, but they are surprisingly similar. You'll notice there is plenty of tie-in to the topics we talked about in leadership style. Here are some of the themes. See if they resonate with you.

Police Your Passions

Founders wouldn't be founders without a certain kind of passion. That passion is often a strength in raising money, closing a key employee, and landing an anchor customer. But the dark side of that kind of intensity is that you might be pretty tightly wound. What that means is that your frustration, your impatience, and your inner anxiety may come across as criticism. Or intimidation. Or, at its worst, bullying. It may surprise you to hear this, but some of the founders who show up this way genuinely didn't see themselves as bullies—it is often a blind spot for them. It doesn't matter. If you're even close to that line you're building a toxic culture (I'll talk more about this in Chapter 4), but I understand that it's unintentional.

You may be frustrated, anxious, self-critical, and impatient. So be it. You need to find ways to motivate your employees, hold them accountable, have straight talk, and even fire them, all without losing your cool. That's why it's important to know what triggers you, and when you can be triggered, so you can self-regulate (which we'll talk more about in Chapter 2).

The other side of that is less common but it does happen: founders who are too emotionally guarded. They never show their emotions, they are hard to get close to, employees don't know where they stand. The area of growth for these founders is to show more emotion, especially positive emotion, so that they are more accessible to their employees.

Say What You Mean. Sometimes

Some CEOs do all their thinking by themselves and often don't communicate or don't do so consistently. Or they may be so terse that employees are busy solving the riddle of what they mean. One CEO I worked with would send a one-word answer, "yes," to an email of a few paragraphs asking multiple questions, none of which was resolved with yes or no answers. His people examined these missives like forensic accountants trying to figure out what he wanted. Trying to be careful of his time—and not wanting to look stupid—they didn't go to ask him and instead spent hours (a) trying to decipher what he wanted and (b) course-correcting their actions when they figured out what it actually was. We spent some effort getting rid of that habit, you can imagine! Meanwhile, some CEOs think as they talk, leaving people confused, trying to figure out what they are supposed to act on and what is just brainstorming. This leads to a reputation of "crazy-making," since you seem like you're constantly shifting what you want, reprioritizing—"moving the goalposts before I even understand the game," as one frustrated executive once told me.

Communication is a whole book in itself (multiple books, actually), but it lives in all the ways you make contact with others: emails, Slack, texts, phone, video, in person, one-on-ones, small meetings, all-hands. Did I miss anything? That too.

Getting excellent at communication means knowing the human being you're speaking to and what they care about. It means listening to what's being said and what's not being said. It means addressing difficult issues calmly, clearly, and positively even when you don't feel like it. It means choosing the right communication vehicle for the right message and—always for you the founder—repeating yourself in different ways until you're sick of your own message.

Let Them Do It. Unless They Can't

One of the CEO's key roles is to set the direction for the team. This shows up in words like "vision" and "strategy." Entrepreneurs have a natural tendency to see the future—that's pretty much what entrepreneurship is! When a start-up is just an embryo in a founder's mind, it's *all* vision.

However, after they start the company, hire some employees, raise some money, they get sucked into the muck and mire of company building. They find themselves running projects, stuck in meetings, dealing with low-level decisions, and handling people issues. And everything else. That's normal and somebody has to do it, but it really cuts into your ability to stay ahead of the market and think about where the industry is going.

As the CEO you have to do some of this (wouldn't it be great if you never got pulled into a meeting!). However, when employees point out that you need to step back, they use words like "in the weeds" and "doesn't delegate enough" or even the dreaded "micro-manager." If you don't delegate because you don't trust your people, you can't think strategically.

On the other side of stepping back, employees might say you're "too high level" and "unrealistic", which means you're setting the direction of the company—which is great—but not creating a mechanism to get things done. I worked with a founder/CEO named Bruce who told me his board informed him that he needed to think at a higher level and be more external facing. He was naturally inclined that way, so it was easy for him to make that shift. He immediately stopped doing any day-to-day operations and started meeting with customers and going to conferences. But, as I pointed out to him, he didn't set up any other system or any other person to run that day-to-day, so his people were lost. This is where it's important to know when to zoom in and when to zoom out, and to make sure other people know what their roles are in coordinating and executing inside of the company.

SCOTT HARRISON
CEO and founder of Charity: Water

I'm not incredibly self-reflective, but I had to go through this experience of reflecting when I was writing my book. And I've been quick to ask for advice and bring on people who have been through this journey before. I'm kind of a pattern recognition learner, and I learn in stories. So I've surrounded myself with people. I got to talk to Reid Hoffman, founder of LinkedIn, about the transition of LinkedIn to Jeff Weiner (now the executive chairman of LinkedIn) through our network. There's a bunch of people that I've been able to ask about different challenges or what's the next upgrade needed for me as a leader, which often is just upgrading the team or giving your team the space to step up and letting them be leaders. So sometimes it's just getting out of the way. I'd say that's probably the biggest learning. Then, I can focus on a few things outside of the day-to-day management of the company that provide the resources, provide the energy, provide the momentum for a really great team of leaders to run the day-to-day operations.

Be the Decider

I think one of the unsung secrets of leadership is that the majority of people want more direction than founders realize. Founders often think that most people are like them—self-determined, passionate about a certain space, not needing someone to tell them what to do. But the truth is that if all of your employees were like that, they'd probably be off running their own company.

This issue is compounded by the fact that a lot of management advice is to seek consensus, to listen to your people. It makes inexperienced CEOs feel like they should be running a democracy. So they endlessly ask others, listen, and try to figure out how to create consensus that goes against their own better judgment. There is more to say about this (the RACI matrix discussed in Chapter 7 is helpful), but on the whole, know that people really want you to clarify who should decide key questions or decide them yourself and let them know what the decision is. They may not agree, they may grouse, but it's far better than the complaining that I hear when people tell me the CEO doesn't make decisions fast enough or doesn't let people know what the decisions are.

At the same time, people also want to feel listened to and respected. They want to feel like their work matters and can make an impact—that's the reason they want to work for a start-up anyway! People want to feel seen and known, they want to be coached, they want an environment in which they can learn, and they want to be helped to align their purpose to the needs of their company and to be able to use their own superpowers.

So finding the right balance in decision-making can be challenging, and that delicate balance changes depending on the situation. But the important elements for you to consciously and methodically figure out are (a) deciding when you should decide versus delegating your decision, (b) deciding how you or someone else will make the decision, and (c) letting everyone know about it.

Praise Is Your Best Tool

This one—give more praise—is a cousin of communication, but I'm calling it out separately because it's so frequent. The most interesting part of the accusation "She never gives us positive feedback" is what often follows—"I mean, *I* don't need praise, I'm fine, but other people need to hear that they're doing a good job." I'm not really sure why people are so embarrassed about needing encouragement. I personally need a lot of positive feedback.

That said, here's the truth: you as a founder may be more internally motivated than most and don't need to hear praise. You also may be particularly attuned to the problems in your company rather than the wins. But your people need positive feedback, and they need to see they are making progress. In Chapter 3, I'll give you some tools to help you do this even if it doesn't come naturally to you.

Run Better Meetings

Meetings are such a thing that I'm devoting a whole section to them in Chapter 7. Meetings don't really come naturally to anybody, and I know that you didn't start your company in order to run a weekly status update meeting, nor are you salivating when you think about the upcoming budget meeting. But just so you know: meetings are a fact of life when you're building a company around that great idea of yours. Meetings easily go off track, and your people often are the ones who pull them off track and then complain that they are a waste of time. You need to learn a few key skills about having a goal for the meeting, guiding the discussion, and having clear takeaways. More on this later.

Be Yourself. Except When You Shouldn't

Ah, yes. I saved this one for last because it's such a polarizing topic. Two camps: "A leader is supposed to be authentic" and "Never let them see you sweat."

Authenticity is complicated. The person who wakes up in your pajamas may be authentically annoyed because something isn't moving fast enough or someone isn't doing her job. If that's so, you need to leave that person at home because her irritation is going to make things worse, not better. If you authentically believe that you can do everything better than everyone else, you can leave that at home too. If you're riddled with anxiety because either the company is facing a set of enormous challenges or you are worried that you have no idea what you're doing—or both—then letting all of that hang out is not good for anyone—not your employees, not you, and not your company.

However, should you show a little vulnerability to your employees at times? Yes. It makes you human, easier to connect to, and it makes people want to follow you. Can you let people know when something is not good enough or that they need to level up? Yes, but not so authentically that your irritation demoralizes them. Is it a lie to paint things in a positive light when everything is blowing up around you? Well, I hope you think you will eventually prevail, and if you don't, you might want to close up shop now. But if you're in the middle of a storm, with faith you'll get out, then you want to make sure your people see the light, not the dark.

So instead of authenticity I like to talk to my founders about humanity. People want to work for someone they know, and they want to know the person they're working for. How can you show up as a human being? By revealing who you are a bit, in terms of your personal life, your quirks, what makes you happy, what makes you sad, by not having all the answers, and by being someone they can contribute to.

That's why you want to show a bit of (appropriate) vulnerability at (appropriate) times. When you act like you've got it all figured out, people often shut down because they don't feel they can add any value. If your people never see a chink in your armor, they also don't see a human being they can connect to. And connection is what yields trust and trust is a massive asset. Trust gives you a reservoir of social capital that is immensely valuable. When people trust you, they will forgive your missteps, they will still follow you, they will still think well of you.

That's why authenticity is so nuanced. It's as much a learned skill as anything else. And yet it does start back at self-awareness.

The work is in you. The work starts with a relentless drive for self-awareness. The work is also managing your impression, the way your words and actions affect your people. The work is not a wholesale personality change—you can't change who you are and you wouldn't want to—but an awareness that allows you to develop tactics and strategies to build supports for your weaknesses and make the most of your strengths. There's always a learning curve, and that's a journey with peaks and valleys. Did I say founding a company is a roller coaster? It is, but there are ways to level out the ups and downs, and that's what I'll talk about next.

TAKEAWAYS

- Self-reflection needs to become a reflex.
- Being CEO is about what the company needs, not what you need.
- Learn what your natural leadership style is and how you need to adapt it.
- Learn what sets you off, what makes you worry, what makes you happy.
- Think about what your people need from you.
- Get feedback from the people around you so you see how you show up to them.

REFLECTIVE QUESTIONS

- How would you describe yourself?
- Your company is a mirror. What do you want to see there?
- Where do you need to dial up or down the elements of your leadership style?
- What are your superpowers and what is your Achilles' heel?
- What energizes you and what drains you?

Endnote

[1] Conley, C (2007) *Peak: How great companies get their mojo from Maslow*, Jossey-Bass, San Francisco

02

Be the Boss of You

Reflective Question: How do you calm yourself down when you feel upset?

In the last chapter we talked about taking stock of your strengths and weaknesses, what sets you off and what makes you go. Now I want to talk about the ghosts that haunt you—your internal voices. You've found that people around you can be quite critical. But not nearly as critical as the committee in your own head.

The roller coaster of a start-up can be traumatic when the downs are happening to you. Add to that all the uncertainty: there is no playbook for your company since by definition you are starting something new. You simply can't know how everything is going to turn out, and you will make a lot of mistakes along the way. All of that together is a recipe for self-doubt. Not only that, but founders are subject to a high rate of depression and anxiety. This chapter will help you deal with all of this.

First I'll take apart what's often called the imposter syndrome and other forms of self-doubt to make them easier to overcome. Then I'll offer some specific strategies and ways of thinking to overcome challenges you face personally. We'll look at how to mitigate stress and the kind of everyday depression that can creep over you in the roller coaster of a start-up. Since you are the most important asset of your company, I'll offer suggestions about keeping yourself healthy, thinking positively, and managing the many demands on your time. Finally

I'll talk about the people who have been where you've been and can help you through it.

How to Deal with Your Demons

Insecurity is almost part of the job when you start a company. You've raised five or twenty or 100 million dollars—that's a lot of responsibility. You've hired a team and told them about the great future everyone will have if you're successful. And yet you often feel severe self-doubt. It may show up as the worry "who am I to make this a reality?" or it may be the feeling that you don't know what you're doing and will sooner or later be exposed as a fraud.

The feeling of imposter syndrome—that your luck will run out—can overtake you regularly or jolt you in certain situations. You read about how famous CEOs handle things, you picture Steve Jobs and Jeff Bezos, and you think you're not doing it like they are, so you must be doing it wrong. Your employees are second-guessing your decisions, the investors are looking over your shoulder questioning you, sometimes kindly, sometimes not. Someone asks you a basic question about your metrics, and you can't answer it off the top of your head. The pressure on you builds, and you often don't get any positive reinforcement.

Not only that, but especially in the early stage, founders imagine this dystopian fantasy when things are bleak: "When someone joins the company, they're doing me a favor. I have to make sure they stay. If one person quits then it will create a cascade and everyone will leave. I'll be all alone with my laptop in the conference room."

My client Matias, who was building a new category of company, experienced this when I was helping him crystallize his vision. He was at a very early stage—he had raised $5 million and had a very small team.

As a way to start the process I asked him just to tell me the vision so we could get it onto paper. This is a common, even vanilla idea—hone the language of your vision and articulate it to your team. When we talked in our coaching meetings, the language and the conviction would just flow out of him. This wasn't hard for Matias. So I was surprised when he narrated his vision to me and it sounded flat. Even boring. Considering how very fresh this concept was and considering how Matias normally spoke about it, this was confusing to me. He tried his "speech" and then tried again. "It just feels like you're reading out of a textbook," I said. "That's not like you. What's up?"

Long silence. Then: "If someone told me about this project, I don't think I'd believe it. I'm not sure if I can really build something that big. And who am I to lead something like this?" As much as he believed in the importance of the project and its value, he hadn't convinced himself that it was possible to do. How could he convince anyone if he couldn't convince himself?

When does imposter syndrome go away? Well, first the bad news: Chamath Palihapitiya, venture capitalist, former Facebook executive, founder of Social Capital, and an investor in Slack and other start-ups, said, "I've struggled with imposter syndrome my whole life. The more successful I am, the more I have imposter syndrome."[1] That's pretty chilling to hear if you're trying to eradicate your own imposter syndrome!

What the phrase "imposter syndrome" obscures is that it's not a single, monolithic thing. It takes many forms and flavors of self-doubt that get triggered in founders in certain situations. There is, however, a way to resolution: tapping into your underlying fears and concerns, using strategies to resolve them, and finding ways to both dance with your demons and move forward anyway.

On the bright side, you are more than capable. Founders are pretty impressive people. You are smart, competent, and energetic. You have moments of feeling like an imposter, but you also have moments of feeling competent, capable—even great! And I know that you have your own superpowers. One founder I coached raised about $30 million in less than three months because he was so passionate, convincing, and determined. He had plenty of self-doubt, but even he couldn't deny that he must be doing something right. Another founder I worked with was an incredible product visionary—I've never seen anyone have such an uncanny dead-on instinct for the shape her market would take. She had moments of real concern about her management skills, but in every fiber she knew she could lead the company to the right answer.

Imposter syndrome is about you, about your self-doubt, which makes you overly self-conscious, too focused on where you might fall short. You have to take yourself out of the equation. I'm going to give you a bunch of strategies to use to handle your imposter syndrome and moments of self-doubt, but I also want to share with you a different point of view from another enormously successful founder: Suzy Batiz, the founder of Poo~Pourri and one of the top eighty richest self-made women in the US, according to Forbes. When I spoke to Suzy about imposter syndrome, she told me, "I don't have imposter syndrome. I AM an imposter! I've never run a company this size before. We're all doing things for the first time and figuring it out." Give yourself a break and embrace the journey. Then try some of these strategies.

How to Be Your Own Best Friend

Jake, one of the founders I coach, was trying to raise his series C round and—let's just say it was not going well. His current investors were willing to participate but not, in their words, bail the company out. They were skeptical about the sustainability of the company's revenue growth and concerned about the cost structure. They wanted to see another investor step in.

This is one of the nightmares of any founder—what if he couldn't raise the round? What if this was game over? These feelings were compounded by the experiences of some of his fellow founders, who seemed to have no trouble raising their rounds, had customers flocking to them, and were hiring seasoned executives from marquee companies. ("We're crushing it" is a Silicon Valley battle cry, which is very often not even true. But it's super hard to deal with the FOMO of feeling like you're the only one who isn't "crushing it.") That's it, Jake thought. They're all going to find out I'm a fraud.

I'm not an expert on fundraising, but I know that his self-doubt wasn't helping. That's the problem with all forms of self-doubt—it's not real, but it feels real. So you have to gather evidence of your actual competencies, not just what your inner critics tell you. Namely, you need to create a highlight reel.

"I can understand you're daunted by being told no a few too many times," I told him. "But that's not the whole story. You've had plenty of successes, including raising a lot of money. Let's write those down to counteract your negative voices."

At first this was a difficult assignment for Jake, but after a little prodding I wrested about a dozen examples out of him. He had raised his initial capital in the first place. He had dealt with one of the executives who wanted to quit with such dexterity that she was now the star member of the team. He had calmly guided the team through a massive product failure and then got the customer to double their order right after. And more. Not too shabby.

"So how about if you try to run your highlight reel in your head when you're anxious? It's not going to solve your problem of the moment, but it will remind you of how capable you are." He agreed to try it. It was not a miracle cure, but it soothed his anxiety and gave him more space to keep going with more conviction and not take every rejection so hard. And, yes, he did land the funding round and started working more closely with his board so they have better communication and a better relationship. (Your board is a whole thing in itself. In fact it's a whole chapter—Chapter 8, to be exact.)

It's helpful for you to challenge your doubting voices when you're in the middle of them, but you can also pull up a story or two from your highlight reel every morning, so that you start your day off reminding yourself of your wins, not just worrying about the issues that lie ahead. We'll talk about this more when we cover rituals and habits later in this chapter.

Another way to challenge your negative beliefs is to picture yourself through the eyes of others. They see your accomplishments and are not privy to the self-doubt inside of your head. Therefore they will see you more impressively than you see yourself—but their view is just as accurate as, maybe even more accurate than, yours when you're caught up in self-doubt.

I was coaching Naz, the founder of a portal of special interest groups. She was a mature leader and experienced entrepreneur—she had grown up in Iran and founded and sold a small company there. Now that she was in Silicon Valley she felt that the pressure was on.

Her company was doing well. She had traction with major customers and landed a few large partnerships. She realized that she would need a more knowledgeable CTO to rearchitect the platform and a VP of finance. She was thrilled to hire two seasoned executives.

Soon, however, she found herself marinating in self-doubt. Not only did they know more about their roles than she did—which is normal—they were steeped in the culture and jargon of Silicon Valley. They were also both men who brought a certain swagger.

One day during our coaching session Naz confided all of her concerns to me. She was self-conscious about her language skills, since English was her third language. She felt out of her depth in the tech world of Silicon Valley. She didn't know enough about technology or finance to judge whether her new executives were doing a good job and—frankly—their comfort in the tech world intimidated her.

It was a lot to unpack, but what came through the most was how differently she saw herself compared with how other people saw her. It was like someone who's six-foot-six looking at a fun house mirror that makes them look three feet tall. I knew for a fact that her investors—well known, highly regarded—thought she was doing a great job since I had spoken to them myself when we did 360-feedback. Her employees were devoted followers and thought she was sophisticated, empathetic, and a visionary leader. Most people thought her skills with language, far from being a hindrance, were a plus. "It makes her more international. We're not stuck in the usual tunnel of the Valley," one of her key employees said. Finally, everyone around her thought that hiring the new executives was just more validation that the company was on the move.

"Your self-doubt is normal," I told Naz. "But can you see yourself through others' eyes?" I asked her to close her eyes and really absorb the massive admiration people had for her.

Armed with this confidence she went directly to her new executives to talk through her expectations of them. After a number of discussions, she found that her CTO was supportive, transparent, and more than willing to tutor her on the tech issues she needed to know, as well as some of the start-up lingo she needed translated. He had joined the company because of her vision, and he was eager to be a partner.

Her VP of finance was a different story. After her discussions with him, she realized that although he was competent, he didn't want to be a part of a collaborative team. More confident in herself now, she fired him.

When you see yourself through others' eyes it helps you view yourself more rationally and, often, more positively.

One of the symptoms of overwhelming self-doubt is very slow decision-making. People often call this "analysis paralysis" and perfectionism. But who can blame a founder for wanting to get everything perfectly right all the time?

A simple (but not always easy) tool is to remember that perfection is not required. It turns out that making mistakes is part of the journey. There is no shortcut, and there are many detours on the way to start-up success. And yet you are still able to get there, one imperfect step after another.

Patrick was a CEO in the UK running a fintech start-up. He had cofounded a company before, but this was his first time being the CEO. In his 360-feedback, his employees said that he was very slow to make decisions, and it drove them crazy and slowed them down.

"It's true," Patrick said glumly. "I start to hedge because I don't know. It's so hard to know which customers we should go after first, how our models will play out, even how many engineers or designers we'll need in the next six months. So I just delay. I just hate the idea of being wrong." I asked him why he hated being wrong so much. He thought a bit and said, "I'm afraid that if I'm wrong it will erode confidence in the team."

I asked him, "Don't you think that hedging also erodes confidence in the team?"

He laughed. "Well, when you put it like that…"

"I think maybe the confidence is only eroded when you don't narrate the story after being wrong," I said. "If you don't explain and then give context, it looks like whiplash. But if you tell them what your assumptions were, what happened and what you learned, and what you're going to try next, don't you think that will build confidence?"

Patrick found that liberating. "I can see that I have this sense of having to be the superman, Yoda, the one who knows all the answers," he said. "Especially since I'm a second-time founder. The idea that I can be wrong and that it would be OK is both terrifying and liberating at the same time. Losing my fear of being wrong would be a big unlock."

Patrick had a breakthrough, which is great. But how is he going to remember to let himself be wrong without beating himself up? How will you?

This leads us to the next strategy: positive self-talk. Before you dismiss this as superficial or woo-woo, just remember that we are all talking to ourselves all the time. When you realize—as many founders do—you're your own worst critic, or you talk about beating up on yourself, that's all self-talk. Intense self-doubt and imposter syndrome come from difficult self-talk. Olympic athletes work not only on their skills but also on their mindset, and much of this work has to do with replacing negative self-talk with positive. So if it's something that world-class athletes do, I think trying it yourself is a good idea.

ALEXI ROBICHAUX
Cofounder and CEO of BetterUp

Self-affirmation and positive self-talk really help focus and steel your mind. Before a big moment, you can visualize how you'll succeed and engage in positive self-talk to focus your energies and mindset productively. We all have a negative script; it's always running somewhere in the back of our mind. Sometimes, it can be hard to stop that script, and I find that focusing on getting louder than that script with the positive-talk track is more helpful. You can say to yourself, "We got this, we're going to do this." Look back at past successes, reflect on that and how you achieved them. Really build a mind state and confidence, not in a conjured-up way, but the confidence based on past experience and based on rational reasons why you have a shot where you can win. That repetition works.

There are always risks. I'm not being naive. This is rational, intentional thought. It's a conscious choice to say, "Hey, I can honor the risk and I can honor my ability as a human to make value judgments, and I'm going to transcend that and choose to believe in maybe the less probable outcome. But my job is to make it probable."

To use this tool, all you have to do is tune into the negative messages you're sending yourself. In Patrick's case, that meant thinking about the script in his head of being wrong or having to change course about a decision he had to make. His natural internal response was, "I got it wrong and I'm an idiot. Everyone is going to quit and the board is going to fire me." (Dramatic, but often that's the real self-talk.)

What could he substitute instead? "When I'm wrong, I just have to remind myself that we learned something, which we always do. The more we learn, the closer we are to cracking the code."

One way or the other, you are not stuck with the self-doubt, self-bullying, and self-criticism. You can challenge them. And you should. Self-criticism is counterproductive. You need to conserve your precious energy so that you can be centered enough to make good choices. You can't be the leader who inspires all the heads/hearts/hands around you if you are filled with the harsh voices of the critical committee in your head.

When It Gets to Be Too Much, Get Help

When I first met Keith he was on top of the world. He was being lauded in the press, and his company had just raised $100 million. We met at a dinner when we were both in Austin and had a nice chat. About eighteen months later, he called, we talked, and I flew out to Utah to meet with him. He sat catty-corner from me in an overstuffed yellow club chair.

He pulled up another chair for his feet and told me all that he had on his mind. It came so fast and was so multifaceted that it was actually hard to follow. But his posture said it all. As he talked,

Keith slumped down more and more in his chair, stretching his legs out even further, until by the end of our chat he was more or less lying down. I'm not a therapist, but sometimes founders will end up literally lying down on the couch.

Keith was depressed. And he's not alone. Founders are 30% more likely to experience depression than their counterparts, so it's crucial to be aware of this and develop strategies in case you need them. The start-up community is opening up about this topic a lot more, which is good, but it still sometimes feels lonely for founders to shoulder this burden. Know that you are not alone.

Depression, anxiety, burnout, and all their cousins come in different shapes and sizes. When one of my clients' company broke their sales records for the quarter, I congratulated him. He shook his head and said, "I don't think about doing well. I just put my head down and get back to work." Founders can get so caught up in what's coming down the road at them, they have so much that's not working, so much they haven't done, so much they still have to do, that they get lost in the fog of it all and lose perspective.

The first thing to say about depression is that if you find yourself thinking destructive thoughts about yourself or anything else, you should get help. If someone close to you suggests that you are hurting yourself, physically or mentally, you should get help. If you're in doubt about it, you should get help. Find a therapist to support you and get you through dark moments.

Ranjit, the founder of a gaming company, worked himself into what even he could see was a bad place. He had moved to Chicago from India, so he had taken himself out of a familiar world and thrown himself into a new one. Dreary days in Chicago will challenge even the most optimistic person, especially during the dark days of being locked down because of the coronavirus pandemic.

At some point Ranjit realized that he hadn't left his apartment in three days. He'd done nothing but work, eat, and sleep. He usually skipped lunch, eating nothing from breakfast until six or seven o'clock in the evening. He wasn't keeping up with his friends because, he said, he became more introverted when he was feeling down and didn't want to talk to anyone. He had gone through a serious depression a few years before, so he knew the danger signals and some things that he could do.

He brought this up with me in one of our coaching meetings. I was surprised at first—this seemingly cheerful, healthy guy was concerned about depression? It's important for all of us to look beneath the surface, to not be fooled by someone's demeanor.

He told me this because he knew he needed help. I'm not a doctor, as I tell everyone, but I do give prescriptions. So I mimed writing a prescription and handing it to him through the video: go outside every single day even for a short walk. Make sure you get some physical exercise—a short run, yoga, stretching, whatever works for you. Call a friend once a day, even if you can't physically see them and even if it's a short chat. Even though you're often stuck inside, figure out a starting point and a stopping point to your workday. And let's talk about finding you a therapist.

Depression is the child of stress and stress is the child of a start-up. Start-ups are extreme environments. You're trying to get your people to do their jobs and dealing with them not doing their jobs. You need to make money, you need to evangelize for your product and see the market at a deep level in the marketplace, and then you need to coordinate all these irascible people around you with all their quirks, with all their peccadillos and all their peopley-stuff. It's a lot to do and it's a big burden. You need strategies to help you deal with all that pressure.

How to Maintain the Most Valuable Asset—You

There's always more work to do, but since you are the most valuable asset of the company, you need to take care of that asset. One CEO I work with said, "It's not just lonely at the top, it's exhausting." That's why, for the sake of the company, you absolutely must attend to your health—physical, mental, and emotional. Your role requires selflessness and self-discipline, not self-immolation. The basics are sleep, exercise, nutrition, and some sort of stress relief. Good maintenance of each and every one of these is not optional. It is not just "eat your vegetables" because "eating your vegetables" somehow gives you the moral high ground. You do these things so that you can cope during difficult times. So that you can make good decisions when your chest gets tight from the uncertainty and pressure. So you can stay on an even keel and act productively in the clutch.

It sounds kind of basic, right? Like, seriously, Alisa, the key to being a good leader is about what I eat for lunch? Yup. Sometimes you have fewer resources simply because you're physically depleted.

I was talking to Tony (whom we met in Chapter 1) about a different meeting that he'd had with his head of marketing and head of product. They were discussing a new plan, and Tony started asking a bunch of questions—he disagreed with the direction they wanted to go in. What I heard from the team was that he "let them have it." The people in the meeting spent the rest of the day texting about "being in the doghouse."

I talked about all this with Tony later. It turned out that he wasn't feeling well, hadn't had lunch, and was running late. Whether or not the executives' plan was the right one, he just wasn't in the right state to have that conversation. Rather than calmly ask questions and pleasantly disagree, his physical depletion sapped his mental state so he blew up a meeting that affected six other people. They spent time licking their wounds rather than putting creative ideas into the company. Everyone's energy well spent is a valuable resource, so this kind of unnecessary blow-up is an unforced error. So, yes, if your hunger is going to cause you to lash out, have a snack.

Down time and sleep are as important as eating. Make your working life distinct from your personal life. Like Ranjit, set a starting time and an ending time. This is particularly important when you work from home, either because the state of the world forces this or because you decide to make your company "remote-first." You have to set boundaries when you live in your workplace.

Give yourself a break and a complete day off at least once a month. In fact, once a week is recommended. Take a quarterly retreat for yourself. People moan that if they take time off, they'll just get further behind, but you can plan ahead to take some time. And the thing is, deadlines make you more efficient. Without a deadline, you figure you can just do it tomorrow, whatever it is. But when you know you won't be in the office next Friday, you plan your week and you're more efficient than you would be otherwise.

Make sure you get enough sleep, and if it takes some time before your brain shuts down for sleep, plan time for that. I tend to suggest to leaders that they set an alarm to go to sleep, which may be even more important than their alarm to wake up. When the "go to sleep" alarm goes off, I tell them, turn off your devices and do something less stimulating, nonwork related. You can watch a junky TV show (oops, I guess that's me) or play a game (but not on your phone). Puzzles became a thing during the pandemic, so by all means work on yours. Read a book. Meditate. All of these things can calm a buzzing brain.

Make sure you get some exercise three or four times a week. There are lots of good sources about all these subjects—this is not a book on nutrition and health—but please know your physical health connects to your mental health, and maintaining your mental health is essential for your company's success.

ALEXA VON TOBEL
Founder and CEO of LearnVest and founder and managing partner of Inspired Capital

I was thinking about "doing the job" 100% of my day, but then I realized no, I need to do better at certain parts of the job so that I can actually make other people do even more. It was a mindset shift. The takeaways that come out of that were: Are you sleeping enough? Are you taking breaks? Are you giving space for everybody around you to really tell you what you need to hear?

None of it was rocket science. It was simple. You're not your best self if you don't sleep. You're not your best self if you're working too hard all the time without a break. You're not your best self if you don't take the time to do what you need to. Again, it really sounds all simple, but you have to make the space to do it. I think making the space to organize to be able to get better was a big moment that I'm really grateful for in retrospect.

The Best Way to Get Through Your Day

If you're like most founders, your day looks and feels like twelve (maybe fourteen) hours of incessant work. The work you have to do, the work you suddenly find your employees didn't do, the surprises from your board, from large customers, from hot prospects, and on and on and on. You're actually too busy to notice, to stop and think, "Uh oh, I'm sort of stressed. I should take a break and maybe walk around the block," or "Wait, I should be having more for lunch than my seventh iced coffee, considering it's 3 p.m."

You need to establish regular interruptions of the endless wheel of work. You need automaticity, which simply means that you should have patterns and practices in place that insert the right behaviors and ways of thinking without you having to think about it or even make an effort.

Enter habits, routines, and rituals. These are forms of training for a strong mental game. Habits are what you do without thinking about it. Brushing your teeth comes to mind, or (for some of us) putting your keys in the same spot every night so you can find them the next day. The point about habits is that they take no cognitive energy to execute. In the words of motivational speaker Brian Tracy: "Good habits are hard to create and easy to live with. Bad habits are easy to create and hard to live with."[2] And Aristotle said, "We are what we repeatedly do. Excellence, then, is not an act, but a habit."[3] Choosing good habits is worth it.

Rituals are habits that you've given a little magic to so that they have meaning to you. Athletes use rituals all the time—you see a batter step out of the batter's box, swing the bat, position his hands, maybe look up to the sky and get back in the batter's box, ready to hit. His little routine is something he's practiced over and over to get into the right mental state. Or you could look at tennis—Rafael Nadal consumes his energy gel, water, and recovery drink in the exact same order every time. It centers him.

You are an athlete too. And when you develop strong habits and rituals you prime yourself for success every single day. In the words of Seahawks star quarterback Russell Wilson, "If I feel good, I'm going to play good."[4]

One of my clients complained that he found himself getting sleepy and distracted in the afternoon. So I had him do jumping jacks during the day. Yes, at first it felt weird to him. But he did it. And the jumping jacks reenergized him and he could get back to work. He was so enthusiastic about them that he would do them twice a day, at 11:00 a.m. and at 3:00 p.m. Others began to join him (you'll see in Chapter 4 how much people imitate you), and it became a quirky thing that some of them did together and laughed about—laughter is energizing too.

Just as you should get some physical exercise every day, you should get some mental exercise that strengthens you for the day. That may take the form of a morning routine—a very popular ritual—or it may be the way you prepare for tough conversations or the way you shut down at night. Find the rituals and habits that support you to be at your best.

I worked with a terrifically capable and personable founder of a consumer app company named Joyce. Joyce was a mother of two and felt like she was all over the place, as she said. She felt like her day started at a full sprint every morning and didn't end until she crawled into bed at night. She felt ragged, exhausted, and it was hurting her confidence.

We worked together on a simple routine that you can try too. Get an alarm clock that is not your phone and keep a pen and paper on your nightstand. When you wake up, take five breaths and then write down five things you are grateful for. Then get out of bed and get ready. Before you start your workday, write down three things you want to get done and one thing you want to let go of. Then read a part of the highlight reel you created—even just one or two of the highlights help put you in a good mood.

Joyce agreed to insert that into her morning every day for a week. After a single week she felt more in control and after one month, she discovered how much better her days went when she started out that way. And she noticed some insights. "I see that even when everything is going wrong I still have a lot to be grateful for," she told me. "And that the thing I have let go of the most is thinking that everything has to go right or we'll die. This whole exercise gives me a lot of perspective."

Try it for yourself. Find your own set of nourishing things you can do as part of your morning routine that will help center you and give you perspective.

You can and should also build routines into the course of your day. There's a lot of glamor around the morning routine that sets you up for the day, and it's important. But don't forget the lowly midday routine where you reenergize yourself (minus the Starbucks salted caramel mocha frappuccino) or the all-important evening routine, where you shut down from work for the day so that you can come back to it renewed tomorrow.

Journaling can be tremendously powerful, and great for a midday routine, especially when it's combined with the self-examination exercise. People resist it sometimes—but it's a great way to get you in tune with yourself. It drives self-awareness and it drives effectiveness—knowing what you want to be doing now, this day, this minute. Take a step back from the chaos and focus on the most important thing.

SELF-EXAMINATION EXERCISE

Journal about the following questions. Don't judge or edit your responses, just notice them. Feel free to jot down notes in response.

1 What am I thinking and feeling right now?

2 What energized me so far today?

3 What discouraged me so far today?

4 What thoughts or feelings did I have during these moments?

5 How did these things affect my actions?

6 Given all that, what should I do right now?

How to Get It Done When You Can't Get It All Done

When I work with founders, I find that sometimes their feeling of overwhelm comes from, well, being overwhelmed. I mean, let's face it, starting your own company is not really a formula for work–life balance, at least at first. So although there are many books about time management out there, I wanted to touch on it here.

The world continues to get more distracting. Phone calls, texts, emails, Slack have now permeated our lives, and if we aren't conscious about it we just react to them. You could spend your whole day just answering emails and Slack! Then there are the detours that waste your time (Did I just pick up my phone and spend fifteen minutes scrolling social media while writing about this? Why yes, I did) and get in the way of the things that actually have to get done, which you feel like someone else should be doing, but somehow it's just easier for you to do. There are always fires, emergencies, and things you have to react to. Hours, days, and weeks go by without you getting your real work done. It's frustrating.

I get it. At the same time, you've got to get a handle on your time to calm your mind and to make sure you're working on the right things. Broadly speaking, there are two key principles to time management: reducing distractions and carving out time for deep work. You often need to do the first before you can do the second. Take as many alerts off of your phone as you can so you aren't constantly distracted by them. Before you accept meetings and tasks, take a moment to reflect on both how mission critical this activity is and who in your company might be able to handle it instead of you. Get in the habit of assuming someone else can do it. Some founders tell me that they are equipped to do everything better and faster than their employees. In the early stage this may be true (but if that's still true a few years into the life of your company, you have a hiring problem), but just play that out in your mind. What's their job and how are they learning if you're doing everything? At some point you have to give things away for others to do, even if you could do it better. Not everything has to be done with the attention and love of a founder.

A simple exercise for you to get items off your calendar is to simply look at your calendar from last week, this week, and next week. Scan all the meetings and ask yourself if (a) the event was mission critical or (b) anyone else could do it.

My client David did this, and he discovered that he was called into meetings to weigh in on product very early in the process. Yes, it was important for him to be updated, but he wanted his team to get further down the road before showing him anything. I encouraged him to raise the topic with his VP of product. David was uncomfortable because he didn't want to give them the impression that he was "too important" to sit in those meetings. "You're not too important," I told him, "but your time is." David finally told his VP that he could be called in later in the process. To David's surprise, the head of product had thought that David wanted to be a part of those meetings. After clearing up this misunderstanding, David got more time back, and his leader felt much more empowered.

If you have too many meetings, challenge yourself to take 30% off your calendar. If people pull you into things that you prefer them to handle, give them the context they need and let them handle it. Block out a few hours a day, and let people know you won't be responding to email and Slack.

Here's something surprising: once you get a better handle on distractions and you carve out a few hours a day of white space (as regularly as possible), you may wonder what to do with your time. That's normal and uncomfortable. (In fact, it's so uncomfortable that you may have been keeping yourself busy so you wouldn't have to confront it.) On the one hand, you have so much to do, and on the other hand, when you have two free hours, suddenly you get blocked. The blank calendar taunts you. It's easier—almost a relief—to fill that time answering email or responding to a crisis of the moment. Do not do that.

I worked with a client, Ryan, who founded a machine learning data company. Ryan was from the South and had a slow drawl and self-deprecating style, but make no mistake that he was intensely focused on his company. We had worked together to clear off his calendar (and hire an outstanding executive team), and now he had a number of blocks of time for deep work. His first reaction was anxiety.

So we used his first few blocks of open-ended time to think through the larger topics he wanted to move forward. We came up with three areas: customer intelligence, company narrative, and thought leadership. He broke those down into more granular tasks, and he put each of them on his calendar as a placeholder for how to use that time.

Think about what your key areas are and make time for them. This might be a great topic to journal about as part of your daily routine: What is the most important initiative I need to land this quarter? And then the follow-up question: How can I move that forward today?

This is a good practice for your employees too. People don't come with factory-installed time management skills. So you need to create a culture where it's appropriate to make time to do more long-term important projects. If you install the ethos of keeping the most important thing as the most important thing and rewarding people who carve out time for that most important thing, you will make progress as a company more rapidly.

It Takes a Village

It's an understatement to say that founding a company is hard. When you acknowledge that, it frees you up to prioritize your mental and physical well-being. And it allows you to look for help.

Peer support is a good tool that every founder/CEO should have. Talking to someone who has been in your kind of situation but is not involved can give you a new perspective. There are all kinds of tricky problems that you can't ask your team to take off your plate. If you have concerns about one of your executives, you can't really discuss it with one of their peers. If you're worried about a fundamental question in your business model, you may want to talk it out with someone else before you bring it up to your board. As I said in Chapter 1, authenticity is great, but you don't always want to show everybody in your company your insecurities and worries.

Your fellow founders and CEOs can relate to what you're going through, sometimes even offer useful advice, and often, most importantly, commiserate with you. Founders like to mentor other founders, even if they're still pretty new to the job themselves! You as a founder benefit a lot from having a network of other founders who can validate what you're going through, make you feel supported, and give you advice from their point of view. They may not know everything about your problem, but you can pick up the phone and talk to them about it. As you talk, you may see a way forward. Or you may just feel better for talking.

It's equally important to know that there are times when you will get the most benefit from one-on-one help with someone who is familiar with all the stresses of a start-up—a coach. (Like me!) We coaches have seen a lot of things inside of companies so we can help you realize what's normal and what's not normal. We talk through issues with a focus on your agenda, not other people's agendas.

A coach can help you adjust your style to the actual experience you're having and also help you walk through the inner issues, the things that are hard to see or just hard to change. When you don't know what you don't know, it's good to hire someone who can tell you. When you can talk out your issues and even shed a tear with someone who is safe, supportive, and nonjudgmental, you can often see your path forward.

Finally, everyone should have mentors—people who have walked the path ahead of you. If you're lucky your board members may be great mentors. But mentors can come from everywhere—other founders, people you meet in the start-up ecosystem, or in any community you're a part of, friends of friends. Feel free to have more than one mentor—one may help you think through strategy and another may have a lot to add about your company structure or culture.

Having a strong network of people around you helps you get your jobs done more efficiently and helps you get support when you need it.

As a founder, you need to be mentally, physically, and emotionally prepared to deal with the problems that you'll inevitably face, and your peak performance can only come from both a combination of physical well-being and a positive mental state. They feed each other, of course, but they are also separate things. You have to nourish yourself physically to have the stamina for the long game. You have to nourish your mental and emotional well-being to keep up your spirits, to help you perform, and to keep your team upbeat. Managing your time well helps you handle your anxiety, and building community around you helps you feel better and get insight to help you.

Proactively take care of yourself in all these ways to be able to handle the long twisting journey of building your start-up.

TAKEAWAYS

- Vaporize the imposter syndrome by coming to terms with your underlying fears and concerns about who you think you are and how your company is doing.

- Take care of the physical you—get some exercise, eat right, get a good night's sleep, impose a beginning and an end on your workday.

- Fight stress with regular breaks—once a day, once a week, once a month get away from your work mind.

- Build in habits and rituals that strengthen your mental game.

- Gather your support groups—mentors, peers, friends, a coach.

REFLECTIVE QUESTIONS

- What ignites your imposter syndrome?
- What experiences have made you feel accomplished?
- Whom can you turn to when you need to vent?
- What habits and rituals do you want to build into your life?

Endnotes

1   The Knowledge Project. Chamath Palihapitiya: Understanding yourself (podcast) 1 December 2020. fs.blog/knowledge-project/chamath-palihapitiya/ (archived at https://perma.cc/YQ5Y-Q4BZ)

2   Tracy, B (2011) *No Excuses!: The power of self-discipline*, 1st ed., Vanguard Press, New York

3   Durant, W (1991) *The Story of Philosophy: The lives and opinions of the world's greatest philosophers*, Pocket Books, New York

4   Dedaj, P (2020) Seahawks' Russell Wilson spends $1M on recovery every year: "I'm trying to play until I'm 45," Fox Business, November 3, www.foxbusiness.com/sports/seahawks-russell-wilson-spends-1m-on-recovery-every-year-im-trying-to-play-until-im-45 (archived at https://perma.cc/F4L3-82Q4)

PART TWO

Managing Them

03

Why Should Anyone Follow You?

Reflective Question: Do you know what motivates your people?

People love to talk about the difference between managing and leading. Entire books have been written on this, and I've been at more than one meeting where people debate the distinction as if it were a religious tenet. Spoiler alert—in these debates, "leaders" are always seen not so subtly as better. People say, as if bragging, "I'm a great leader, but I'm a terrible manager." I do love a good leadership story, but I think it's important to recognize that the day-in, day-out grind of management is what actually gets things done.

Leaders can't entirely avoid the managerial work of making work work. Both roles aim at melding you and your people into a cohesive and harmonious unit. Leadership is setting the vision and direction and motivating people to go do the job. Management is doing the traffic-cop stuff—making the systems work, setting clear goals and giving feedback about them, and giving people the right incentives to meet their goals.

You as a founder have a certain set of priorities. This company is your baby. Your entire waking existence—and maybe some of your sleeping existence—is focused on your company.

Your employees are not like that. Early employees may feel like founders, with that primal sense of being fused with the company, but as you get bigger—and you want to get bigger—your employees are not willing to sacrifice their lives to the company in the same way you are. They may have a lot of passion for your vision, a lot of passion for you, but they don't have that "this is me" feeling that you have.

In order to orchestrate their work, you need to know who they are, and they need to know what you want. Don't assume they know what's in your head. You need to communicate with them in a way they understand. So get curious. Who *are* these people? What motivates them? What sets them off? What are their priorities? Once you know all this you can better motivate them, influence them, guide them, activate them.

In this chapter I want to talk about five foundational things you need to learn and embody as you start to build your own leadership style: creating psychological safety, using positive attention to motivate, setting clear expectations and holding people accountable, and delegating.

How to Create Safe Space

Google conducted research on what makes teams most effective and famously popularized the most important element: psychological safety. (Harvard Business School Professor Amy Edmondson first coined this term.) This is simply the not-so-exotic thought that people should feel safe at work. They should not be afraid that they will be bullied, disrespected, harassed, humiliated, or anything else. You'd think this should be obvious, right? Just read the news.

In the stresses of a start-up it's easy to lose your cool. I understand that. But people don't do their best work when they're anxious. They can't be resourceful and creative in solving problems when they feel they're being picked on. As the leader, you're the ultimate role model for how people create the right team environment.

We'll talk about this more in Chapter 4 when we address culture, but psychological safety starts with you. In Chapter 1 we talked about getting to know your style, your quirks, and your triggers. This is important because without this self-awareness you may not realize that you respond to stress by exploding at people. (It may not feel like that to you, but it does to them.) Without that kind of reflection, you may not see that your normal go-to when you're a little irritated at someone is to make sarcastic comments or that when you get bored you tell a joke at someone's expense. That might have worked for you in college, with your friends, or even in your first jobs before you were a leader. But right now you're the boss and making fun of people or worse gives others the green light to do the same. And ultimately it makes people watch themselves before they say or do anything.

SUZY BATIZ
Chief Visionary Officer and Chairwoman of Poo~Pourri

The biggest part of management for me was really increasing my communication. One of my triggers from childhood is when something chaotic happens, I can get really triggered. For example, there was an issue about the warehouse. Nobody seems to know how much inventory we have, and I'm freaking out a little and my VP of operations says, "Okay, I hear that. You're triggered." And I'll say, "Yeah." So we've developed very open and honest communication skills. He understands that when I'm triggered, it's not about him.

This is an old pattern. People go through management and professional training and really, we're just a bunch of children being triggered, triggering each other all the time. So the more that I can be an example of how to have that conscious conversation the better. And my team can have the same conversation. Basically the one thing that we've found is that honest, raw communication is the best for conflict. My team has that language—they can go, "I feel scared," but it's okay. You can feel scared and you're not in trouble.

If you think you're under surveillance in just a run-of-the-mill meeting (and you are), imagine how much your behavior carries when you and the team are under pressure. How do you act then? Do you lose your temper? Do you make snide, sarcastic comments? Do you blame your team in the middle of trying to fix it? Or do you calmly reassure the team, maybe even cracking a joke or two to break the tension? Do you compliment the fixer even if he's the one who broke it?

One wonderful role model is my client Suzanne, the founder of a networking company. When I met her, the company had about 600 employees. One afternoon she got a frantic and angry call from a customer about a massive outage. Her team already knew about it and was scurrying to fix it. She worked through the night side by side with the team, had pizza brought in for them, and any time someone snapped (which does happen in those circumstances) she brought everyone back to the present state with her mantra: We have to fix this problem. We can fix this problem. And we will fix this problem. Yes, she was intense, but she stayed calm, focused, and positive. As one of her employees told me later, "She kept the wheels on the bus. It was a very daunting problem with a screaming customer and tight time frame, but she didn't make a single comment about blame. She showed us she had faith in us to deliver, and I think that's why we moved mountains to get it done." That's psychological safety in action.

You need to exercise emotional self-control so that you can choose a response instead of having a reaction. Remember that your behavior is the baseline of a high-performing company.

Praise Is Your Secret Superpower

There are many ways to motivate people, but I often see founders ignoring a tool that is easy, free, and requires no special equipment. It drives me crazy so I am excited to address it here.

It's simply using praise to motivate people and build social capital—the loyalty you need so that people will follow you through walls even when things get tough.

I know this is counterintuitive for you. No one tells a founder/CEO on her hard days that she's doing a great job. In fact, in some ways you can only become a founder if you have an overdeveloped sense of internal motivation. Think about it—isn't it so much easier to go work for IBM than start your own company?

As the CEO, you take the brunt of your team's defensiveness, their worries, their insecurities, their annoyances. Founders have to deal with that all the time, so it's not as if your head snaps up and you say to yourself, "Oh I need to praise people." But you do and you should.

In fact, all those gripes and doubts your employees generously share with you are actually more about them than about you. Your people are looking for markers from you. "Am I doing this right?" "Is this what you want?" They won't say these things out loud, so you have to think consciously about giving praise and then tell them. You might think, "Oh, this is great" when someone hands you the spreadsheet that you asked for, but if those words don't come out of your mouth, nothing is gained and something may be lost. That employee may walk away worrying that the spreadsheet wasn't right somehow, but he doesn't know how and he wastes the next hour looking at it again trying to figure out what he should have done differently.

Or even worse, praising with faint damns. Say your employee unveils the new website to you, and you think it's pretty good but you have a question about the cover photo. If you start out, "How did that photo get up there?", no matter what you say after that, believe me, you've lost. Instead say, "Great job! I love it! I'm so impressed! Can I ask you just one question?"

As the CEO, you don't always see the hidden cost of lack of praise. But as the coach, I do. One of my clients, Lindsey, is building a skin-care empire. Her packaging designer, Wilson, is brilliant and also high strung. I happened to stop by Wilson's office one day, and he was in a bit of a funk. He had heard from the COO that Lindsey didn't like his new design. He got a little heated defending it to me. Then he added, as if in a non sequitur, "I think I'm doing a good job. I mean, I know I'm not perfect, but I think I'm doing a good job. I mean, I'm sure she would tell me if I wasn't."

I could see he wasn't sure, and that was actually confusing to me because Lindsey loves Wilson and thinks he's a creative genius. I couldn't hold myself back. "Wilson, let me stop you right there. Lindsey thinks you're a genius at what you do. I hope she's telling you that."

Wilson actually got weepy. "Thank you, thank you for saying that. It's really meaningful."

This is not a one-off. The tears might be extreme, but the sentiment is normal. That's why you have to stop and remind yourself to verbalize positive things even when they seem obvious or ordinary. And you certainly should overemphasize things that are really good.

Your people get worn down from the grind of a start-up. There are ups and downs and always something more to do, so it's hard to see progress. When they only hear criticism or problems coming from you, they get a lopsided view—they feel like they're failing even when they're doing well. That uncertainty costs you because it embeds itself into their heads as self-doubt and that makes them a little less safe, a little less energetic, and, as a result, a little less likely to offer a revolutionary idea.

Another super-important part of your job is to show your team the progress they and the company are making. You should help them bite off milestones and then celebrate their wins so they can get a feeling of success. They'll be more steadfast in the face of obstacles and keep up better morale in the face of the difficult work you have to do. And they won't feel like they're failing. (More about how this builds culture in Chapter 4.)

Sometimes CEOs will say, "If I'm not talking to you, you're not a problem." That's not helpful. People actually need positive input so they can measure success for themselves and can also stay motivated for the difficult journey ahead. Like Wilson, many people have said to me, "I guess I'm OK because she doesn't come and talk to me." But they don't actually know.

The work is in you. You need to understand your employees and to recognize that they are not in your head. And they do look up to you and to you for cues.

This too may be counterintuitive, but praise is an effective tool even with employees who aren't doing a great job. There's a story I love in Michael Lewis's *Moneyball* about a ballplayer named Scott Hatteberg. Billy Beane, the general manager of the Oakland Athletics baseball team, had just traded his first baseman, and he needed someone to replace him. Beane wanted a great hitter, and that's why he chose Hatteberg, who had never played first base in his entire life.

It was left to the infield coach Ron Washington to turn Hatteberg into a first baseman. It did not look good. "The guy stinks," he said to the entire management team. (He actually used more colorful language.) But to his face, Washington was 100% encouraging. "That was a great catch! You're amazing, look at you. Fielding *machine*!" After a while, Washington's encouragement made Hatteberg believe in himself and turned him from completely unskilled into a pretty good first baseman.

We think we have to constantly correct people and get them to see the error of their ways. However—surprise!—you actually can get more out of someone when you praise them for what is working. That builds their confidence and makes them feel appreciated, which in turn makes them feel more motivated.

If you're running a small company, you probably can't start out with the best, most experienced executives. You will get talented people who are raw and need molding, guidance, and support. It can be frustrating, which is why you need to know how to manage your triggers so that you can manage your people well. They're like a candle: easy to snuff out early, but if you protect them and support them, they can burn into a good flame.

CEOs worry that if they praise their employees too much they will get big heads. Or that if they praise their employees when they do things that are wrong, they will keep repeating their mistakes. Of course you have to steer them in the right direction, but nothing good ever came from making your people feel stupid or like failures. Blame and shame are not helpful learning tools.

When you're unhappy with a team member's work, help them solve the problem. Don't attack the employee. Contextualize the situation. "OK, we missed our sales target. We're going to have good months and bad months. You tried some new things, and that's good." Bring her into the solution: "Was our target number too high? What's the number we can actually accomplish?" Look for the facts: "We need to quickly do some research and some experiments to find out what's working and what's not."

Frame it as a learning journey, which it actually is. If your employee gets defensive, check to see that they feel safe. You can say, "I just want to emphasize that I think you're great and that I know you are trying hard. Let's figure out together how to crack this code." If, over time, your employee shows over and over again that she can't hit her goals, then of course you have to make some changes. But remember that the clearer you make the goals (let's discuss that below) and the more you make your employees feel safe and have a record of building their confidence with praise, the quicker and more easily you'll be able to resolve what's getting in their way or figure out if you have to part ways.

Positive attention is more than overt praise. There are lots of ways of delivering that encouragement: celebration and personal attention, appreciation of how much they've achieved, marking a milestone. Positive attention is also commiseration, a personal acknowledgment, even just sincerely saying, "How are you doing?" It's anything you say or do with an employee that recognizes their humanity and makes them feel seen and successful.

Many founders I work with deemphasize this kind of celebration and positive feedback. It's understandable—you're busy running a company and anyway, as a founder, you're not necessarily aware that others need positive feedback. It sounds nerdy, but you can use a spreadsheet to keep track, at least as you're teaching yourself to do this. List all your executives and other key employees and make sure you give them some praise or connection twice a week.

I work with a technical and quite outgoing CEO named Jae. Jae is already on his fourth company. When he hired me he said that in his previous companies, he saw his job as more or less just yelling at people to get the job done or yelling at them if they didn't get the job done. His first companies were very successful but, he said, "They were all afraid of me." He also thought that if he had focused on building his team, he could have gotten more done.

I asked him to set a goal for how many positive interactions he had with his employees and to use a spreadsheet to keep track. (He's an engineer so that made complete sense to him.)

He started by going to the work area of a junior-level employee and simply asking her how she was doing. After chatting for a few minutes he then asked, "Is there any way I can help you?" She told him about a problem she was having, and he helped her solve it. After that, he said, someone who used to be afraid of him was seeking him out because she finds it so valuable to talk to him. He told this to me with a huge smile on his face.

He's made these check-ins a regular practice. He started skip-levels, calling the junior employees and getting to know them better: where they grew up, what their family is like, what are we doing well, what can we be doing better. To his surprise he's found that with this kind of attention people turn into much more talented employees than he realized. People he thought were good, but not great, acted differently and worked better when they got more positive feedback, especially from him since he was the founder. I'm not asking you to build a better relationship with your employees to make you a better person—although it's fine with me if it does. Your employees will become more valuable to your company.

To be clear, as the CEO your job is *not* to manage all the junior employees and solve their problems yourself. As the company gets bigger, Jae—like every one of you—will not be able to talk to each employee or even know them all. He'll have to hire other managers and make sure they are handling the team (see Chapter 6). But remember this foundational element of your job: creating the conditions for people to do their best work and contribute the most to the company. That requires you to find tools and time to appreciate your employees and to get your leaders to do the same.

Say What You Mean and Mean What You Say

Now that we've talked about psychological safety; now that you're walking around reminding everyone what they're doing right; now we can talk about expectations and accountability.

I'm a big fan of accountability. I think everybody is happier when they know what's expected of them in specific, well-defined ways. And great people want to drive for goals and work with other people who are driving for goals.

There are good ways to handle accountability and bad ways.

Let's start with the bad ways.

I coached Carol, the CEO of a small but fast-growing training start-up. She had asked her head of marketing to focus on hiring someone to build a new version of their website to capture leads better. That would give him time to concentrate on social media marketing, which they had agreed was their most fruitful channel for the moment. He didn't do it. She redirected him. Twice. So the third time, she just snapped.

Carol was working on her ability to bring people along rather than just dictate orders, so it was a good example to unpack. We talked through what happened. How did she feel before she snapped? "It was like an attack," she told me. "It was this build-up of tension inside of me. Have you ever smoked?" she asked. No, I admitted, goody-two-shoes that I am. "Well, I used to smoke," she said. "And there would be this build-up inside me telling me I needed a release and finally I would go outside and pull out a cigarette, light it up, take that first puff and suddenly I could breathe again." Wow. I thought she might take a cigarette out right then!

(That's actually great self-awareness. Being able to tune into your body and your feelings is very helpful when you're trying to figure out what's going on when you lose control.)

I like to debrief conversations with a recipe—G-O-D: goal, outcome, do-over. What did you want to happen? Goal. Did that happen? Outcome. If you could do it over, what would you change? Do-over.

It was obvious that when she lost her temper with her head of marketing she had no goals, she was just angry. I asked her if she got the outcome that she wanted. Obviously not, she admitted. "What's the do-over? If you could cut and paste your actions, knowing what you know now, what would you do?" To me, this is the key question. You can't actually do it again, but by examining what happened, rewinding the tape, and doing something different, you can actually re-groove your mind and your behavior. You're more likely to do the more productive thing next time.

When she talked about the cut-and-paste, she addressed it in a more or less enlightened way: be curious about why he was saying one thing and doing another. Ask him what it would take for him to do this. Get his commitment and a time frame. But she was still angry. And even as she gave me the "right" answer, she came just short of asking—with some heat—the real question on her mind: When can I punish him? She stopped herself from saying it, but there was clearly a desire to have the satisfaction of rubbing his mistakes in his face.

Be honest—if you search your heart, you know you've felt that way yourself.

Leading is frustrating. People are endlessly confounding. But here's the truth: it rarely helps to make someone feel bad when the only point is to make them feel bad. Actually the best way to hold someone accountable is to make sure that they *don't* feel bad. Feeling bad won't help them honestly reflect on their behavior, but it *will* make them defensive, destroy their confidence, and drain their motivation away.

Your goal in debriefing misses and redirecting people is to help them get their jobs done better, to help move their goal forward, and to help the company win. That's it. Difficult conversations will result from that, no question, and you'll lose it because you're only human, but you don't want to or need to scold, blame, or punish.

So here's the right way to think about accountability: first do all the things we discussed above to create psychological safety and make sure you spend some time investing in praise and affirmation. Holding people accountable is just a conversation about negative unexpected results. And it starts with making sure that the expected results are transparently clear to everyone involved.

Even seasoned founders miss that sometimes. Recently I was talking to Mika, a three-time successful entrepreneur. She was building a direct-to-consumer business for hair care. By using clever Instagram marketing and strategic influencers she had tapped into a nerve in the market, and the company was growing fast.

Mika was complaining about her team not "getting it." (CEOs complain to me all the time. They really don't have anyone else to talk to.) I asked her what she meant exactly, and after a lot of discussion she finally boiled down what was in her mind: the merchandise was routinely late and the marketing team didn't know what products to feature until the last minute so there was always this scramble to get everything up in time, and therefore they made a lot of mistakes.

I asked her what her expectations were for the process for the merchandising team to get the information to marketing. What was the time frame they had agreed on? When did they sync up?

She was silent for several seconds as she thought about that. And then she realized that she hadn't really told others what she expected. She just assumed that her leaders should know that they should come up with a schedule and a process together.

You know, she's right. They should. It's just that I find more often than not in the high-growth environment of a start-up people often don't realize that things have changed around them. The informal way that the head of merchandising and the head of marketing coordinated used to work for them. Then the company got bigger, they each had a larger team to manage, the demands sped up, and they didn't regroup how they worked together. Mika assumed they knew what the expectations were, but I knew that she hadn't clarified them for herself because it took her quite a bit of time to go from "they don't get it" to "they aren't coordinating together seamlessly." The gateway to that was her realization of "I have expectations that I haven't fully articulated to myself or them but I know something's wrong."

Although this situation was indeed annoying, I asked her to think of it as an opportunity to practice clarifying expectations and then holding people accountable. (When I ask founders to think of a problem as an opportunity, they often find it annoying and I don't really blame them.) She had to start with her own mindset. (Remember that we talked in Chapter 1 about getting a handle on your triggers? This is a good moment to be on top of yours.)

The phrase I like to use to give people some perspective is simply "problems, problems everywhere." My clients enjoy this because it just reflects their reality. There really are problems everywhere! And when you solve these you'll have new ones tomorrow, and that's the game. The good news is that you chose to start a company, so you chose these problems. (If you don't like these problems you can always go get a job at IBM. Then you'll have different problems.) So it's helpful for you to come to terms with it and calmly (maybe joyfully?) accept these problems. That's important because when you address accountability you definitely want to have an even keel. Unchecked, your irritation will make other people defensive or shut down, which will just make things worse.

You, the founder, need to say explicitly what you expect and meet with your leadership team regularly so you can calibrate on a regular basis expected outcomes versus actual outcomes for both business goals and behavioral goals. That's pretty crucial when it comes to addressing accountability. We'll focus more on systems and meetings in Chapter 7, but overall it's helpful just to make commitments visible so you can look back over them and troubleshoot what went wrong.

It's *Not* Better When You Do It Yourself

Once you've established psychological safety, built social capital and good juju with your team, and learned to set expectations and hold people accountable from the right mindset, you finally get to focus on that last foundational skill: delegating.

Delegating work and responsibility are basic to your business. You almost begin your business by delegating. Having a cofounder, asking a friend to work with you, hiring your first employee are all delegation, at least in the sense of dividing up the workload. You can't do everything yourself. Your company can't grow unless you delegate, and neither can you.

There is a great blog article from First Round Capital that sums this up: at some point you have to give away your Legos.[1] When you start getting bigger, you have more infrastructure, you have more people, so you have to give away the parts of the day-to-day. That should be good, but often it's bad because you think that nobody can do it as well as you and it really lights you up. You love to design. You'll have to give a lot of that up. You love to tinker with the technology. You'll have to give that up. Maybe you're one of those salesy founders that likes to go see customers. That's fine, but who is running the company while you're gone? There are so many other things to do. Giving things up can be hard for founders to do, but it has to be done and done right.

Delegating is one of those nuanced topics that takes some thinking through. It's not giving up—"Hooray, I don't have to do that anymore!"—that's abdicating. It's not giving in—"Now that I don't do that, everything will get screwed up." It's certainly not holding on—"Do this but tell me everything you do"—that's being a bottleneck and a micromanager for good measure.

Most of all, delegating is not about you. It's about them. It's about assessing their capabilities, giving them the right guidance and context, and then trusting them.

I hear somebody in the back of the room muttering, "I did that. And then the so-called expert I brought in to run sales ruined the things that were already working and didn't build anything to replace it. How can I trust them when they're not trustworthy?"

I know! It's hard, right? Experts let you down. People tell you they got it, but they don't. You need tools to figure out who you can trust and for what. How do you do that?

Start by determining what you're actually delegating and to whom. One of the founders I coach, Jack, needed an analysis of the competitive landscape. He asked his office manager, Chris, to take a crack at it. That's not necessarily a bad idea—Chris was bright and ambitious and volunteered for this—but Jack just handed it off without any context or suggestions for how to get started. You can see where this story is going: Chris was overconfident in his skills. He approached it in a convoluted way. He asked a few executives to get him some information. They, thinking that it was something Jack wanted them to do, spent a lot of time getting him what he asked for. By the time it came back to Jack, it was an overly complicated and quite unhelpful analysis that had to be done over by someone else. Jack was super frustrated and used it as an example of why he doesn't like to delegate unless he has to.

I can understand that—Jack is not alone—but let's see if we can approach this in a more enticing way. At some point you're going to have to be a master delegator.

DENNIS CROWLEY
Founder and Executive Chairman, Foursquare

You'll find out you've just got to learn to delegate, and you've got to learn to trust people, and you have to understand that when you trust people, sometimes they'll do the right thing, sometimes they'll do the wrong thing. Sometimes they'll do the thing that you're imagining, and sometimes they'll do something totally different. If they did something totally different, it's probably your fault for not effectively communicating, and that's challenging.

I think the first thing that we had to delegate at Foursquare was we hired our first general manager. I was delegating parts of the operational part of the business. At first it was stuff I didn't want to do anyway, like I don't want to pay the Amex bill, I don't want to worry about health insurance, or order office chairs. I don't want to worry that the payment will happen on time. Eventually that turns into delegating hiring decisions and strategic decisions, and you put someone in place that you trust to do the job, and then you hand them harder and more intense and meaty little projects and challenges.

As those people succeed at those jobs or succeed in answering or solving those problems, you continue to trust them with the power even more, like running teams, hiring their own teams, doing their own things autonomously. That's a big part of it.

There are a lot of different styles of CEOs, and some of them are the finance CEO, the sales CEO, the BD CEO. I was the product CEO. I was very passionate about the products that we were making and why we made them and the story they told, and how they looked and acted and worked and how they made people feel. We hired our first product folks, and now you're really delegating that thing you feel super passionate about, and that's really hard. When you delegate the thing that you feel like you're best at, it's challenging to live with that, in order to coexist with the people that are making those decisions.

I like the framework developed by Ken Blanchard. He called it "commitment and competence," what most people now call the "will and skill" framework.[2] It aims to determine how willing and able someone is to take on a new task.

Will: Does your employee want to do it? How do you know? Have conversations with him, not only about the job you're delegating but about what makes him excited. Does he ask insightful questions?

FIGURE 3.1   Will and Skill Matrix

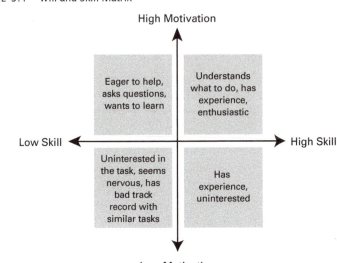

SOURCE Jon Hugo Ungar (2021), jhungar.com

Does he add ideas and information? Does he have a sophisticated understanding of what you want? Does he seem burdened by and buried under the work he has now or does he have time for more things?

Skill: Does your employee have the skills to do the job? Keep in mind those skills that relate specifically to the job in question. Talk through what the job requires. Does she have a plan to achieve it? Ask her for a story that illustrates that she has done something similar before. Do you think that she can handle this with a lot or a little guidance from you? Is this a stretch for her and maybe even slightly out of her comfort zone? That's OK, but just know that she might need extra guidance or more time.

You can also get a sense from the people around her. If you're thinking of promoting someone to be a manager, for example, check out whether her peers enjoy working with her, spontaneously go to her with their questions, and generally look up to her.

Once you assess someone's will and skill, you'll have a better sense of how much you need to explain and direct. You'll know if you can leave them alone to figure it out or if you should help them plan it out step by step.

Delegating is also about delineating. Good delegating helps define where someone's swim lane ends and where somebody else's begins and how you expect your people to work together. That can be hard because roles by nature are interconnected. You should know who has final say over the website, for example, but also who is supposed to weigh in. It's also about who has the final say when they disagree. If the head of product and the head of marketing have different points of view about the direction to move in, they should know who ultimately gets to make the decision. (As I said, we'll talk about the RACI matrix for assigning responsibilities in Chapter 7.)

Delegating well is the only way you'll get leverage as a founder. It gives others structure about what they're supposed to do and helps you focus on the most important things for you to do. What's your highest and best use as a founder? What is the thing that most needs to be done that only you can do? What are you really suited for that nobody else can do as well? When you delegate, you can focus on that. And that's what building a company is all about.

Leading others is often frustrating and annoying. You wanted to build a product, and you find yourself pushing the head of sales to get his job done. You want to spend your time talking about the road map, but instead you are painfully managing how to get the most out of people who are, at times, falling short. You're trying to remember to praise people while solving problem after problem.

I know. It's not easy. At the same time you need to lead (and to manage) to be able to get your baby out in the world. On the bright side, it's kind of amazing when you are able to orchestrate a team to work together as one or support someone who accomplishes feats that surprise both of you. Being a coach and getting the best out of others is pretty awesome (I know I'm biased). And trust me, it's very satisfying to go through the personal journey that you'll take to learn the leadership and management skills that allow you to build a successful company. Once you embrace that journey of personal growth for yourself, you can turn your attention to our next topic: building a healthy culture.

TAKEAWAYS

- Make sure your people feel psychologically safe.

- Praise your people proactively, more often than you think you should have to.

- Make sure your team knows what's expected of them.

- Hold your people accountable, calmly.

- Learn to delegate properly to give you leverage.

REFLECTIVE QUESTIONS

- How do you respond when someone makes mistakes?

- When was the last time you gave positive feedback to each member of your executive team?

- Which of your people is ready to take on more responsibility? Which are already overwhelmed by their job?

- What do you need to work on to become a master delegator?

Endnotes

[1]   First Round Review (n.d.) "Give away your Legos" and other commandments for scaling start-ups, First Round Review, https://review.firstround.com/give-away-your-legos-and-other-commandments-for-scaling-startups (archived at https://perma.cc/ZY8M-9WSL)

[2]   Blanchard, K and Johnson, S (2015) *The One Minute Manager*, William Morrow, London

04

Cultural Conceptions
(and Misconceptions)

Reflective Question: How much have you thought about the culture you want to build?

Culture. How can a word used so frequently in the start-up world mean so many different things? People go out for beers with each other and work long hours together, and we call it culture. People have to "bring facts not opinions" to a meeting where they then try to one-up each other, and that's just the culture. Employees share or hoard information and give each other direct feedback or shy away from doing so because of culture. Some managers intimidate or even scream at people, and if you allow that, it becomes part of the culture. And then there are the ping-pong tables and snacks in the kitchen.

When I conduct 360-feedback for my clients I talk with the executives and employees. One of the questions I ask is, "What's the culture like around here?" Often people will hesitate and not quite know what to answer. Someone might say, "We care about results," and another will say, "We all like each other." Often there isn't any consistent experience of culture—each group has its own microculture led by their own manager who is either intentional about building a certain culture or, sadly, not. That plays out in the experience that employees are having at your company. To say nothing of your customers.

Many founders don't think about culture. As far as they are concerned, the culture is something they'll think about... well, later. Not now. Culture, they think, is nice to have, a good decorative addition you can make as your start-up starts to get successful and scale. It's actually the opposite—setting culture early and intentionally helps your start-up scale successfully.

This chapter illuminates cultures both good and bad and gives you the interlocking structures necessary for building a culture that can empower your people: a narrative that employees can rally around; values that guide you and them in making decisions and surviving calamities as you grow; and rituals and stories that connect your people, galvanize them, and help you build culture.

News Flash: You Already Have a Culture

If you're a founder/CEO you are starting or leading a company with a culture. You may not have identified or articulated that culture. You might want to change whatever culture you have. But you have a culture, whether you wanted one or not.

Culture is a mix of qualities that guide how your people are expected to behave and make decisions. Ben Horowitz in his book *What You Do Is Who You Are* calls it "the set of assumptions that your people use to resolve the problems they face day to day." He goes on to say, "If you don't methodically set your culture, then two-thirds of it will end up being accidental, and the rest will be a mistake."

He adds a few questions that can only be answered by culture, for example:

"If I know something is badly broken in the company, should I say something? Whom should I tell?"

"Should I go home at 5 p.m. or 8 p.m.?"

"Should I stay at the Four Seasons or the Red Roof Inn?"

"Should we discuss the color of this product for 5 minutes or 30 hours?"

"Is winning more important than ethics?"[1]

Your job as the founder is to embrace the need to think about what you'd like your people to do and how they should treat each other. You have to take responsibility to communicate that to others and make sure you and everyone who hires new people keep those cultural traits in mind. Your job is also to reinforce the behavior you want to see and correct the behavior you don't want to see. (We cover accountability and giving feedback in Chapters 3 and 6.)

The culture you wind up with is a complex chemistry of your own personality and preferences, the way you communicate and behave, the people you hire, and, importantly, your consistency in reinforcing the behavior you want to see. You have to have a strong vision of the behavior that represents your company, but you also have to be open to the fact that your culture can and should evolve as you grow, as your business shifts, and as you bring new people on.

JON STEIN
Founder of Betterment

I probably over-index on culture because in some ways, I started the company because I wanted to build the culture. I have a metaphor that I probably didn't come up with, but I've been using it so long, it sort of feels like I did. When people ask me about what's the Betterment culture, I answer with, "It's a house." Values are the foundation. They're super-important, but you never see them. The best values are ones you don't have to talk about all the time. You just know they're down there, underneath everything. Without them, you don't have the rest of the house, but what you see all around you is not the values.

What you see is the weekly team meetings that we do, the weekly show-and-tell where we talk about our work. The structure of regular events throughout the year: the winter retreat in February, the anniversary party in May, the summer retreat in August, and Betterment Thanksgiving in November—the weekend before Thanksgiving, we throw a big potluck that we invite families to. You see the communication infrastructure. What document format do we use? Is it standardized or is it do whatever you want? Do we actually care about the objectives and key results (OKRs)? What's the review process? We have a daily ticker-tape email that shows how assets are growing and which products are growing and how customers are behaving.

There's a weekly report that all the heads of functions write in a Slack channel. There's the monthly operating review and all the process that goes into that. The quarterly board meetings. You see all of that reporting and infrastructure. You see how we foster relationships. There are the "bands" that we have lunch with once a month. We have this whole thing around the design of our pods, the way people sit in the office. The design of the office, all of the things you see, they're like the furniture and the walls of the house. They are essential, visible every day, and the way that we get our work done well. That's important stuff, but what really makes the culture is the people. When my roommate in college and I moved to New York we lived in this gross cheap apartment. But we had good times there. And I remember him saying often, "People make the place." And I think that's really true. And so ultimately it's about the people you hire and are they amazing, great talent? High-horsepower, passionate, and open-minded are the three things I always look for. And if you have that, you're going to have a good culture, ultimately.

"Culture eats strategy for breakfast" is one of those quotes that people like to claim as their own, and I wish I had said it too. But the wise management guru Peter Drucker gets the credit.[2] What it means is: you can have the most elegant business model, the smartest strategy, and even the best technology in the world, but it's the conditions you create for the people who execute on your vision that will bring it to fruition. If you hire smart people who are prima donnas and can't work together, you won't achieve the plan. Or if you have a company that creates endless process and makes few decisions, your people will get tired and leave or, worse, stop trying but stay. If you want people to "ask forgiveness instead of permission," you'll probably move pretty fast, but if you don't have a mechanism built into the culture to sync everyone up you'll create an "us and them" mentality inside of your company. If your employees all think it's OK to spend money whenever they want and assume that finishing things tomorrow is just as good as today, you'll possibly run out of money or get overtaken by another company before you have a chance to be successful.

So it's a good investment of time to investigate your culture to figure out how your people view it. Survey your people. Do kind of a

360-feedback process for your company. Don't directly ask your people to describe the culture. It's an abstract question, and the only answers you get might be those they think you want to hear. Instead ask questions that will give you more information, for instance:

- Who are the people here that you think are the most successful?
- What qualities do they have that make them that way?
- What are the things you like most about this company?
- What have been some of your peak experiences here?
- What have you experienced in past companies that you're relieved you don't have to deal with here (or, sadly, do you also have to experience here)?
- Which of the people in your personal life would be the best fit into our company and why?
- Who would not be a good fit here and why?
- What three words would you use to describe our company?

Now don't walk around and ask people these things randomly. Think about the context, sequencing, and structure. First you might want to ask those questions of yourself. It could be your journal prompt for a day or two. You should also ask the questions of your executive team, since they will have their own take on it as well as some insight from the employees they manage. You can have a mini-offsite or a long management meeting to discuss these questions, which could be the jumping-off point for some good conversations about the company overall.

Then you (or your leaders or your Head of People) can ask your employees. The best way to do that is to divide up your employees into a few small groups. If you are a company of 30 or 100 you can certainly do this with all employees. If your company is 200 or 300 that's going to be tough, and with more than that it may not be practical, so just choose a subset of people.

One group to include for sure are the folks you see as the cultural stewards, the spiritual leaders of your company. Bringing them together as a group and having a long conversation about culture will give you some great insight and also lift your spirits—both of these are great things! But also include some workshops with more random employees to discuss this. It will be interesting to see the differences among these groups.

Remember that the purpose of these discussions is to gather data. Once you sift through all the words and the insights from the discussions, you'll have an understanding about the air your company is breathing—what the culture is now. Then you can also ask people to weigh in on what they think the culture should be.

In one company I work with, the cofounders met to discuss how they saw the culture. As we talked they realized that their most productive, high-performing employees all had significant outside interests. One was a furniture maker and spent weekends in a cooperative with other creators. Two were in bands and played multiple instruments. One was on her way to becoming a yoga instructor.

"What does this tell you about your culture?" I asked them. "That we value commitment," one of them said. "And curiosity," the other chimed in.

When they discussed the question of culture inside of a few groups, these same topics came up. Employees talked about being able to learn from each other by talking about their hobbies and that supporting each other in their outside activities helped them feel connected. They also realized that many of their pursuits were team-based and helped them all build skills to work as a team, which strengthened their ability to work across disciplines and negotiate conflict inside of the company. So "multifaceted people with commitment, curiosity, and a collaborative mindset" became a pillar of their culture. They used these "3 Cs" as a framework to hire new employees, and the founders and leaders made sure to reinforce those qualities inside of day-to-day work.

Unintended Toxic Cultures and How They Got That Way

Now let's open up that uncomfortable topic of toxic cultures. We've seen plenty of news reports about start-ups that became toxic. Certainly women, people of color, and others feeling unsafe in the

Silicon Valley culture is extremely problematic. It's also important to note that both men and women are accused of bullying their employees, playing favorites, and other truly awful behavior, and that they often do so at companies that were founded on lofty principles. (Enron anyone?)

These obviously toxic cultures make an easy target. But how did they get there? Everybody "knows" that bias, favoritism, intimidation, and bullying are wrong. It's easy for founders and CEOs to dismiss the headline stories, easy to say, "I don't do that stuff. I'm not a bully or a racist," or "I treat everybody equally." Nobody starts out hoping to create a toxic culture that demeans, degrades, or discriminates against their employees.

But I've known founders who started a company believing that their job is to drive people hard and don't realize the negative impact of biting or sarcastic comments. I've worked with CEOs who wanted to examine every spreadsheet and second-guess every decision. They did that because they were anxious, driven, and focused on success, not because they wanted their team to be worrying whether they were doing the right thing or, alternatively, not doing much of anything because they knew they would be criticized. But that's what happened. And that culture is not sustainable in the long run—the employees will quit or do as little as possible to get by.

Dysfunctional cultures are just as likely to be generated by leaders who would never utter a sarcastic word or a gratuitous criticism. Because they haven't been focused on building culture, dysfunctions simply spring up around them like weeds in an untended garden. Here are some examples of errant cultures that well-meaning leaders can inadvertently create.

The mirror culture. (1) The founders hire themselves, and (2) everyone emulates the founders. That can be great when they model founders' wonderful qualities like quiet confidence or ability to bring people together. But it's destructive when they emulate behaviors that don't play so well, like not communicating to others or an inability to make decisions without perfect information. This kind of culture is downright toxic if it means employees amplify the founder who, on a bad day, loses his temper. The mirror culture also creates cliques of people who are like the founder, perhaps spend time outside of work with the founder, and overall seem to be favorites. It's demoralizing for the others to feel like second-class citizens.

The "polite" culture. When I use it, the word "polite" is never a compliment. A culture that is too nice is another way of saying that people can't tell each other the truth, can't manage conflict constructively, and are busy making sure they don't hurt each other's feelings. The outcome of this is always that things move slowly and important problems don't get surfaced. I worked with a CEO who presided over a polite culture. He was a doll! But since he couldn't bring himself to broach tough topics with people, building the new version of the company's product ran more than eight months late. Employees model the founder's behavior, so they didn't address other company problems with each other, and they sure didn't bring them up to him. (They did talk about them behind others' backs—a polite culture tends to cause a lot of underground noise.) By the time I started coaching him we had a lot to untangle.

The conflict-avoidant culture. This is a cousin of the too-nice culture, but it's worth calling out separately. This means that employees (probably starting at the top with the founders) go out of their way to maintain harmony and, as a result, not have hard conversations. An extreme of this was one founder who hired an entire shadow tech team rather than risk conflict with his CTO! Massively delayed projects and burning way too much money is the price you pay when you're not willing to pay the price of learning to have uncomfortable conversations in a way that doesn't alienate people.

JERRY COLONNA

Executive coach and author of Reboot: Leadership and the art of growing up[3]

When a leader is so driven that they are almost demonically possessed by a desire to succeed, and there is no conscious conversation around it, the danger is great. And the likelihood is high that everybody around them is suffering. And that's needless. It's hard enough to do the work that's needed; don't add needless work.

There are lots of examples, oftentimes associated with the viral videos of people just yelling and screaming and being aggressive. And then you've got the corollary of racial identity discrimination, gender identity discrimination, sexual harassment, and abuses of power.

And then there are the covert expressions of toxic leadership, like conflict avoidance or passive aggressiveness. If we look at something like conflict avoidance, what we often see is that there is a lot more going on under the surface. Maybe a founder has an irrational and unpredictable key person on the team. This creates a toxic environment where everyone has to walk on eggshells around this character to avoid upsetting him. The founder is frustrated and has had it, but he's afraid that if he loses this person, he won't be able to raise money, for example. And when you unpack it you often see that he unconsciously hired this person because it reminds him of the way his mother was or the way his father was. And so there is more to the conflict avoidance than just being afraid to lose an important employee.

The reason I highlight that is that we often think of toxic leadership as somebody picks up a chair and throws it across the room. And of course that's awful, but that's actually easy to manage—as long as you have power, you say, "Get the hell out." The problem is the insipid, continuous, persistent toxicity that comes from a lack of consciousness. And until a founder is conscious of this tendency inside of themselves, they are going to keep repeating this error.

The friends culture. This culture stems from the founder hiring friends or cofounding with a friend. Either way, your employees somehow feel there is an untouchable class of people: the friends. The friends may not be doing a good job, but nobody says anything to you because they're your friends! They believe either rightly or wrongly that you already know about the issues and aren't addressing them. If the friends you've hired or cofounded with act inappropriately inside work (bullying people, not setting deadlines, hardly coming to work) or outside work (drinking too much at bars or other bad social behavior), people tend to gossip about it behind your back. They also work around the friends. All of this is distracting and, to say the least, slows work down.

The slow decision culture, also called analysis paralysis. The CEO needs more and more data before making decisions, and that affects the ability of executives and the other employees to make their own decisions. I don't have to tell you that this makes for a slow-moving team in a fast-moving industry.

The extroverted culture. The culture is built on spending a lot of time together and going out for drinks after work. This is great and can be a lot of fun and very unifying! But unless the CEO has an ample supply of self-awareness, the team can devolve into an in crowd and an out crowd, with status dictated by how often you hang out in a bar with the founder. Over time as your start-up grows, you will tend to hire more seasoned people (or your original employees grow up a bit themselves) with families. You'll have to find ways to stay cohesive even when people can't go out as much. Also, not everyone feels comfortable going out drinking. One start-up I coached dealt with this by having biweekly lunches they called free-for-alls. The idea was that they created an environment where people just hung out together, no agenda, to mimic the way they used to hang out in bars (without the alcohol.)

The bifurcated culture. This one shows up when cofounders—usually when there are just two of them—have effectively divided their roles. That's good. But not if they seem to be running two different companies. When I did 360-feedback for two cofounders of a communications systems start-up in Miami I discovered this. The CEO was an engineer, an intensely hard worker, and a high-strung person. Naturally he ran the engineering team. They put in long hours and lived by their project plan. They would brag about how much time they put in. The COO, on the other hand, was not only more laid back, he also came from the world of sales and liked the camaraderie of going out together and celebrating wins big and small. He was not that focused on details, and he was better at intuitively managing his team than overseeing the sales pipeline. The employees felt very bonded to their own area but very wary of the others, which they actually called "camps." We had to work to get the founders more aligned and the culture more unified so the team could work together.

The hard-driving culture. The founder sees her job as driving her people hard. She sets a very fast pace herself, so in that sense she leads by example, but most of her employees can't keep up. This culture is often unaccompanied by any praise or rewards; sometimes it's combined with an overly harsh tone and maybe temper eruptions. Either way people feel like they can never get enough done and what they do get done falls short. This can backfire, because if people never feel like they're making progress or that the expectations are impossible to meet, they check out, gossip behind your back, or finally just quit.

Creating the Culture You Want

Now that we've listed a whole set of cultures that you want nothing to do with, let's focus on creating and nourishing the kind of culture you do want.

Tactically speaking, culture grows from three things: your company story, the bigger picture of the vision and purpose of the work, and a set of values that are important to you and your people. Then you ensure your behavior matches those things, and you talk about them all the time. You can employ rituals that come organically from you and your people to make your place unique. Culture comes from your weaving a complex tapestry of these elements with a little bit of *je ne sais quoi* for good measure.

How Did You Get Here?

In the beginning, there is the founding story, a narrative about the genesis of the company, the old days. That story gives people a north star, an embodiment of what the company is, its reason for being. It builds community and camaraderie. People will fondly recall the founder story even when they joined five years into the life of the company. It helps people feel connected to purpose to being a part of something bigger than themselves.

A founder's story is a tool for galvanizing people inside and outside the company about its purpose. You can't get people to run through walls for you with just data. They need a story that gives the facts context, the sense of mission. It puts a name and a face on your goals so that the people you bring in can see it clearly. You have to hire people, and they naturally have their own issues, families, interests, and dreams. But somehow you need to focus them all in the same direction and work hard. Without a narrative, people run out of steam.

Airbnb has a legendary founding story. Joe Gebbia and Brian Chesky decided to found a company together but didn't have a concept. They noticed that during conferences, hotel rooms were always scarce, so they cooked up the idea to host people on airbeds in their living rooms, throwing in an airport pickup, breakfast, and a tour of the city. Many ups and downs ensued, along with a colorful story of the side hustle of making cereal for the political conventions (Obama O's and Captain McCain's), which they used to raise the $20,000 they needed to pay their maxed-out credit cards and get media attention for their burgeoning company. You can see this story on the Airbnb website: the first entry of "our story" is Brian and Joe hosting their first guests.

The founding stories are a great touchstone for your employees. They are some of the foundational elements you have to knit employees together. Without a strong narrative, people can get siloed into just thinking about their own job or dragged up into infighting or lose the meaning of what they're doing.

What's It All About? Purpose and Meaning

When you need people to bear down even in the face of daunting odds, you need to envelop them in purpose and meaning. Purpose and meaning aren't always about curing cancer or saving babies— although those are good things to do. People get purpose and meaning out of understanding how their jobs fit into the bigger picture, how the work of their hands is a crucial part of energizing your team to do their best work.

And on the other side of that, people get turf-focused, defensive, exhausted, and even ornery when they don't reacquaint with purpose and meaning.

A few years ago I worked with a biotech company in Boston, and as it happens, they literally were curing cancer. I gotta say that it wouldn't take the leader of the year to figure out how to emphasize purpose and meaning. Unfortunately part of the reason I was brought in was because the CEO—for all his personal passion—didn't spend any time reminding the employees or his executive team about the reasons they were doing this. He was very brilliant, very quiet, and extremely critical. As a result he trained his people to only focus on the negative and never celebrate wins. Four years into the life of the company the business was doing great, but his executives were exhausted and his employees demoralized. There was a real threat of missing deadlines without a change in culture.

The company had doubled the number of employees in less than a year. Naturally that led to a need for a lot of training, which put pressure on HR. I was leading an offsite of the executive team where all of our discussions led to one place: our employees need more training. The vice president of HR was—understandably—getting more and more defensive as we talked.

I did what we coaches do: I called a break to give him a moment. He and I went for a walk. He vented for twenty minutes about a number of things, including his frustration and disappointment about running a hiring process for the COO and then another when the first didn't work out. He railed about the lack of respect from his peers and about his employees dropping the ball. Oh, and by the way, he hadn't taken a vacation in over two years.

I got that he was overloaded, and I sympathized. Then I asked him about our offsite: "What do you think about the issues with the training capacity?" He snapped at me. "I am down two people. I am working over sixty hours a week. I finally had to learn to say no to all new training."

"I totally get the need to set limits," I assured him. "How do you think that strategy is working now?"

"It worked," he told me, sort of frantically and sort of desperately. "They stopped asking."

Wow.

That's what happens in a company when you see your job without keeping the greater goal in mind, without a reminder to explain where you're going. By putting up a massive roadblock the head of HR was protecting himself and his team. No one was reminding him of the bigger picture, his role in the larger view, and helping him find a different strategy to get what he needed and also get the company what it needed. Without connection back to purpose and meaning he just shut down rather than work with the other team members and bring creativity and resourcefulness to a shared problem.

Values: Your Culture's Building Blocks

Another way to build purpose and meaning along with team cohesion is with your values. Values are what matters to you in your company. The more you clarify your company's values and act on them, the more fulfilled and engaged the employees are—even when they don't share each and every one of them. Even when things are changing, even when there is the normal chaos of a start-up, even when there's a pandemic, they trust their leaders.

A company in Dallas that is building robots to use in hospitals is an outstanding example of how to think about culture up front. The company was started by two first-time founders sitting in the upstairs bedroom of one of their parents' houses for two years, not taking any salary, planning their company. They both had been in companies where they didn't enjoy the culture. So in addition to figuring out the technical specs of the product, they spent time and energy talking about the kind of company they wanted to have. They built the values before they built the website. They thought deeply about what would produce a culture where they'd love to come into work every day, and they came up with three principles: "Our passion combines drive for the business and caring for each other. We see humor as a gateway to intelligence. We celebrate our wins and always seek what's next."

What was impressive and quite unusual was that when I was doing 360-feedback for them, their team could rattle off those principles off the top of their heads. They didn't have to consult a little diagram or look at a laminated sheet of principles pinned to the wall. They didn't forget a single one. Everybody knows these principles, remembers them, lives them. When employees interview potential hires, they think about these ideas and ask new employees to talk about how they combine drive and caring. People actually think about whether they laughed at all in the interviews. They use these words when they talk about performance. The founders refer to the values all the time. They point out examples of drive and of caring, especially when they are combined. They end their all-hands meetings with two sections: "What wins are we celebrating this week?" and people will share the milestones they hit. They then ask, "What comes next?" and people will talk about what they're working on. The values permeate everything they do at the company, and you can see them in their employees and their commitment to the company.

It's important that the values that you express are values that are relevant to the work of your company and its people. And that they are distinctive—the best cultures are opinioned, have high conviction, and are a little bit quirky.

MAXINE CLARK
Founder and former CEO of Build-a-Bear Workshop

We were trying to reinvent retail. Make it an experience. We were trying to be a company of the twenty-first century, we had to be more flexible. The teddy bear was our guiding light. What would a teddy bear do? I know that sounds crazy, but you know, it's humanity. It's: Are you treating people respectfully? Are you listening to them? A teddy bear will always listen. It just made common sense to me. Sometimes if we didn't have a solution, I'd say, "What would a teddy bear do?" A teddy bear would want to come up to you and hug you, and say, "OK." That is, they would just look at a problem differently.

It was really thinking about philosophy. You don't always have the answer. There's not always an answer but is there another angle? We created our bear-isms, we called them. Like, "It takes a village to raise a bear" and "You're not born a bear, you become a bear." Things like this became part of our way, our philosophy. It was on the walls. It was in our stores. I was the Chief Executive Bear, somebody was the Chief Financial Bear. Everybody had bear titles. It just made us more human. And it immersed us in the business of being there for children. Just not to take ourselves so seriously.

Sarah, a founder of a consumer app company, totally bought into the notion of surfacing the things that were important to everyone. She sent a bunch of her people offsite to come up with a set of values for the company. They came back with a list of things like "integrity," "dedication," and a bunch of other vanilla words. There is nothing wrong with dedication or integrity! It's just that they could be bolted onto any company. There was nothing distinctive about them at all.

Sarah and I talked more, and one thing she said to me sort of "oh by the way" was that the most successful people at the company showed their dedication through their intensity and, sometimes, salty language. She told me that she values both respect and intensity, so she's always joked with her employees "you can swear *with* others, but not *at* others." Now *that's* distinctive and says a lot with a little. It's also opinionated—if that's the kind of company Sarah wants to run, then people can self-select if they want to be a part of that. Values need to rally your people and give them guidance about how you expect them to show up to work.

As you clarify your values and define the culture that's important to you, you have to create structures to model, support, and reinforce it.

The starting point of that is to model the culture yourself. If you want proactive people, start taking initiative in your own role. As the founder/CEO, initiating things may come as second nature to you— that seems obvious, right? But what do you do when people come to you with problems? Do you give them the answer? Do you grill them tersely about what they're doing and make them feel like a dummy? If you're doing either of these things, it may explain why you're not getting people to proactively reach for solutions.

Instead, you can teach them to be proactive by asking them coaching questions such as "What have you already tried?" and "You may not know the answer, but what do you think is the next step?" You'll be surprised how often someone can answer their own question once you've shown them how to think through to a solution. And then you may be surprised at how much initiative they will take.

Say you want people to take risks. Make it safe for them to do so by celebrating their attempts when they do, even when they get it wrong. One company I work with has instituted "screw-up meetings" for people to share the risks they took, how they went wrong, and what they learned. Leaders share first to make it safe for the employees to contribute. The message they send is not that anyone is trying to make mistakes, but that misses are inevitable if you take risks and that the point of reviewing these issues is both to make them OK and to take away valuable lessons.

If you want quick deciders, then be a quick decider, even if it goes against your nature. Praise people for being quick deciders. Even if their decision doesn't pan out, as long as they made it on the basis of the values and goals that you've expressed, praise them for it. Start talking about it and celebrate people who do that.

Celebration is key. If you are great at ideas but not systems, you may praise people who offer great ideas. But if you want to build more "operational excellence" in your company, you have to remind yourself to publicly praise people for their systems thinking and attention to detail.

JON STEIN
Founder of Betterment

I love the team. I love events. That to me is a big part of happiness in life, is creating community, having good friends and family. It's super satisfying to me. I think if you just pursue pleasure in itself, it can be an empty existence. If you're just throwing parties all the time, that doesn't feel right, but if you're celebrating milestones or "We're doing this," that feels really great. And so it was always a big part of our culture. I think of my mom, who always said, "You have to celebrate occasions." It's just ingrained in me. The office space was part of it. From the early days we would order in, and somebody got to pick where the team lunch came from. There was a rotating winners kind of thing where people would get to choose. We did happy hours in the office, and we included friends in addition to colleagues and I loved that time.

That may sound obvious but I worked with one founder who had this blind spot. He said he wanted people who were more focused on processes, but what he did was (1) break the processes all the time and (2) say flippant things about the COO he had brought in to manage the systems of the company—calling him a bean counter. When we discussed it, he told me he was just kidding, but he didn't realize that his words and actions reinforced the old culture of "just do it" and went against the culture the company was trying to build of "routine excellence."

Ultimately, your people are going to take their cues about culture—like about everything—from you. What do you want to communicate about culture with your words and behavior?

I can't tell you what the right culture is for you—it really depends on the unique alchemy of the company you're building. But one thing that's important for all healthy workplaces: the more you can create an environment where people feel comfortable bringing themselves to work, the more they will be able to give you their best selves and their best work. People are not as successful if they feel they have to hide a part of themselves.

In Chapter 3 we talked about the importance of psychological safety for creating high-performance teams. That just means an environment where you can be yourself, make mistakes, even act a little goofy, and you won't be teased or criticized. This lets people feel comfortable saying what is on their mind and trusting the people around them, which means that people will feel comfortable collaborating and will bring all their creativity and resourcefulness to solving problems. It also means your team will be able to raise and resolve conflict with each other and be able to hold each other accountable without having the discussions topple into blame. Your people will give you all their ideas (yes, you'll get plenty of bad ideas that way, but you'll also get way more good ones) and also stop you from marching off of the metaphorical cliff. So no matter what kind of culture you decide to build, make sure it contains psychological safety for you and for your employees.

Rituals Connect Your Culture

The CEO of a data storage company sends out a weekly email that compliments the team and shares his reflections, his concerns, and what he's learning from customers. He explains how the company added value for the customer and calls out specific people and their wins. He also shares what he's concerned about and what he wants to make sure people stay focused on.

Those weekly emails have become a ritual. Like your personal rituals, a ritual is a company activity that happens regularly, like the same day every week or the same time every day, and so gets infused with meaning above and beyond the thing itself. As Erica Keswin says in her book *Rituals Roadmap*, rituals are more than habits and routines.[4] Rituals are personal, purposeful, and powerful. They bring people together in real, authentic ways that deeply matter. And in the workplace they can be the glue that holds your workforce together.

Founders have to come up with creative ways to inculcate the company values. One founder I work with created "Wednesdays are Winsdays"—every Wednesday afternoon people gather to announce their own milestones and get cheered. Everybody learns what others are working on and sees how their part fits into the whole. When they do this every Wednesday at the same time it turns into a time the people can look forward to. A VR company I work with started issuing an "immersive" award for outstanding contributions. The office was across the street from a toy store, so they began to give people a ridiculous plushy toy, accompanied by a fun ritual. Then they went remote during the pandemic, and to continue to support their local toy store, they had the store ship the plushy toy to the employee at home.

The important thing is that the values are recalled and repeated so that they become part of your team's DNA.

Another really helpful ritual one of my clients uses is having people gather in weekly lunches in small groups called pods. These weekly cross-functional lunches facilitate communication among people who have no reason to meet inside of their day-to-day. The pods are a group of about six people from all parts of the company—

cross-functional, cross-level—who have lunch together every Friday. So maybe a shy junior engineer has lunch every Friday for six months or so with the head of marketing, a sales guy, a woman from design, and someone from HR. At some point he might have a question. He may not be comfortable calling someone from marketing whom he doesn't know, but he will feel comfortable bringing it up to the head of marketing over lunch, since he's come to know her. This kind of ritual knits the company and builds social ties that help get work done.

Ping-Pong and Other Perks

Finally, at long last, let's talk about ping-pong tables. Should you have perks? Sure—once you've created an environment that embraces all the things we've been talking about here.

People need a place where they can socialize informally. This helps people get to know each other, and that makes them feel good at work, helps them feel like human beings among others who care about them. More practically, when people have social ties at work, they are more willing to ask each other questions and get help from each other, and they are much more able to resolve conflict with each other.

Once you have this kind of environment—where you encourage people to get to know each other and where you showcase that results matter as well—then you can decide whether or not you want games. I've seen employees work out conflict over a sort of friendly game of ping-pong. I've seen creative people make up a whole new campaign while playing air hockey. I've seen engineers brainstorm through playing cards. Games can be a great tool to help people socialize, and play can ignite creativity. If people are playing games and not getting their work done, you don't have a game problem, you have a management problem.

Have snacks—fed people are happy people. Treats make people happy, and who doesn't want to hang out with some chocolate in the middle of the day? Parties after work are great as long as alcohol isn't the only refreshment and proving how much you can drink the only goal. The big picture is that you want to create the informal ties that bind people together so that they will work for each other as well as working with each other. But remember that these are frills, things that you add after you've done the deeper work of intentionally thinking about and creating your culture.

You Built It. Culture Will Help You Grow It

As your company grows, culture is the foundation you build on and also the foundation that you build out on. The company you started with five, ten, or twenty people becomes a very different place when there are eighty people, or 800 or 8,000. That means it's essential that you make room for new people, physically and culturally.

Shana founded a sports and leisurewear lifestyle brand of women's clothing. Her early employees were friends of hers and intensely focused on her, the brand, and their customers. This is great, and they were definitely the kind of folks you want on your team, especially in the early days. Working together in the intense pressure cooker of a start-up they bonded even more. They knew each other's quirks and made allowances for weaknesses. It was great—until that clan turned into a clique. The old guard didn't always welcome new people or let them in until they proved themselves, based on criteria that were unstated and even unconscious. New people were subtly assessed and judgments meted out. They didn't feel comfortable.

That caused, of course, a hit to productivity and teamwork. It was painful for Shana to see this and even more upsetting to recognize that she had to change the culture to make it more collegial to new people and to separate her team's social life from its work life. In a series of difficult and sometimes awkward conversations, Shana impressed on her long-time team that they needed to be more open and collaborative or they would have to leave. Not everyone responded well to these discussions. Some of them left, which meant that new people came in who were more open to the kind of culture that Shana envisioned, a place where people could be more straight-forward with each other, celebrate together, and work together to achieve the company's goals.

This comes back, again, to self-awareness. Since founders often hire people like themselves, it's crucial that you know who you are so that you can add people to complement and compensate. As your start-up grows up, you'll need to find people who have done the job before. They may not be as freewheeling as your initial hires. They may not want to mix their work and personal lives as easily as the employees in the early days, and, candidly, they may be a bit older and have families and other priorities. Not only that but your company may need to adjust its culture and priorities. One company I worked with realized that its focus in the early days was about product and experimentation but that to win it would have to add more of an emphasis on customers and predictability. That required a new way of working together, and so culture naturally had to be adjusted.

You need to be situationally sensitive not only to where you are in your culture but also with where you want to go and how you can meld new people with the old people. The other edge of that sword, however, is that no matter who you bring in, if they are any good at all, they will change the culture. Making sure that your current team understands the mission of the company, knows where they fit, and knows how their work contributes to the big picture plays a huge role in keeping the transition as smooth as it can be. If your people know that they are relevant, valued, and that their work contributes to the bigger picture, they will feel less displaced when new people come in.

Hiring the right new people is, of course, foundational, and I'll go into that extensively in the next chapter. But when it comes to culture, the deeper you can align your values with the people you hire, and the people they hire, the more successful you will be at growing your company and building the kind of culture that puts you in position for success.

When all of this is true—everyone knows what they are supposed to be doing, is more or less doing it, people are working together constructively, and you're all having fun—that's what I call a winning culture. Not because you're winning at all costs, but because you're winning in the right way.

TAKEAWAYS

- Define your culture intentionally and identify elements which are unique to your company.

- Investigate what your people think the culture is.

- Use stories, values, and rituals that help you build culture.

- Celebrate the people and events that support the culture you want to build.

- As your company gets bigger, make room for new people to shape the culture.

REFLECTIVE QUESTIONS

- What's your culture? Can everyone in your company articulate it?

- Who among your people are the best fit for the company and why?

- What rituals do you have to reinforce the culture?

- Do people feel safe in your company? How do you know?

- How do you make sure you hire people who will build and expand your culture?

Endnotes

[1] Horowitz, B (2019) *What You Do Is Who You Are: How to create your business culture*, Harper Business, New York
[2] Drucker, P (1959) Work and tools, *Technology and Culture*, 1(1)
[3] Colonna, J (2019) *Reboot: Leadership and the art of growing up*, Harper Business, New York
[4] Keswin, E (2021) *Rituals Roadmap*, McGraw-Hill Education, New York

05

Hiring and Firing

*Reflective **Question:*** *Which of your employees would you hire again and why?*

One thing about hiring is very consistent: most people do it wrong until they get it right. There are a few categories of bad hiring, but a consistent issue is that often people hire based on the criterion of "liking." As in, "I liked Beth. Did you like Beth?"—"Yeah, I liked her. Not John."—"I know! I didn't like John."—"So let's hire Beth." I don't mean to say that everyone who is hired is incompetent, or that this is the entirety of the hiring process—it's not—but let's face it, very often hiring comes down to intuition, and those inklings most often come from whether or not you enjoy your time with someone. Add that to the fact that many people don't know what to ask about, and you come up with a process that is, shall we say, unscientific.

The same is more or less true about firing: it's usually done badly, and although that's more understandable from a human point of view—no one likes to do it and no one is happy having it done to them—there are better ways and worse ones. More important, there are ways to see in advance when an employee has passed their expiration date and how to handle it.

So in this chapter, I'll tell you what you should think of before you hire and whether you need to hire at all. If you do have to hire, I'll outline how you should go about it and what you should do after your offer is accepted. I'll also talk about how to tell when you need to make a change with someone, either to move them to a different job or to part ways with them.

Hiring the Right Way

When founders start a company, they don't know what they need except that they need people. They just need butts in the seats. That's where things start going sideways. They don't think about two of the most important things in hiring: (1) who they are looking for in their company—what kind of values, motivators, and habits they expect to see in their employees, and (2) what specifically they want people to do and what abilities and experiences the want-to-be employee will need to do that job.

Hiring Right: Values

Jocelyn was the founder of a healthcare start-up. She knew she needed a lot of domain knowledge, and she wasn't trained herself, so she hired doctors, as many as she could. As time went on in our coaching process, she shared her frustration. "The docs are smart, but they aren't working together. They also are not great at meeting deadlines for complicated projects, and I constantly have to follow up. They have no management skills at all, and their teams are confused and at cross-purposes. It's like I have the best rowing team in the world, but they are not rowing together. The boat is going around in circles."

Jocelyn hired for the right domain expertise, but not the right leadership skills. When she interviewed people, she didn't ask about their management skills, their work styles, and how they got things done, and she didn't talk through her vision of culture with them.

The moral of the story is that you need to think about the qualities you want to see around you. As we said in the last chapter, culture is critical and the only way you'll build a good culture is to be intentional: think it through then hire for it. If you want people who will not only work hard but also naturally solve problems together with others, ask them about times that they approached a really hard problem. Did they sit at their desk and try to reason it out, or did they call together a small group and work it out together on a whiteboard?

If you want people who want to find a brand-new path rather than just do the tried-and-true solution, ask them about a time that they shucked the conventional wisdom in favor of exploring a hunch. Want to hire people who are proactive? Observe them during the hiring process to see how much ownership they take.

ALEXI ROBICHAUX
Cofounder and CEO of BetterUp

We have six values. Three of them are about peak performance, and those are grit, courage, and craftsmanship. We also wanted three values that honor both the squishiness of humanity and what makes life worth living. Those values were empathy, zest, and playfulness. Most people are going to think these are completely contradictory and make little sense together. We try not to hire those people. If they can't look at these values and see the beauty of the creative tension, the opportunity for transformation in that polarity or dialectic, and that these things can be actually realized in our lived experience, then this company isn't a good fit for them.

For grit, we'll ask people: Tell us about the hardest thing you've done. Something where you had to persevere to figure out or succeed.

We'll look for personal agency and responsibility. I'll often ask folks, "What's a time you've been slighted, or you felt that an injustice was perpetrated against you in the workplace?" Then I want to understand how they constructively confronted the person and constructively resolved the situation. You find out really quickly if someone's able to empathize. Can they see the other side of things and see beyond their own emotion and feelings, even if they were wronged? Can they step out of themselves and say, "What's best for my team, my company, or a larger unit?" That's a sign of extreme ownership, which is another key behavior we look at when hiring at BetterUp.

Aneel Bhusri (cofounder and CEO of Workday) and his cofounder interviewed the first 500 employees themselves, and Reid Hoffman (founder and former CEO of LinkedIn) recommends doing this as well. Eddie (cofounder of BetterUp) and I committed to do that after being inspired by their practice of doing this and their successes. The first 500 employees are your "cultural cofounders." You should view them as cofounders. If you believe in the inevitability of your success and you're going to be 10,000 people, it's a fraction of your eventual workforce. We've committed to doing that. So Eddie or I do the final interview with everyone who gets hired at this company. It's cool for them too, because they get to meet a founder and we don't talk about their job. I don't even understand half their jobs anymore. We just talk about them: their mindsets, motivations, and what makes them tick as a person.

We dig into: Why is this company special to you? How do you think about hiring as a future hiring manager, since they're certainly going to be hiring one day? And we really try to understand their mindsets and their motivations in a profound way and that's really helped. About a half of finalists don't make it past a founder interview. So there's still significant contribution to the hiring process even at this late stage.

But even before the founder, I learned this one through Josh Reeves (cofounder and CEO of Gusto), he personally trained a cohort of people to interview for the values and that aren't on the job description. So basically, we have a group of people in the BetterUp world, we call them our balloons, and every interview process has a balloon. And a balloon is like a blind interviewer who doesn't know anything about their job but just focuses on mission, stage, and value fit for BetterUp.

If you're an engineer candidate, you will not have a balloon as an engineer because then they could ask you about your job. For example, you're going to get someone who's in marketing. And they are only there interviewing for mission mindset and motivation. So everyone in the hiring panel could be like, "This is technically the most brilliant engineer in the world. We're going to hire them." But if the balloon says, "Yeah, but they don't align to our values or they don't seem mission-driven," it's a veto. We don't hire them.

Hiring Right: What's the Job?

Your company is winning, but you need to go faster, so you think that means hiring more people. Not so fast. Sometimes the first step in hiring is not hiring. That may seem counterintuitive, but the most important part of hiring is to have the discipline to get clear about what you actually need done.

I worked with a CEO, Nelson, who had a small auto parts store in Michigan that slowly turned into a larger auto parts store. He had a director of operations who was great and had been with him for seven years. She kept track of inventory, leases of new stores, purchases of buildings and equipment, and all the other unglamorous things that make businesses work. Every time the company took on a new commitment, she would add it into the spreadsheet. When they got large new customers, she would add them to the spreadsheet. She kept track of employees and payroll on her spreadsheet. All good.

But over seven years, with all the growth, the properties, customers, and employees, spreadsheets became unmanageable. She couldn't hold all the information in her head like she used to. So she told Nelson she couldn't handle all the work and wanted to hire an assistant.

I don't want anyone to feel overworked, but what she really needed to do was to research and use easily available software tools and easily knowable systems to help keep track of things that she used to keep in her head. Because she had sort of grown into the role, she didn't stop to step back and think about a different way of approaching the job. This is not unusual for someone who's outside their area of expertise or their depth. And you, the founder/CEO, since you've never done this before either, also don't know that such a program exists. But if you had hired someone who knew the job to begin with, they'd say, "Hey, I'm going to buy and implement this program. It's cheap and it will keep track of all these things automatically and give us a heads-up in advance when we need to do something. It will also save me a ton of time so I can do other things." You want to squeeze all the juice out of the lemon by adding automated tools and implementing well-known processes before you hire new people. But you, the CEO, are not the person who should be figuring out how to squeeze. You do need to make sure that the people you hire are on the lookout for ways to do their jobs more efficiently and, at some point, find someone who has a knack for evaluating and implementing systems and processes for maximum efficiency.

There are two takeaways from the story. First, when you have a specific, discrete job to accomplish, make sure someone does some research to find out if there is a way to do it without hiring someone new. If that job is something most companies do, then there may be no need to create something yourself. Speculate with your employees and executives about the existence of systems that can be acquired, and push people to find new ways to do things rather than just hire more people.

The second takeaway is that if you determine that you need to hire a person, you need to know specifically what you want them to do—what you really need, not what you've seen in all those job opportunity ads you see on LinkedIn. People advertise or go to a recruiter, and they spew out some generic thoughts, such as: "I need someone with exceptional communications skills!"

I ask them what they mean by that specifically and they say, "Written *and* verbal!"

What does that mean? Think about it. Communicating with customers, for instance, is very different from communicating with investors or communicating to engineers or to your peers to influence them. These are all very different functions of communication. So define your needs as specifically as you can. If what you really want is for this person to be influential with their peers, to be able to make goals clear, and to bring people along to them, then go to the trouble of clarifying what that means to you.

Think of three stories of success that you'd like to see this person accomplish in six months. Imagine him or her talking to the team and reaching a goal. What is it? The clearer you can see it, the better. Think of yourself as a video camera recording behaviors. If you can see it, then you know what it looks like. You want the new hire to influence peers. Can you see them taking controversial topics and thinking about trade-offs and making deals with peers that are a success for both of them? You want someone who can effectively manage direct reports. Imagine them meeting with their direct reports, understanding their skills, strengths, and weaknesses, putting them in a good spot, and helping them to get back on track when they get off. Take into account the cultural attributes that are important as well.

Now that you can see what you're looking for, then you collect evidence. How do you do that? There are three ways. First, in the interview: you ask them to tell you some stories. "Tell me about a time when you brought peers along on a controversial topic. A time when you were wrong about something and had to go fix it. A time when your direct report was not really on board with something and you either got them on board or had to part ways with them." When they tell you one story, ask for another. Collect stories that you can tell other people. The point is not to overwhelm anyone with surprise gotcha questions in an interview, but to gather tangible examples of how they approach scenarios and how they think.

The second way to gather evidence is to check references. Don't bother asking about their strengths and weaknesses. Just ask for facts. If you need them to be able to influence their peers, ask for an example of the applicant doing that. If you need them to be super-organized, say, "Can you tell me a time when they organized chaos?" You need them to own up to mistakes and fix them: "Can you tell me an instance of when they screwed up something but fixed it and moved on with their life?" And the acid-test question: "Would you hire this person again? For what role? What kinds of roles would you *not* hire them for again?"

Finally, see if you can find anything in writing about them. Have they published anything? Have articles been written about them? Have they won any recognition for the work you're hiring for? There's a lot of information online, and though you can't always trust everything, you can check up on it if you find it. And of course, these days, you need to know if they've done anything embarrassing or insulting online.

How detailed you want to get and how much information you need to collect depends on the position you're hiring for. With an executive, you want to get really detailed. With a manager, you want to get some convincing detail. With an individual contributor you might be more willing to hire for potential, especially if they will have a strong manager.

At the same time, especially when you're hiring for executive positions, be aware of who you are. Founders tend to replicate their own personality and strengths and weaknesses in the people they hire. If you know that you tend to avoid conflict, you may naturally gravitate to people who can't handle conflict, and that trickles down to the rest of the organization. And then when someone who does engage with conflict is hired by you or anyone else, the organization can't really tolerate them.

The opposite can be true, too. Another human error is to assume people are like you. Another founder, Jared, who was building a healthy snacks business, complained to me one day that his people weren't "driven." I asked him if he had hired for "driven."

"My executive team are drivers, that's for sure," he said. "But maybe they didn't hire their employees for drive. I think we just assumed everyone is as driven as we are."

It's natural for founders—for the rest of us too, for that matter—to assume that the qualities that motivate us are going to motivate other people as well. You may not probe enough about their values and their motivators, and so you, like Jared and his executives, assume that everyone who works for you is the same. The people he hired were driven, but they didn't know how to hire for driven. So when you're hiring someone who's going to hire other people, that in itself is a job skill you investigate.

Finally, keep in mind that you're hiring these new employees to create something new. I'm sure the company you're building is a massive opportunity. Of course there will be growing pains, but there will also be peak moments. As I've said, I've met many founders who think that the people they hire are doing them a favor, and so they get too nervous to ask too many questions during the hiring process. This is connected to imposter syndrome, and it's something you should get over. Your company will have ups and downs like any other company, but remember that you're offering the person the opportunity to be a part of a journey unlike any other in their lives. You should absolutely vet people carefully and make sure they have a skills fit and a cultural fit. You should then fully expect them to fulfill their responsibilities even if there is some uncertainty, a change in direction, and anything else your start-up goes through. That's normal, and when your people sign on for a start-up, that's what they're signing on for too.

THE HIRING CHECKLIST

1 Decide if you need to hire someone.

– Research to see if the job can be done without adding head count.

– If it can't be, outline the specifics of the job that needs to be done.

– Determine what you want them to do and how you will measure success in the first few months and first year.

2 Collect evidence on candidates.

– Ask candidates to tell you stories about related experience.

– Check references.

– Review online reputation.

3 Once you find the right person, welcome them with communication, support, swag, and specifics about day one.

4 Onboarding.

– Establish their priorities and scope of job.

– Document what success looks like in thirty, sixty, or ninety days.

– Give them your personal operating manual.

– Ask them for their personal operating manual.

– Help them achieve some quick wins.

– Adjust for remote workers.

Hiring Right: Mixing Friends and Business

Most founders hire friends, certainly at the beginning. It's natural. You're comfortable with each other and know something (but maybe not enough) about each other's work and habits. That doesn't mean you don't face all the problems of any hire, and in fact, you face a few more. Noam Wasserman, author of "The founder's dilemma" and a professor who has researched the field of entrepreneurship extensively, says that you can hire a friend, but you have to accept that you will probably end the relationship as friends.[1] It may not end up being that extreme, but be aware that it's a possibility and that you may have to decide between your friendship and your company. There are other things to think about as you hire friends.

Have a formal interview process. Just because she's a friend, don't skip the basic steps that go into hiring someone. Make the job requirements concrete and specific to the job, and get the evidence in a way you can present to your team. This is crucial when you're hiring friends, because you want to make sure the team is bought in to the value she can bring, not just that she's your friend.

Discuss with your friend how you're going to give him feedback if he's working for you. You have to be as straight with him as any other member of the team, and he has to be able to deal with this input the way he would in any other job.

Have the success conversation in the beginning. You should do this with everyone, but especially with your friends. It goes like this: "I think you're great. I'm so excited that you're joining the company. If we're successful, which I hope we're going to be, there's likely to come a day when I'm going to tell you that I want to bring in someone more senior above you. At that point, I'm going to make sure this is someone you can learn from, and I hope you'll see this as a good thing, because it means we have grown to the point that we have outstripped your experience level and have gotten into a whole new well of success." People will have trouble with it, but at least you've said it and you both understand what the deal is when the time comes. (There's a script for hiring friends in the Sample Scripts at the end of the book.)

An extra item on your checklist for friends is have the conversation about how the relationship is going to change when you hire them. If you're used to hanging out together, that may still be fine, but be aware that others may see it differently. People see that you two are buddies. They're going to think you will defend your buddy and protect your buddy. They won't want to tell you what's really going on with your buddy. A good check is to make sure you have somebody in the company who will tell you the truth about your friend. And you should be aware that the truth may not be what you want to hear.

The takeaway here is that hiring is a system. The first step is not hiring: try to squeeze more operational efficiency out of what you're already doing. The second step is clarifying what you're hiring for and what you want them to do. The third step is interviewing. The fourth step is the formal mechanics of hiring, like an offer letter, a start date, and sending swag to your new person.

The fifth step of hiring is onboarding. Think about onboarding when you're clarifying what the job is. What are the things that will determine success for this new person in the first thirty or sixty or ninety days? You should definitely talk about this with your candidates before they are hired, and once they join, immediately ask them to come up with their start plan. So let's turn to onboarding.

You Hired Them. Now Help Them Start Strong

OK, you found someone who looks terrific. Your job's not done. You need to get this person into the work. For anyone remotely senior, you must have the conversation about what you expect your sparkling new employee to accomplish in the first thirty, sixty, and ninety days.

Get clarity on the roles. Let your new person know: "I want you to know what's in my mind's eye about what I think are your top priorities and what you should be working on. And I want to know what's in your mind's eye."

After he founded a community platform for musicians to share their music and find their audience, Martin hired his buddy Colin as the head of product. Colin was an experienced and talented designer, and they had worked together before, but they didn't think to get really clear when they talked about what head of product actually does. Colin saw his role as being visionary. Martin saw himself as the visionary and that Colin's role was to run the product team and make sure people were doing the right things at the right times.

Since they hadn't clarified their roles, Colin, in his words, "couldn't win." They butted heads regularly over product direction (Colin wanted more say) and about the deliverables of the team (Martin wanted more predictability and accountability). Ultimately, and sadly, Colin left the company in less than a year, and naturally his friendship with Martin was frayed.

It didn't have to be that way. These are the conversations they should have had during the interview process and during the first few weeks of onboarding. What will success look like? What are Colin's top priorities? What will a "quick win" look like after thirty days and what should he plan to accomplish within ninety days? That would have surfaced misalignment quickly and also given structure and guardrails as Colin got up to speed.

In the precious and delicate early days for the new hire, she, of course, needs to gain credibility with the executive team and the CEO, but also with her team immediately. This is particularly important if this executive is the one who comes in as the new leader who "layers" other people on the team. One way to get traction with the team quickly is to engage with them and get their take about what's going on. You as the CEO should support this process and encourage the new leader to interview everyone on her new team. She can ask the same questions of everyone. For example:

1 What are the most important things I should do in the first thirty to ninety days?

2 What are you most concerned I will do?

3 What are you most concerned I will not do?

4 Who are the people who know everything around here?

5 What should I know about how you're wired and what's important to you?

She can use both the process of doing that and the content she gleans to get to know her team quickly and figure out some things she can do quickly to gain traction with them.

Your top job when you bring in senior hires is to ensure their success. Initially you should meet pretty regularly to transfer context, get them embedded in the culture, and help them understand the world they are operating in. Help them understand how to get things done, who the key people are, and how they can get a win as soon as possible so everyone around them can see that they bring value.

A great way to get your new executives up to speed on you, the CEO, is to create and share a personal operating manual. A personal operating manual is a description of how someone can work best with you. It describes how you know you are: what you are best at and what you need others to do to fill in your gaps. How you like to be contacted: Do you want a heads-up before someone calls you? Do you like things in writing before discussions or would you rather talk it out first? What kind of data do you want before making a decision? Do you tend to mull over decisions or make quick decisions? When do you change your mind?

That's not an exhaustive list, but you get the idea. Writing an operating manual is a good exercise for everyone, and your new hire should produce one too.

On to one of my favorite topics, quick wins. I can't leave this section without making the case that quick wins are one of the most important parts of onboarding.

Quick wins are, just as they sound, positive things your new employee accomplishes—that's the win—which are visible and sometimes symbolic or even superficial—that's the quick. These are important for people taking on a new role—like managing a team they used to be a part of—and even more important for a new leader coming into the company. Most of the time your new executive has something to prove. You might have gone through an expensive and extensive search process to find her, and she may be coming in over someone who has been at your company a long time—what everyone calls "layering." So her team (and especially the person who was the stand-in manager) needs to see her value immediately to begin the process of accepting her. The same is true for her new peers—they need tangible things to point to so that they can see her value.

The "win" part has to be in the eyes of the people around the new leader. For example, if the new hire thinks that his first step is to examine and update all the systems, think about how that will be perceived. Even if that is a good thing, even if you brought that person in to help your company get organized, that's simply not an initial win. People hate change, and if your person moves too quickly, he will get organ-rejected. Instead, what's an interim step? It might be, "I'm going to go talk to everyone and find out what they hate the most about the current process and give them a time line for fixing it." Yes! I often recommend bringing cupcakes or candy, too. People love to complain and feel they've been heard—listening is always a win. So are chocolate and other snacks.

When You Have to Part Ways

Let's face it—firing someone is hard, especially if the person comes with pedigree, great recommendations, and all the trappings of a successful career. I'm not going to pretend to you that firing is easy or obvious, but I am hopefully going to help you see the signs that you should fire someone and give you some strategies to do it.

Nobody sets out to hire the wrong people, obviously. Kevin certainly didn't. Kevin was the charismatic founder of a collectibles marketplace. Kevin was like a pied piper—he raised a lot of money and was able to get top executives to join his team. These are amazing qualities for a founder/CEO!

As the company grew, Kevin knew he needed a technical executive to rearchitect the product to get ready to scale. He hired a CTO who looked great on paper. Sean had worked for the fancy companies in Silicon Valley. He came highly recommended with references from those same fancy companies, and Kevin thought he had found the answer to the question of how he was going to scale to millions of users.

All seemed well for about a year. Sean got his arms around the problems in the technology and hired a team. Kevin thought it was an awfully big team, but Sean convinced him that was what he needed to rearchitect the site. After those twelve months Sean told Kevin that the work was more extensive than he had realized and that he'd need another three months to complete a solution. At the end of those three months, Sean said he'd need another three months.

By this time Kevin had, understandably, lost trust in Sean. However, rather than addressing Sean directly about why he was slipping deadlines and finding out what the real problems were, Kevin had a side conversation with the VP of engineering, who reported to Sean. Kevin asked him to take on a special project to check Sean's work, and to keep it secret. This VP of engineering hired other engineers and before you know it, they had a shadow team of thirty trying to check the work of the formal engineering team.

Does that sound like a mess? It was a mess. Kevin ended up firing Sean anyway, and it took several years to unravel—years of precious time fixing issues rather than moving forward. Kevin could have saved himself a lot of time and money if he had fired Sean earlier.

The brutal truth about firing is that most often by the time you get around to firing someone you're probably months late. That means it's become apparent to multiple members of the team that the person isn't doing their job.

How You Know They Have to Go

There are a few different flavors of having to fire someone. One is when you have to part ways with someone pretty early, like maybe in a year or less. This means that you made a hiring mistake. You made the wrong hire, or didn't give them clear direction or set them up for success.

That's different from firing someone who over time hasn't grown with their role or the company. Someone you hired in the early days of your company, your first executives, may not be able to make the leap to their role inside of a larger environment. For example, maybe your VP of product was great at managing the team that was focused on one product, but he doesn't have the skills or experience to handle a larger team building multiple products.

Although this is uncomfortable, it's normal. Every eighteen or twenty-four months is a good time to do a sanity check: Are these the right executives for the company right now? Is anyone a gating factor? Has everyone grown?

If you have good systems to capture goals and track progress, they will tell you when you need to make a change. A retail company I worked with that specialized in children's clothes is a good example. The CEO hired a fantastic designer, Katrina, who produced wonderful, whimsical clothes that became very popular. The company did well and so did Katrina—she hired a few other designers, and they continued to produce great work. As the company grew and opened more stores and built out their online store, Katrina had to manage her small team and help them plan much further out. They had to deal with a more complicated workflow: navigating with the merchandising team to make sure their designs could be manufactured in time; working with the marketing team to get a more refined handle on what their customers wanted. Katrina was also a part of the leadership team where they talked about longer-term strategy, something she just didn't know much about or care about learning.

Markers soon appeared that things were not right. Her team missed deadlines. Merchandising couldn't make sure the clothes were done in the right time line. Her team got into serious conflict with other employees and each other, and she didn't know how to handle it. Other executives began to work around her, and a slight sense of awkwardness and tension descended on executive meetings, since nobody felt comfortable bringing this up to Katrina or to the CEO. The pace of growth slowed way down.

When you don't address situations like this because you don't quite see the root cause (and believe me, although it seems obvious as I lay it out for you here, when you're in the middle of it, it is far from clear) or you don't know what to do, the issue festers. As the CEO, you will probably get frustrated with your executive who is not performing and either seethe silently in resentment or blow up at her. Your other executives will definitely start wondering why you're not doing something about this. What you may not quite realize is that the underperforming executive herself will know she's not keeping up but not know how to solve these problems. You may have to part ways with her, but before you do that you should have a straight conversation with her.

BRIAN BERGER
Founder and CEO of Mack Weldon

I think about the first key person I had to fire. We needed somebody to focus on finance and operations, we needed somebody to do a lot of the complicated modeling and analytics that we needed for the business, but also to showcase to investors. And there was somebody who came up who really had an unusually ideal profile for what we were looking for and had a real familiarity with our business. And so on paper, he was really good. And there were aspects of him that were really awesome. But he was a really, really tough personality. And I didn't want to believe it, even though multiple people told me. My cofounder used to say all these "isms." And one of the things he would say is, "If there's doubt, then there is no doubt." And multiple references for this person indicated that there was doubt.

I thought, "It will be different this time. I'll be able to manage him." So we hired him. Anyway, long story short, he was exactly as advertised. Very competent in the technical and operational things that we needed him to do, but a cancer of the highest order to the small culture that we had at the time. And so I had to deal with firing him. Then I'm worried that he did our whole financial model. I hadn't been involved with it. How am I going to back-fill this? So I just had to get comfortable with the fact that no single person is ever really the only one. You always think that they're a really critical person, but if you can make the decision and have a plan to back up the areas that are going to be left alone, then it's always better to do that than to keep somebody around who isn't good for the organization. And there's never been a situation, by the way, ever, in the eight years of doing this, where that was not the right call. If you think somebody has to go, the sooner the better.

It's Not Easy to Tell Someone They're Not Doing Their Job. But That's Your Job

Very often, even when the CEO knows that there are problems, he doesn't quite know how to address them. He hopes the executive will figure things out. He wants to help her solve the problems. He dreads her defensiveness. He's afraid that if she leaves maybe her team will leave with her or maybe the company will lose some important institutional memory. He doesn't really want to hire some-one new, given all the other things he needs to do.

I get it. But there comes a time when you have to address these issues and the sooner you do the better. You'll need a plan to handle this. First try to assess if this person wants to do this job (will) and can develop himself to do the job (skill)—the framework we talked about in Chapter 3. Be honest with yourself about this, since it's going to form your performance conversation with your employee. Think about the things we talked about in hiring—what the job is exactly, what qualities it requires, and what specific goals you want this person to achieve. In some ways, this is like a hiring process—you're contemplating "rehiring" your executive and therefore resetting expectations. If you approach it that way, it gives you the freedom to think through what it's going to look like if the executive in this role is working better. Remember it's not about the person. It's about what the company needs. Talk to people who can give you fair observations of how she manages and interacts with other execu-tives. Think about how the person is going to respond before you have the conversation. What if she gets defensive? What if he honestly admits that he doesn't know what to do?

When you've prepared, you meet with your employee and give him feedback that is candid and compassionate. Share facts, not emotions. Don't say, "People aren't happy with you." Say things like, "The feed-back I'm hearing is that there's a lot of conflict on the team, and they don't see you stepping in to resolve it." Or "People see you as work-ing at a level of task, not of strategy." In Katrina's case, for instance, it was not an issue of her design sense—which was impeccable. It was about her lack of strong management of her team and her peers.

Especially in the first sit-down, ask the employee what he is think-ing; you want to know how work looks from his side. Tell him that you don't know if you have the whole picture and you need to gather the facts, but also let him know that there's a perception out there that there's a logjam in his department and perception is reality in these cases.

Give her some specific ways to improve: "Delegate more and manage at a higher level so that people know what to do." Or "Tell your team how you expect them to manage their conflict or get involved yourself to help them." Or "Sit down with your peers and listen to their concerns and let them know how you plan to address them." At this stage it's helpful to be prescriptive. Get specific about what you want to see done differently.

You might brainstorm with this person about how he can change to do what you and others need. Would a mentor or a coach be helpful? Do we need to have more frequent meetings? You may not want to have more meetings, but that's your job at the time with this person. Plan to have back-and-forth discussions—like everything else, it's a process.

Make sure that the person understands clearly this is urgent and what specific things they need to fix immediately. Make an agreement with them, and ask them to check in with you on progress at a certain point, a week, thirty days. (They check in with you, not the other way around. This is their issue to fix, not yours.) If they need help, you will get them help, but change is not optional. (There's a script for this conversation in the Sample Scripts at the end of the book.)

You do have a few options that don't include terminating your underperforming employee. If she is fantastic and open to growing but not at the job she has, there might be a better fit in your company. Or this person could do very well if she had a manager over her to provide the training and experience she needs. As long as you're legitimately bringing in a good manager, it's a great opportunity. You can say, "One of the great things about start-ups is that we can grow and change. We think you're great, but the company has reached the point where we need to bring in more experienced executives. What I'd like you to do is hire a more experienced executive to run your area, who you will be the right hand of, and who will teach you the things you need to know." I'll talk more about layering in Chapter 6.

These are great techniques for someone who has the will but not the skills to learn how to do his job. It's more problematic if he doesn't have the will. I should point out that I don't mean they're just lazy, since, after all, there aren't a lot of lazy people in a start-up.

I mean they don't see themselves as needing to be the kind of person who does the job they have.

I once worked with a CEO who had a very strategic head of product named Zak. In fact, Zak was so strategic that he couldn't get all that much done. He loved sitting at his computer and creating wonderful PowerPoints. His passion for the product and the company was off the charts. Everyone liked Zak and was in awe of his intellect, but they were also frustrated that he never got back to them on time and didn't share with them what he was working on. The product managers he was supposed to manage learned not to turn to him for help, and they became increasingly out of step with the efforts of the company because there was no executive coordinating their efforts with everyone else.

When the CEO finally had a conversation with Zak, there was already a lot of irritation around him. The CEO and he had a series of discussions that let both of them see that he could add a lot of value, but he was in the wrong role. The CEO hired a new head of product and moved Zak to a more creative and strategic role that didn't require so much coordination with other people. That did the trick to unblock the flow of work and let Zak's great energy and passion be channeled productively.

Sometimes people simply aren't inclined to do the work needed to do their job. I was talking to an employee inside of a fast-growing company who had been promoted to head of marketing. She was frustrated that the CEO wanted her to create a plan for product marketing, but that was not in her wheelhouse from her past marketing experiences. I found out that there was a two-day training coming up in a few weeks where she could learn some of the basics of product marketing. It wouldn't be a master's level or anything, but at least it would be a start. I was very excited about this opportunity for her! She kind of shrugged and said, "I don't really like going to conferences." So, in turn, I shrugged. I knew how this movie was going to end, and sure enough the CEO hired a new head of marketing within six months. If people don't have the will to learn how to do their jobs, there's not much you can do to help them.

How to Fire, Whom to Tell, and When

By the time you are ready to fire someone, it's probably too late. So you have to move quickly. Of course, you need courage. Remember that your decision is based on what the company needs. If the company needs someone new in that role then you really have an obligation to the company—and to the success of every single one of your employees—to tell this person it's time to part ways.

The specifics of how you do it depend on the person and the situation. Should you ask them to stay for a few months and transition, or should you insist that today be their last day? Should you give them severance and give them extra time to vest their options? Is there anything they were promised when they were hired in case they got fired? Make sure you decide all this in advance. Work out your plan before you actually do it, not only about what you are going to say but what happens before and what happens after. If there's a contract involved, be sure you know what its terms are. (There's a script for firing your friend in the Sample Scripts at the end of the book.)

There's no way to do it painlessly. Don't pretend that it's not dispiriting and awkward and painful. You have to make peace with that before you do it. On the bright side, let's be honest, it will be liberating. If you've been spending extra hours trying to make a situation work but it just doesn't, at least you'll know that it will be something of a fresh start. Whatever happens, it deserves a moment of reflection.

As with all things, the effects are not limited to you and your departing employee, and you've got a series of decisions to make. Should you tell the executive's peers before or after you do it? In fact, should you get their opinion or buy-in, or is that inappropriate, since they are peers? When should you tell the person's direct reports? Should you make a company announcement? Sometimes one person's departure makes a reorganization possible, or if not a reorganization, a redistribution of work.

Every case is different, but in general, you should tell your inner circle on the executive team so that they can be ready to tell their teams. Get your HR person involved if you haven't already. There may be one or two trusted executives you want to discuss this with to make sure you're not crazy and to get their take on how their peers and the rest of the company will react to it. You can tell their direct reports afterward, or you can give her a choice to do so. You should tell the whole company either by email or in the next all-hands meeting. You can also call a quick sync—please don't call it "an emergency all-hands" (I'm speaking from experience here)—depending on how large you are.

If your company is notable enough that the press is involved, have an external communication plan. Let people know what happens next—who will take over as an interim person, or who the new executive will be or when she is taking over. Remember that this is a normal part of your company's growth. New people will come and old people will go, and the company will change and evolve. Sometimes dramatically. Take a long view, and see this as one in a series of actions that you take on the way to victory. (There's a script for firing an executive in the Sample Scripts at the end of the book and another for delivering bad news at an all-hands meeting.)

When You Have to Live Without the One You Can't Live Without

The text came in at noon. "Arnold quit. Talk to you at 2. I'll be drinking scotch." Uh-oh. Arnold was Sara's CTO. He was leading a massive rebuild and had only been with the company ten months. Sara had spent a lot of time coaching him to get him settled in and connected to the team. I knew that she felt betrayed and put upon: it's not easy to hire a new CTO.

It's painful, it's frustrating, it's maddening, and it's inevitable. At some point in your company's growth the one person you can't live without will resign. You will get emotional. But you will get through it. The key is this: have your emotions, but don't let them have you. When you make your choices, make sure they are business decisions, not emotional decisions.

When we met, Sara was indeed drinking scotch. "I don't want to be like 'after all I've done for him' but dammit, after all I've done for him! I spent hours working through his conflict with the product folks. I let him hire all the people he wanted. I had him over to dinner. I honestly can't believe this."

I let her vent. CEOs have nobody else to talk to. Sitting with them as they vent is part of my job. Then I suggested she focus on the mechanics. "It's a math problem," I told Sara. "What's on his plate? How much time does he need to resolve all of this? Whom can he transition things to? Count up those hours and figure out what time line you need from him. And then let's get the search going."

People often ask me, "Is it better to have someone finish up quickly and move on, or is it better to have them complete as much of their work as they can?" The answer is, it depends. How much do you trust them? Do you have a good relationship with them? How likely are they to operate at a high level even as they're walking out the door? What is the mission-critical nature of their projects? Is there a successor in house, either interim or long-term?

At that moment, Sara was raw and angry and needed to process, but eventually I helped her see that Arnold leaving, even in the middle of a major project, gave her an opportunity. Instead of blowing a hole in the company, Arnold was opening a door. In her heart she'd had concerns about the way Arnold was managing the team, and it cost her a lot to keep smoothing over his relationships with the other executives. Also the company had grown and changed in the ten months since Arnold had joined. His resignation gave her a moment to reflect on the profile of a new person who would lead the tech team in a better direction. Which she ultimately did.

Again and again, I've had founders come to me and say, "So-and-so just quit," in a tone of voice that suggests the world is about to end. Again and again, the world has failed to end. And often, it's had a new beginning.

Downsizing with Dignity

There's no good way to soften the blow of a layoff. At the end of the day, people don't have a job and it sucks. Just accept that. It's tremendously hard on the people who are leaving. It's hard on you, the CEO, and it's hard on your executives who will have to make the granular decisions about who will be laid off.

People say that a layoff can be productive because it helps you take care of your performance problems, but that's not a great way to do performance management (which we will cover more in Chapter 6). You should have taken care of those problems before you have to lay people off anyway. However, it's true that your business almost always runs better after a layoff because it's tighter. You probably weren't rigorously careful about hiring to your needs before the layoff, and in the same way that hiring can slow a business down, reducing staff can make it move more efficiently.

Before you do your layoffs, don't forget to consult with your attorney—this is one of the times that legal advice is critical. Then, remember that you have to manage the people who are staying. They will be upset because their friends are leaving, and they will be nervous that they could be next. You, the CEO, need to talk to your managers, figure out who on the remaining team is at risk and who's not, who needs more encouragement, and who needs to get more onboard. Remind everyone of the big picture.

How you deliver the news is crucial. Founders have to say that they are focused on the health and welfare of their people, their customers, and their business, and the layoff helps ensure the welfare of those customers and that business, unfortunate as it is. Here is a script you can use and adapt to your needs:

> This is not easy news to share, but I need to let you know that we parted ways with [a specific number] of coworkers today.
>
> Here's the background: in order to be financially responsible, we had to take a look at our expenses. Because of the uncertainty ahead of us, we needed to make the difficult decision to lay these people off. I want to stress a few things:
> - We are done with layoffs so don't worry about your own jobs.
> - I have thanked every single one of them for their work with us—they have helped us get where we are today.
> - They did nothing wrong and we are parting ways because, unfortunately, we need to do a reduction in force in these areas.

- We have mechanisms in place to help them find new jobs, and we will do everything we can to help them. I am personally putting them in touch with my network and am reaching out to friends for them.
- Please feel comfortable getting in touch with them and offer to help them. They are part of our extended family, and you don't have to feel weird about being in touch.

[If appropriate] We are reducing emphasis in this area but, as we talked about in our company strategy meeting, we are increasing our focus in a different area. So it may sound strange, but I want to be up front with you that we may hire people with different skills. I don't want anyone to be surprised by this.

As the CEO it pains me massively to do this. It just sucks. I wouldn't do it if I weren't 100% certain that it was necessary for us to achieve what we hope to accomplish. So I didn't want to leave this meeting without sharing what I see in store for us and why even despite this difficult moment I am so positive about the future. [Share some thoughts about the strategy, the vision, the plan, why you see a bright future.]

If you have any questions about this, talk to your manager or I'm always available to talk to.

(There's a script for announcing layoffs in the Sample Scripts at the end of the book.)

Have your executives and manager meet with their teams either in a group or in one-on-ones right after to check in, express empathy, and see how they are feeling.

You can't build a company without employees, and when you have employees, you need mechanisms for hiring, firing, onboarding, and everything else. You may not have given this too much thought before you started your company, but you'll have to get up to speed pretty quickly. To be honest I hope your start-up is so successful that you'll need to deal with the issues of fast-paced hiring as you scale. To integrate all this smoothly, you'll need to take a new look at structure and the way people manage, which is what we'll cover in Chapter 6.

TAKEAWAYS

- Before you hire, identify the specific job you need done.

- Get specific evidence that candidates have those skills and experience.

- Hire for values as well as skills.

- In onboarding, make clear what you expect of your new team member and emphasize quick wins so your new person gains early traction.

- When you identify issues with someone, address them as soon as possible.

- Terminations and layoffs are really hard. You will get through them.

REFLECTIVE QUESTIONS

- For your next hire: What are the values and specific skills you need to test for? How will you test for them?

- Have you thought about the social and tactical needs for onboarding someone?

- Have you defined some quick wins for your new hire? Remember that quick wins look different to different constituencies.

- Are there people on the team you can say you would not hire again? Why not? And why are they still with you?

Endnote

[1] Wasserman, N (2008) The founder's dilemma, *Harvard Business Review*, https://hbr.org/2008/02/the-founders-dilemma (archived at https://perma.cc/M32Q-UG8K)

PART THREE

Managing the Company

06

Growing and Growing Up

Reflective Question: Have you worked with your managers to help them manage better?

Congratulations, your company is growing. You've gone from start-up to scale-up. You've followed the advice in this book, so you're managing your psychology and have integrated healthy habits. You're serious about creating psychological safety and an intentional culture. And it's all working! You've got more customers, more business, more funding. You've also got more people. You're way past hiring your friends and turning more and more to experienced people who have done this before. Hiring is still a headache. Some of the first people you brought in—the OG (the old guard, or as some say, the Original Gangsters)—are managers, but you have the sense that they're struggling. Some of the early employees who aren't managers are clamoring for promotions. You don't think they're ready for it, but since you don't have a formal feedback and appraisal process set up, it's hard to have a rational conversation with them. People are also asking for more company kinds of things, like a better health plan, a career path, and, surprisingly, performance reviews.

You've hit the bend in the road where you have staff and need somebody to take care of the staff. It's time to step back and reflect about where you're going and how to get there—again. In this chapter, I'll tell you why you need a Head of People to help and what that person should do. I'll talk about what your managers should be doing and how you can help get them there, coaching with useful performance feedback and appraisals, and providing career development. I'll emphasize why and how your people should cascade information up and down the ladder, and the need for clear goals and productive accountability.

Getting the Right People Person

The good and the bad of joining an early-stage start-up is that everyone is kind of making things up as they go. There is something exhilarating about that! And super creative—fresh eyes and energy can achieve remarkable things! And it begins to work. You create your proof of concept or your minimum viable product (MVP). You get some customers and achieve your targets. Things go well and the company gets another round of funding, or, as I often tell the CEOs I coach, you earn the right to play again. Success is never a destination; it's always just a leg of the journey.

Now you have fifty or sixty people—way too many for you to manage personally. People need roles and goals. They need managers to teach them, coach them, unblock obstacles, coordinate their work, and help them prioritize. You need managers to share the bigger picture with them and to reinforce your messages about direction and purpose. But you may be suspicious of how valuable management really is. The company needs structure, but you probably don't know how to build structure. And as a founder you may be allergic to structure (what is this, IBM?).

This is where it often starts to get messy. Many CEOs get the office manager to assume the role of Head of People. In fact she—nine times out of ten it's a she—may have taken the job of office manager as a way to get her foot in the door to something else. She has a great personality, she likes people, everybody likes her, and they get in the habit of telling her all their problems. It seems like a perfect fit!

At this point the CEO isn't thinking of either HR or management as jobs that require specific talents and experience or training. The managers don't know how to manage. They may be too lenient, conflict-averse, or soft and don't address deadlines and issues inside of their teams constructively. Or they are too tyrannical, power-hungry, or rigid and bully their people or force them to work around their mood swings. Things play out fairly predictably from here. In both cases employees shut down, gossip among themselves, or quit. Work slows down, people are confused, and deadlines get missed. One dramatic example of this was a CEO I worked with who was ambushed by his team—he went out to grab an iced coffee, and five people on his team followed him. Standing right outside the office door, they aired their grievances to him about the way things were working in the company.

At the same time, the former office manager turned inexperienced HR manager has challenges. She doesn't focus on building HR processes like performance management, career ladders, and trainings. She's not thinking about instituting a 401(k) plan. She wants to work on the softer and more fun stuff such as culture, one-on-one chats, and engagement surveys. And who can blame her? She's doing her best and doesn't have anyone to teach her.

The lack of HR tools and processes hits home as people demand more feedback and an understanding of where they are and their career path. That means they need training, another growing gap.

Your new HR manager is hearing everyone's complaints, but she's not experienced enough to redirect them or take what they say in context. Well-meaning, she feels she has to fix everyone's problem by serving as a go-between or advocating for promotion for them. With all this chatter, she grows increasingly concerned and spun up. She comes to you to tell you her take on what's going on and her conclusion: everyone is going to quit. Here is that nightmare again—you, sitting alone in a conference room with your laptop. So you get spun up too.

This is avoidable. You have to realize that you're building a business. The business needs goals, hierarchy, and coordination of various parts. You'll need a system to handle all that, and you'll need management capacity—trained managers and a reasonably capable HR person—to operate that system. You need to get organized.

Structure Is Sexy

Many founders start their companies with idealistic visions of what company life will be. A lot of the founders I've coached have been inspired by well-publicized examples like the Netflix culture deck or the idea of "holocracy" at Zappos. If you want to experiment with various leadership practices, go right ahead. I genuinely think it's helpful to be a bit skeptical about conventional management practices, since they get passed down in a confused, nonsensical, corrupted way. As you investigate these practices, you and your team will certainly learn something, and—who knows?—you may invent a new system of leading. You'll probably reject things that make no sense and adopt practices that will work for you. You'll absorb the nuances and subtleties of managing people, and I guarantee you this inquiry will make you a better leader and manager.

However, this I know: at some point you're going to have to create structure to get all these folks working together. And structure requires—like it or not—hierarchy. You (hopefully along with a few of your wise leaders) need to assign employees to rational and manageable teams. Spotify called them "squads, tribes, and guilds." Hubspot's sales team is organized into "pods." My clients have implemented "tiger teams," "e-teams," and "bands." You can adopt these concepts or find your own organizing principle. Once you figure it out, the org chart is where you formalize it.

The point of an org chart is not for some bean counter to be able to check the box. It's actually more for the employees than the manager. They want clarity about what they are supposed to do and who to go to if they have questions or something getting in their way. Emotionally, employees want to feel like they have a home, that they are part of a small tribe. That's what teams, squads, and pods give people.

Once you have all that set up, people want to be managed, not in a toxic, dictatorial way but in a way that helps them be their best. Your managers should play a part in creating the environment of psychological safety that we discussed in Chapter 3. People often think it's HR's job to manage everyone, but it's really on the manager herself to take responsibility for her people. You as the CEO can and should lean on the managers and also HR. The two work together to create a strong system of management inside of your company.

What's a Manager to Do?

To say that managers manage may be accurate but not helpful. Your managers need guidance about their job as manager, especially young managers who have never done this before. I once worked with a company in which the young, newly promoted engineering manager didn't give any work to his employees at all—he just couldn't bring himself to delegate and didn't know how to set deadlines. For months he stayed in the office until 10 p.m. doing almost everything himself, while his team hung around until 5 with very little to do.

Your HR person (especially if you hire the office manager) may not know how to help, and she herself may think it's her job to manage, not quite understanding that her job is to help the managers do the components of management as a part of their jobs.

So step one for managers is to realize that they have to undergo a big shift in mindset in how they get satisfaction. When you're an individual contributor you get your satisfaction from getting things done: finishing a project, solving a hard problem, launching the website, whatever it is. When you're a manager, your fulfillment comes from getting results through others. They are the ones who do the work. You, as the manager, coordinate the work. When you're an individual contributor you get work done. When you're a manager you create the conditions for others to get their work done. It's a big difference.

New managers often find this challenging. They are used to getting the high of completing things themselves, and they're probably good at it, but that strength doesn't always translate to helping others get work done. Designing the website or coding your part of the platform is completely different from coordinating the efforts of a small team and answering their questions. Not only that, new managers (and even seasoned managers) feel like they don't have as much to do because they're not doing the work themselves. So they feel guilty or insecure, and that might cause them to meddle in the work of their employees.

When managers don't understand their roles and don't know how to do them, they can easily descend into toxic managers (see Chapter 4 about toxic culture). They swoop in, micromanage and don't delegate. This is annoying and completely disempowering to capable employees. Or the manager feels competitive with their employees, and then there is an underlying fight for credit. Or they feel like they have status and power, and sometimes this triggers bullying. That is unacceptable, and if that's happening inside of your company you must root it out and put an end to it.

What your managers should be doing while letting their people do their jobs is building cross-functional relationships with their peer managers to make sure process and turf issues between the teams get solved. They need to be available to unblock obstacles for their employees, coach them, give them feedback (sometimes in a super-supportive way and sometimes in a tough-love kind of way), hold them accountable, and other managerial things. That requires an interpersonal dexterity that takes time and effort to develop. In other words: all roads lead to manager training.

At some point you will certainly start hiring more experienced managers, but until then, you have to (1) promote people inside your company with natural instincts for managing and (2) help them learn how to be great managers. As you'll see, your HR person has a role to play here as well. But let's start with the core skills you should discuss with your managers. These are: role modeling, cascading information, coaching, giving feedback, helping with career development, and goal setting and accountability.

Your Managers' Job 1: Modeling Behavior

I've emphasized that you, as the founder and CEO, are under surveillance. Guess what—so are your managers. Their stage may not be as big as yours, but there is no time like the present to get them adjusted to the fact that being a manager requires more intention and attention than being an individual contributor. Think about it—on Friday they are one of the gang and suddenly on Monday they are the boss. But they're the same person and so are their former peers. That's quite a change!

So they need some advice on how to handle this. They have plenty to learn (training!), but in general the starting point goes back to the mind shift. They need to realize that they are the manager now. Sure, they may still go out to a bar with the team, but when they do, their job now is to make sure everyone on their team is included (remember that people want a home). They also need to keep their behavior in the bar under control and remember that this is actually a work event and they are the manager. People are watching them, and they set the standard of behavior. That may feel weird to them at first, that they aren't being authentic. Then you can discuss what it means to be "real" inside of playing a "role." (See Chapter 1 about authenticity.)

Obviously this goes double for behavior inside of the office. If they are moody, remind them that they need to be upbeat and positive at work if they want to get the best from their people. If there are messages that you the CEO want to make sure everyone hears, their job is to embrace the company message overall, not just the bits and pieces that resonate personally with them. Managers have to own the decisions the company makes, which can be hard to get used to. You should definitely bring the managers together in a meeting regularly to help update them on the bigger picture and see where you and the leadership team are heading. If they want to have input or just complain, they can do that in that kind of meeting. But in the end their job is to think about things increasingly from a company point of view. If they simply don't want to do this, they may not be manager material, and that's important for both you and them to come to terms with.

When I started working with Mikael, the CEO of a media start-up based in Stockholm, he was struggling with a long-time employee, Gus. Gus had been promoted into the role of VP product. Now he was managing his former peers. Gus had a lot of great ideas about product and definitely got the overall vision. As a member of the OG he had plenty of great relationships. But the very first conversation I had with Mikael was about Gus. Gus could be moody. Gus went out for drinks with his team, but only the ones he liked, and then would openly joke about the ones he didn't like. And when Gus didn't agree with a decision that Mikael and the other leaders made, he would tell his team, "Listen, I don't like it either, but I got outvoted."

It didn't take me all that long to help Mikael diagnose this lack of management skills. After Mikael had a straight conversation with Gus about the role of a manager, after Gus tried to explain to Mikael why he was wrong, and after they had some additional chats, Gus and Mikael agreed to disagree and part ways. Sometimes that happens, and when it does, you'll find it will be a relief to your employees and most of all to you.

When you promote someone to manage former peers, they'll probably need help addressing this with their former peers. It's awkward, right? Here's a little script you can give your new managers to help them address this with their peers.

> Listen, I know you heard from the CEO that I'm now going to be running engineering and thanks for the email you sent congratulating me about this. I'm really looking forward to helping us continue to move in the right direction.
>
> I thought I would just talk through what this means with everyone and also get advice from each of you. First of all it might be a little awkward that suddenly I'm your manager, so let's try to get past that. I don't want to be all bossy with you, which would be weird anyway. I do see my role as setting direction, with your input; coordinating the work of the team; unblocking obstacles and communicating our issues to others if necessary; and making sure that the CEO and the leaders take us into account when making decisions.
>
> Let's face it—I'm a new manager and I have a lot to learn. I will try to learn quickly, and I hope you'll help me by giving me honest feedback. I also hope you'll cut me some slack when I make mistakes, which I know I will.
>
> Now, I'd love to hear your suggestions so I know what you think. I may not take all your advice, but I'd like to know what it is. What are

a few things you'd like me to do pretty quickly and a few things you want to make sure I don't do? And is there anything I can do to make your job easier or better right now?

Your new managers can and should adapt this to their own situation, but having a context and structure to address it will help them set up the right environment for success. (There's a further discussion and script for career development in the Sample Scripts at the end of the book.)

Your Managers' Job 2: Spreading the Word

When your company is small, you manage everyone yourself. When you have something to tell people you just swivel around in your chair and say it. It's easy to stay in sync. But when the company gets bigger, it's much harder to stay on the same page. Communication has to be intentional. You have to let people know what's going on. For you the CEO, that's about pulling your people together so that they're making sure that all of their people are pulling in the same direction.

How can you manage people you don't have that much direct contact with? Bring your executive team in for regular meetings. (We'll talk more about the executive team meeting in Chapter 7.) Update them about the company, talk about the company's dashboard, whether you're meeting goals, and if you're thinking about changing anything or iterating the strategy. Have them update each other—social game developer Zynga used to have two leadership meetings per week, one with the CEO to talk about ideas and strategy and one without the CEO so that managers could get on the same page about what they and their teams were doing.

In the leadership team meeting, decide together the message that you want the whole company to hear. If you've been working night and day for a launch, it might be, "We've been working hard for six weeks, and we should acknowledge the team's extra work during this intense time. We'll definitely give you time off, and we appreciate your sacrifice." Or it might be, "We're going to expedite our new feature to have it in time for the fall, so it needs to be ready by July rather than next September." Or it could be something like, "We're going to send out a culture survey, so give people a heads-up and encourage them that we care what they think." Make sure they know that it's part of their job to make sure their people hear these messages.

One of the key roles of this leadership team is to cascade information up and down. The leaders relay the message back to their people—in groups and in one-on-one meetings, in the hall, and over coffee. They share and reinforce key messages and then listen to their people. If only one person objects to something, he may be an outlier. But suppose a lot of people say, "We can't do that, we've got too many things on our plate," or "We don't have enough people to do that, and we can't hire enough people in time." Then that executive can relay that back to the executive team: "I told my people about this, and they really pushed back, said they needed more help. Is anybody else hearing that?" Other leaders might say, "Yes, we're hearing the same," or "No, but if your team needs help, you can use some resources from our team."

There could be a real problem, one that nobody was aware of, that gets cascaded back up to the executive team. Or an issue that's built up under the radar for a while—maybe everyone is complaining that it's the sixth time you've changed the feature requirements in the last three months. And when that comes back to the executive meeting, the CMO might say that his people are really tired of rewriting the website, and the head of sales agrees that the sales team is confused and that some of his people have heard from customers that they aren't sure that you know what you're doing.

The meeting then becomes useful in fundamental ways instead of being just a flow-through pipe. The leaders can look at the problem all together and see that the project was more difficult than everyone thought or that a few little drifts have led to more change than people can easily take on. The CEO knows what people are thinking and she'll address the topics that are on everyone's mind at an all-hands. Information flows up and down the ladder, and everyone knows what's going on, people feel like they are part of the process, and the company can react with a real understanding of what needs to be done.

Sadly, this is often neglected. I was once in a meeting with a CEO and her team. It was clear that people were not on the same page, which was strange because the CEO and I had talked about the need to communicate to everyone. I asked her if she let everyone know what was important to her and she said, "Yes, I sent everyone a Slack."

She is not alone. CEOs often don't realize that they have to communicate, and they have to do it *all the time*. They need to tell people they need to communicate "in small groups, in large groups, in all-hands, in one-on-ones, over email, over Slack, informally, formally." I say it a little bit sing-songy—I can be quirky like that sometimes. When my clients (and my poor friends who are the recipients of gratuitous coaching from me) repeat it back to me in the same exact sing-songy way, I know they've gotten the message. It's the same for you: you probably aren't really being heard until you're sick of hearing yourself say the same thing. When you hear them making jokes about what you say and how you say it, or when they say it to you before you say it to them, then you really know that they've heard you.

It's not a democracy. It's not management by consensus. But people have to understand and buy into what's going on, and when you have a common theme of something not working, you should pay attention. And sharing information with people, building rapport and trust, and giving them the big picture and context means they're a lot more likely to go through walls for you.

Your Managers' Job 3: Coaching

As a coach myself, I'm biased. But I also know the power of coaching and how it helps people grow. Just think about yourself: Who in your life has been a coach, a mentor, or a loving critic and how has the person helped you grow? That's a great question for your new managers, by the way, and a great model for them to use when they are approaching their employees. A great manager is a great coach. You should coach your leaders, and you should expect them to coach their people.

A couple of things get in the way: (1) they lack experience, so they don't have the confidence or skills to do it, and (2) they are managing people who are older than they are (maybe even more experienced), which further eats away at their confidence.

All roads lead to training (have I already told you that?), but you can help them gain confidence in their role as coach: coach them yourself on this topic. So here is a super-light crash course on coaching.

The most important part of coaching is to create a strong relationship with your employees. Get to know them, appreciate them, and let them know that you're on their side. This is the power of chit-chat: you create a bit of a bond when you shoot the breeze with your folks, ask them how their weekends were, follow up about something they were upset about, praise them. You get to know them better, and they feel that you care about them. That sets you up for everything you need to do as a manager, including coaching.

There are many tools of coaching and many ways to coach, but I think people benefit from structure, so I'll share with you here the GROW model first developed in the 1980s by business coaches Graham Alexander, Alan Fine, and Sir John Whitmore. I like the GROW model because the heart of it is asking open-ended questions. That's great for you and your managers because it frames your coaching role as a facilitator, not an expert. That means you can help your employees explore ideas and get to solutions without knowing all that much about their functional areas. Briefly GROW stands for:

- Goal—what do you want to have happen?
- Reality—what's the present state?
- Options—what are some things to try?
- Will or Way Forward—what should you do?

A big part of coaching is asking open-ended questions, which helps people see a bigger picture and triggers them to think more deeply. So you can use this framework to structure your questions. Here is a very short list of great coaching questions:

- What's the goal? What do you want the outcome to be?
- What have you already tried?
- What are some of the things that you see in the way?
- How could you resolve those obstacles?
- What are your options?
- What are you afraid of or concerned about?
- What advice would you give a friend about this situation?
- What is your next step?
- How can I be helpful?

Your Managers' Job 4: Giving Feedback

Feedback is different from coaching because it's more focused on offering observations and getting someone to see how they are coming across—whether it's how they intend it or not.

You often want the employee to use the feedback to make changes, but that said, we often only think of feedback as "constructive"—as in "cut it out and shape up." So I want to remind you that positive feedback—also known as praise—is super-important. (We talked about this in Chapter 3.) Your real power as a manager comes from people wanting to follow you and wanting that in part because they see you care about them, and a simple way to care about them is to point out all things they are doing right.

For example, one of the CEOs I work with learned that he needed to say things like "I can tell that your team loves you, and I know you've worked on that—great job" to his vice president of sales. To his vice president of marketing, he'd say, "I appreciate that you bring creative solutions, and also you are very operational when it comes to executing them. That combination of skills is very valuable." You don't have to wait for someone to win the Academy Award—just point out a few things they're doing well. Your managers can and should learn to say the same kinds of things to their people.

A reminder: the other benefit of positive feedback is that by definition it means people don't only hear about problems. When your managers (and you) get in the habit of giving people positive feedback, you build up a sense of good feeling. Who doesn't want to be praised? Who doesn't want to hear about the good things they are doing? When there's a reservoir of that good feeling—I like to call this a balance in the emotional bank account—you can draw on that when you give constructive feedback, which you inevitably will have to do.

I think the word "constructive" is more accurate than "negative" because you are truly bringing it up to make them better—not to insult them, not to demoralize them. You are giving them candid input plus the willingness to work with them to fix issues. All of us need that kind of attention to get better—to show us our blind spots and to give us new ways of approaching things. How do we learn without feedback?

ALEXA VON TOBEL

Founder and CEO of LearnVest and Founder and Managing Partner of Inspired Capital

In your normal life, very few people give you feedback. Very few people take the time to say, "Hey, what you just did is ridiculous." Or "The way you're doing that makes people feel this way." You have a few very close best friends, or spouse, or family members who will happily give you feedback all day long, but in your working life, not everybody feels that they have the emotional space to do that.

So one other thing that I started thinking about is feedback really is a gift. When people give you feedback, they are doing the harder thing by telling you these things. It's not mean. They're actually doing something that's really, really kind to you because they're telling you something that you should know so that you can get better. I genuinely believe that feedback is a gift.

Many managers are squeamish about giving constructive feedback because they don't know how. They put it off until the person keeps doing the thing over and over, and then the manager explodes. Or when they give feedback their employee gets defensive, they have a very bad conversation, and the manager learns yet again that giving feedback is really unpleasant. The answer: training. For everyone. Both in how to give and how to respond to feedback. In the meantime, here is a model I created to help you and your managers structure your feedback. It's called the COIN model—think about it as a way to give you currency with your people. The letters stand for:

- Context—this is the context, like "during the meeting" or "while you were working on the website redesign."

- Observation—this is the fact-based observation. For example: "During the meeting I saw you sit back, fold your arms, and look down." Or "While you were working on the website redesign, you were supposed to make sure you got input from the other teams, but as far as I know you didn't."

- Impact—this is the impact of the behavior. "During the meeting I saw you sit back, fold your arms, and look down. It made me think you were shutting down and tuning the rest of us out. I'm not sure if you noticed, but after that we stopped having constructive dialogue because people seemed wary of your body language and so we didn't get to a great decision." Or "While you were working on the website redesign, you were supposed to make sure you got input from the other teams, but as far as I know you didn't. That means that you are about to put up a website for our entire company that not everyone is bought into, and in fact people may not agree with or know about that content. That means that we are risking issues with our internal team, and we are also risking sending out misinformation to our customers."

- Next step—this is either a suggestion from you or, even better, a suggestion from them about what they should do.

So here we go, the complete feedback example:

> During the meeting I saw you sit back, fold your arms, and look down. It made me think you were shutting down and tuning the rest of us out. I'm not sure if you noticed, but after that we stopped having constructive dialogue because people seemed wary of your body

language and so we didn't get to a great decision. In the future I'd ask you to check in with yourself when you're feeling frustrated in meetings and constructively share your concerns so we can address them, rather than shutting down.

Or:

While you were working on the website redesign you were supposed to make sure you got input from the other teams, but as far as I know you didn't. That means that you are about to put up a website for our entire company that not everyone is bought into, and in fact people may not agree with or know about that content. That means that we are risking issues with our internal team, and we are also risking sending out misinformation to our customers. What do you think you should do now to correct this and in the future to make sure it doesn't happen again?

Even if you have executed the model flawlessly, here is the truth about people: they may get defensive. They may cry. Be prepared for that and stay calm. Here are some little speeches.

To a defensive employee: "I didn't mean to insult you or make you feel bad; trust me, that is the last thing I want to do. I would only share these kinds of topics with you because I know how great you are, and I want you to have the opportunity to improve. I know that I've personally benefited because someone gave me some hard truths over the years. If we need to stop this meeting and revisit this topic, that's fine. Do you want some time to go away and digest what I've said, and we can discuss it again next week?"

The version for an employee who gets teary is essentially the same, but I mention it because many people are very uncomfortable with tears. Men especially get uncomfortable when a woman cries. You can handle it. Use the script. This one starts by recognizing that the employee's tears are a perfectly human response that deserves consideration. They are not a ploy or a diversion. So it begins, "I didn't mean to upset you, and if you need a minute I understand. The last thing I want to do is make you feel bad!" and continues the same as the previous one.

I was working with an executive team of a biotech company, and one of the leaders pulled me aside. She was very frustrated about one of her managers. "I gave him the feedback," she told me, as if that was the end of her job. Feedback is never about the feedback itself. It's about the behavior change that comes with feedback, and that means that at the end of the feedback discussion you need to get a commitment from your employees about specific changes they will make and when you will assess the results. (That's the "next step" in the COIN model.) "What are you going to do differently?" and "When should we have a follow-up conversation to check in about this topic?" are great questions to ask at the end of a feedback discussion. That will make the conversation you just had more tangible to them, and the new behavior will begin to take root. Helping them think about the problem is fine, but it's even more powerful to help them to the solution.

Your Managers' Job 5: Helping Employees Grow

When you are an individual contributor, you have to focus on growing yourself. When you become a leader, you have to focus on growing others.

If your managers embrace their role of helping their employees develop, your company culture will take a gigantic step forward no matter what. This is often a completely missing piece in start-ups. Which makes sense. In the early days the mission of your start-up is front and center. Nobody is thinking about career development. As you begin to add more hierarchy, you tend to have first-time managers who simply don't know that this is part of their job. The work itself is nonstop, so nobody takes time to do the important but not urgent work of planning out where employees want to go. Inexperienced managers worry they won't be able to promise the employee the new role or even know how to help them get there, so it doesn't even seem like a useful path to pursue.

CHIP CONLEY

Founder of Joie de Vivre, Strategic Advisor to Airbnb, and author of
Peak: How great companies get their mojo from Maslow[1]

Personal development and corporate development ideally are on parallel paths. And if you create an environment where people are developing themselves as humans, you create not just better humans but better leaders and better people in a company. So [at Joie de Vivre] we created something called Joie de Vivre University, and our requirement was that half the classes had to be personal development classes. Lifestyle enhancement classes. And half were specific to work. It was really the epitome of *Peak*. *Peak*'s model is basically taking Maslow's hierarchy of needs and applying them to employees, customers, and investors. So, in essence, at the core of that book, and of my leadership philosophy, is that understanding the hierarchy of needs for anybody is an important talent of a leader and understanding that at the bottom of the pyramid are the commodities, the tangible commodities, but what's at the peak of the pyramid is where the gold is.

I understand. However, as you begin to put people into manager roles, make sure they know that a key part of their job is to help their employees grow and develop their careers. It's not that complicated. They can schedule a discussion with their employees a few times a year exclusively to focus on career development. Here is a little script they can use with their employees:

> I think that part of my job as your manager is to help you develop your career, so I want to talk with you about what your career aspirations are. You may not fully know what they are, and that's OK. And honestly, we're still a growing company, so we may not be able to accommodate what you want immediately. However, I'd love to at least get you thinking about what you want and where you want to go and then be on the lookout for opportunities to help you get the right job assignments, training, and mentoring to get there. Let's plan to have this discussion a few times a year so we stay synced up on this. It's easy in the busy day-to-day of work life to put this off, but I want you to know that your career is important, and we will make time for it.

First of all, has anyone said that to you? Probably not. Can you imagine how an employee on the receiving end of this speech feels? Hopefully pretty cared for and pretty seen. That's almost the most important part of this process anyway.

After that setup, the manager's job is to listen, ask questions, and think with their employee about creative solutions. I remember a discussion I had with Paula, a new manager at a start-up that was just taking off. Paula was managing a group she knew a lot about—marketing—and a group she knew very little about—product management. Her employee, Sanjay, was proactive and ambitious and wanted to build a career in product management. Paula was concerned she couldn't help since she didn't have any background, but we quickly saw that Paula had a lot of tools. She could introduce Sanjay to more senior product managers in her network who might be able to mentor him. She could encourage him to investigate training opportunities and join a peer community of product managers. And she could be on the lookout for him to present to the all-hands meeting so he could get the experience of presenting and the exposure to the rest of the company. That's a great example of a manager helping her employee with career development even outside of her area of expertise.

Your Managers' Job 6: Setting Goals and Accountability

I put this one last because everyone thinks of it first. Helping your people set and reach goals is certainly the work of management! And holding people accountable is essential. In Chapter 3 we talked about your role of setting clear expectations and having follow-up conversations to make sure you build a culture of saying what you mean and meaning what you say. (In Chapter 7 I'll talk about one of the popular tools start-ups use to do this: objectives and key results [OKRs].)

Just like you, your managers should help set clear goals and help people stay on track with good accountability conversations. But also just like you, if your managers just do this without all the warm-up I laid out above, they'll be less likely to win the hearts and minds of people when they begin to get into the real discussions of goals and accountability, which can at times be tense and frustrating, especially in the heat of start-ups. When they focus on the big picture and the right tools of management, your managers will have earned the right to set goals and hold people accountable for reaching them in ways that motivate them.

So Why Do You Need HR?

You might think that if all those things are the managers' jobs, why do I need a Head of People? Well, let's talk about it. People make fun of HR (getting HR right is an entirely different book), but there are some incredible human resources professionals I've met who really get it. Carl, for example, was an HR leader I coached when he moved from a large bank to a small blockchain start-up. Carl was wise, thoughtful, and structured. We worked together to help him adjust his style to what he called "the Wild West" of a start-up that was also experimenting with decentralized management. He quickly found ways to be influential to the CEO and other key leaders, and he was one of the driving forces in the company scaling from 400 to 2,000 employees in two years. How did he do it? Well, he focused on the key things a great HR leader does, which I'm about to tell you.

HR's Job 1: Training

Have I already mentioned training? It's surprising to me that start-ups focus so little on training. They have this incredible resource of eager-beaver, smart talent but they don't give them training to point them in the right direction.

Your Head of People should take charge of training. That's why you need to hire someone who is experienced enough to recognize this gap and effective enough to advocate for it convincingly to people who may not see the need, including you.

Your managers need training to help them develop and hone the skills I talked about. "Training," however, does not always have to take place in a formal setting. It might include some skills sessions as well as some talks from guest speakers you bring in. Your managers can find training videos online, which they can watch on their own, or during monthly group meetings they can self-organize to talk through management challenges. Your employees need internal training on the company's values, strategy, and vision. That could come with a regular fireside chat that you do.

One CEO I work with was disturbed that in a company survey, people were clamoring for career development. He and his Head of People quickly pulled together a career panel with their more senior people and some executives from other companies to talk about strategies that employees can use on their own to build their career.

My point is that training may sound cumbersome and one-dimensional, but there are a lot of ways you can make sure that employees and managers are getting developed and building their skills while also building your culture and team cohesion. Your Head of People is the person to lean on and to remind you that this is important.

HR's Job 2: Make Sure People Know What They're Doing and How They're Doing

Among these great people in your start-up, you can tell that many of them are doing great work. And then there's Eddie. You have a sense that Eddie isn't cutting it. You can't really tell what Eddie is doing or what he's producing. You see Eddie chatting with other employees all the time—you want people to like each other and you don't want to run a sweatshop, but you also need them to get their work done. You don't exactly have clear goals, so you can't actually redirect Eddie. And everyone likes him so much that you don't want to get into a tough conversation with him.

Or take Angela. Angela does a terrific job in her role in marketing, and her manager can't believe how fast she produces content. But her peers across the company can't stand her. She never helps, she always points out what they are doing wrong, and she is a roadblock to others trying to do their jobs.

Or Sandy. Sandy is proactive, enthusiastically volunteers for special projects, and is a wonderful cheerleader for people on the team. You think she's great. She wants to run the entire department. She's insisting that she wants a promotion. You're afraid if you don't promote her, you'll lose her, but you don't know if she has the skills or temperament to run a team and there is nobody to train her. (There's a script for talking to someone who wants a promotion they're not ready for in the Sample Scripts at the end of the book.)

In other words, by the time you realize that you need to implement a performance management system, it is well past time. And hopefully your Head of People can advocate for it a little bit sooner than you might yourself.

It's not sexy, but a performance management system handles these issues. You need to figure out if people are meeting their goals (or if they even have goals) or missing them. If they are missing goals, what do they need to get things done? It will help you figure out who is ready to be promoted, who needs specific training, and who your underachievers are. It will help you with if, when, and how you are going to fire some employees. If you don't implement a system, I guarantee you're going to have a bunch of people who used to be great but aren't anymore, and you have no good options about how to handle them.

The centerpiece of this process is performance appraisals. These get a bad rap. They feel like corporate red tape. Employees did not come to work for your company because they wanted to get a performance review like they were at IBM or something!

Nevertheless, there will come a time when you realize that you don't know who your strong performers are, who isn't productive, or which managers are good. You need to step back and look at performance. You will be surprised to find out—either through informal conversation or through a survey you do—your people actually want performance reviews! Some will begin to make snide comments like, "We don't even have performance reviews around here."

As bizarre as that may sound, let's unpack what it means. Employees want to know how they're doing, to have a sense of progress and guidance about how to get ahead. Most people don't have much language for this except to say they want a performance appraisal. So let's go with it.

I'm putting this section into your Head of People's camp because it's his job to make sure performance management is happening. Managers need training in how to conduct an awesome performance review, and HR should make sure they have these skills and a good form to do it. (Please don't copy a large company's multipage form and ask people to spend hours filling it out.) HR folks should also step back and think about the purpose and value of a performance review.

If a performance review is conducted properly, it's an opportunity for the employee and manager to reflect on the year (or the half-year or the quarter) and talk about the highs and lows. It's a moment to highlight the employee's strengths and accomplishments, to look at areas for development and help them make a plan, and to think together about where they want to go in their career and how they can get there. Sometimes it's a safe space for the employee to vent.

Above all, a performance appraisal is not about gotcha, not a blame game, and not even a grade. No smart adult is motivated by getting a B, and when a manager starts grading, thinking of herself as evaluating, the appraisal turns into this weird power dynamic. It becomes about the grade.

A good performance review gives the employees direct and diplomatic input to help them grow. The form itself is not the most important thing. Here are the aspects to a good performance appraisal:

- What the employee accomplished. For example: launched these four products, built a customer service team that would handle all the customer service issues in a systematized way, or met sales goals.
- What the employee's strengths are: proactive, solutions-oriented, job functional skills, great communicator.
- What the employee's development opportunities are: learn to speak up more clearly in a meeting, learn to work better with cross-functional peers, meet deadlines.

- Your tone as the manager: educating, inspiring, and empowering the employee so that people feel built up and not torn down. Candid and also compassionate.
- Your job together: leave the employee feeling inspired to do even better, fix problems, and continue to build their relationship with the manager and the company.

Managers can also get input from a few of the employees' peers to get their take on how the person is doing. They can do this by using a survey tool or having an informal chat. Remember that this is also not a grade, it's simply data so the manager can expand her line of sight into what an employee is doing.

Your employees should not hear difficult feedback or big problems for the first time in the performance appraisal. There should be no surprises. One of the weird aspects about performance appraisals is that people save up their feedback for the review. It's the worst idea. Managers should be having conversations throughout the year, giving continuous feedback. Nobody should be surprised at what's being talked about at the performance appraisal.

If there's a problem, address it and bring the employee into solving it. Ask, "How can I help put you in a better spot to succeed? What's in the way of you achieving your goals? What do you need to build in yourself? Where do you want to go in your career? Do you think your performance this year is going to get you there?" You have to have the conversation, even if it's difficult. And you have to decide ahead of time what you're going to do with this person. Are you going to put them on a performance improvement plan? Are you going to give them specific goals to be achieved in a specific time frame? Stick to the facts and the data with honesty and empathy.

Over time, when you have consistent ways to measure performance, you'll be able to figure out if you need to fire Eddie (sometimes you might) or how you need to handle Angie's relationships with her peers. You'll be able to give Sandy a clear road map to how she can get promoted. And overall, your employees will feel more comfortable that they know how they're doing and where they stand.

HR's Job 3: Growing Your Org Chart as Your Company Grows

As you reach milestones, raise more money, and begin to take on all the trappings of being a real scale-up, it's a heady time. And yet, as you solve some problems (how are we going to survive?) you cause some new ones (we need to build a large customer support team in multiple geographies and we don't have anyone to run it!). The truth, again, is that these "wins"—which are fantastic!—simply earn you the right to play again.

One of the traditional milestones is when you start to bring on seasoned executives. It's wonderful when your start-up is on the map enough to be able to attract more experienced talent. They bring the wisdom of years—sometimes decades—in the trenches. You won't need to tell them what to do; they'll be telling you what to do—how refreshing! They'll bring great strategic ideas and maturity to your executive team, and the ability to manage and coach their own teams. What could go wrong?

Hiring them is only the first step. You have to then get ready to integrate them, to stick them into the soil of the culture so they can take root. (See Chapter 5 about onboarding.) We already talked about the need to make room in your culture for the new people. When you bring new people in, you want them to be enough of a fit for where you are now, but also bring enough new people in to get you where you need to be. You also have to have the conversation with the employees who are getting "layered," as we call it when a new boss is put above them. (There's a script for this conversation in the Sample Scripts at the end of the book.) When you're layering, you may find that someone who is used to attending the executive meetings is no longer at that level. Then you have to have the conversation with them about taking them off the executive team. (And there's a script for that conversation in the Sample Scripts at the end of the book.)

One social media company I worked with, for example, had a lot of talented, scrappy, hard-working, loyal employees who did great work! Their young marketing group built an impressive events process and were very responsive to the needs of sales. As the company grew, Erica, the CEO, realized that they were going to have to come up with a more strategic approach to marketing and went out to look for an experienced CMO. After a long search she found Charles, a marketing pro who had decades of experience in large companies. He had also led marketing at a few start-ups and even served as COO in one of them, so he brought a lot of know-how to the team. He was also a wonderful cultural fit—he cared about people, he was laid back but intense about work, and funny.

The only issue was how to break it to the director of marketing, Diana, that she was going to have a new boss. Diana was ambitious, proactive, and everyone liked her. She had done more than was expected of her, but she just wasn't ready to lead the team. It was a hard conversation to have (and I've given you a script in the Sample Scripts at the end of the book to help you when the time comes), helping her come to terms with her own gaps (no fault of hers, she just needed more time to develop) and reporting to someone else (she felt she was being demoted—she wasn't; the company was growing, and she was being put in a position to succeed). Having these delicate conversations with your employees can be difficult, but your job is to communicate transparently what's going on, see the bigger picture, and help people adjust to their new position.

Your Job Changes Too

I was talking to Daniel, the founder and CEO of a fintech start-up in New York. He was instituting a pretty good-sized reorganization that included bringing in a few seasoned executives and promoting his vice president of marketing into the CMO role. We had spent a few hours talking about the onboarding process for each of them and how he would make sure they could integrate and be successful in their new roles.

"And how about you?" I asked him after we had discussed everyone. "How are you going to re-onboard yourself?"

He nodded slowly. "Yeah. I hadn't really thought about it, but you're right. After we do this re-org my role will change a lot, and I probably need to think about how I'll handle it." He was quiet a moment. "It's changed a lot in the past year anyway," he added.

This whole chapter is about the change and growth of your company. And you've changed too, even though your title hasn't. You're no longer personally overseeing everybody, and you barely even know some of your employees. Your company has grown from a start-up to a scale-up, and your role has changed from leading and managing everyone to leading and managing leaders. You're probably handling some things more skillfully and delegating more projects to (hopefully) an increasingly sure-footed team. You've hopefully freed up your time to focus on other things, like building a longer-term vision, reiterating your message to a larger and increasingly diverse company, and playing a larger external-facing role. Your job has changed, and it's a good habit to reflect on how you now define success in your role and where is the best use of your time.

Your growth is a time for celebration, but as new issues emerge, it doesn't always feel that way. Take solace in the fact that these are the right problems to have and that there are tools to solve them.

Remember that what's past is not necessarily prologue. People who are good at designing product are not necessarily good at managing designers. People who were good at another company may not be able to work within your culture. As your company changes, your culture, your structure, and people's roles—including yours—will change, but your self-awareness, clarity, and conviction will guide and support that change.

TAKEAWAYS

- At some point, you will need to manage the management of your company, and you will need managers to do that.

- Your managers need to learn the multifaceted set of skills required to manage.

- You have to make sure that the structure of your team is getting built as you scale.
- The Head of People is a real job that requires skills, and that person can be a tangible help to you.
- As you scale up, you will have to make tough choices about which of your executives needs to be replaced or layered.

REFLECTIVE QUESTIONS

- Which of your executives is a good manager? How can you tell?
- As your company doubles and doubles again, which of your executives will have to be replaced?
- Do you know how the employees are feeling about their careers?
- Do your employees have a good sense of their career trajectories?
- What do your employees need training on?

Endnote

[1]   Conley, C (2007) *Peak: How great companies get their mojo from Maslow,* Jossey-Bass, San Francisco

07

Smooth Operations

Reflective Question: How do you know that your projects are on track to meet their deadlines?

You may be the kind of founder who was hoping to not have to have "forms" and meetings and red tape, but at some point—quicker than you think—you have to create ways for people to do things efficiently at scale. That means that you need a standard way of doing things that will lead to predictable outcomes. And it also means that you have to embrace meetings, which can actually be inspiring!

Systems, metrics, and processes may feel boring and bureaucratic, but they are essential to running a growing business. They drive operational excellence—the efficient, predictable running of the business—which is what you have to have when you're running a big enterprise. Operations is about giving your people a structure and keeping track of everything.

Well-structured operations lets your people know where things are, what you're all shooting for, and who needs to know what to make it all happen. Operations ensures that the right people do the right things at the right time, and the right people know what happened. When there are just fifteen or twenty of you, that's not much of a problem. Your file retrieval system may consist of "Hey, Megan, where did you put that customer spreadsheet?"

But when there are fifty or sixty of you, that's not an efficient system. And when there are 500 and then 5,000 and more, it's not even an option anymore. At that point there will be multiple Megans, and none of them will know where the customer spreadsheet is, and anyway, different people are keeping different lists for different purposes. Add remote work into the mix when you can't even walk over and ask her, and you're lost before you start. The more successful you are, the more you need good operations and people who understand why they are necessary.

So it's time to get organized. Probably past time, but there's no time like the present. I'll talk about why metrics are so important and why they are about people, not numbers. Then I'll discuss a few key systems and processes and how they can help you run the company. And I'll convince you that meetings are the magic that keeps it all working together.

What to Measure and How

The concept behind metrics is simple: they measure your progress and guide your way. But metrics are not just about numbers, they are about people. Bear with me and we'll get there.

There are a few metrics that are useful for almost every start-up, and there are also some that are specific to your business. You need to know what they are and what they mean. Many founders underestimate how much employees are motivated by knowing what the goalposts are. When they know that, it shows them where they need to focus and generates good conversations about performance and accountability without making it personal.

Many founders aren't that excited by metrics, and who can blame them? They are caught up in their vision of the product that they're making, and honestly, they're excited about any progress at all. Especially in the early stage, it's hard to predict, for example, how much they will sell or how many new users they will gain, so selling more this quarter than last by any amount looks good. But think about this: What if you could have sold even more? Metrics help you consider that and get everyone on the same page.

Nat was the CEO of a company in Los Angeles that enabled sourcing and giving creative presents to others. It had started out as a business app to build customer loyalty, but Nat saw the opportunity to evolve it as a consumer app and open it to the masses. As a product CEO, he enjoyed sculpting the design of what they were building. He went to his board, eager to share his vision of the nuances of the new strategy and his new designs. The board surprised him by pushing him—hard—on the change in direction. "Look at your projections," one board member said. "You're not meeting your current targets. And look at your headcount and your operations; you're way over budget right now. I think you need to focus on getting this business working right before you think about developing a new business line."

"It was bracing, and not in a good way," Nat told me. I nodded sympathetically even though we were on the phone. I know what it's like. "I feel resentful," he went on, "like 'I can't believe you're not giving me credit for all the things I've done. Don't you even want to see the new designs?' But after I thought about it awhile, I realized they were right. We aren't doing a good enough job at simply selling and managing our expenses." In the absorbing day-to-day of solving all the puzzles your business throws at you and getting excited about new ideas, it's easy to lose sight of what a business is supposed to do, which is to make money.

You need to start managing your industry's key drivers as soon as you can, because there's always a learning curve. When you do something new, expect to do it badly at first, but as you do it more often, you get better at it. You probably know some of the metrics from your personal experience, but that doesn't mean you shouldn't do your research. You can find out more from your peers, and your investors can be helpful. There's also an enormous amount of information readily available online about your business, no matter what it is.

Cash Is King for a Reason

The most basic measurement to watch over is your cash. Whether you've raised a $250,000 seed round or a $45 million series C, it seems like that much money will last forever. But then you rent office space, hire a team and buy supplies, pay for lunch and snacks, and before you know it, you've burned through half of it and you haven't made as much progress as you thought you would.

Nathan, a CEO of an AI start-up in New York, raised $17 million. He knew what his priorities were, and then he and the team went out to hire. It goes without saying that hiring is important, and after you raise money a normal thing to do is hire. (We talked about hiring in Chapter 5.) They had a well-thought-out plan to hire, and they filled all those roles. Good. Then his VP of product said he needed someone else to do data research, which made sense, so they hired that role, then they found someone else who was great and hired that person, figuring they'd find a good role for her. The VP of sales said they could get more done if they had an extra person to handle sales ops, so they hired that person. The CTO needed two extra people to rearchitect the system, something they hadn't anticipated. He also wanted to upgrade and add more servers to have capacity for growth. After a few more moves like that, suddenly they had all these extra people they hadn't budgeted for and at the end of the year had a lot less of that $17 million than they thought they would.

It came as a surprise to this CEO, but in retrospect it was perfectly predictable. None of these ideas was bad by itself—in fact they were pretty reasonable—and all the hires they made were good. But they made each decision in a vacuum, without looking at its effect on the overall plan, forgetting to track a key metric, the budget. Their next hire? A CFO.

Learn to Love Dashboards

In addition to a budget, you should get in the habit early of monitoring your projects and milestones and creating a dashboard so you—and everyone else—know where you are according to plan at any given time. A dashboard is simply a document that captures the status of your most important metrics, hopefully on one page, and compares them to what you had expected. The most important metrics will change over time, but the process of monitoring them shouldn't.

For example, I worked with a company which focused on last mile logistics, helping their customers convert a sale to a delivery much faster. They used the data they garnered from their implementations to help their clients get to know their customers better and to apply the best solution for their needs. When I started coaching Alex, the CEO, the company had only about five salespeople and five product people, and what they needed was proof of concept and referrals from customers to be able to branch out. So their key metrics focused on the number of customers and, more importantly, successful implementations.

After their fourth year the company really took off—an 85% increase in sales. Their goal in the fifth year was to double that. That was a clear goal that everyone could rally behind—much better than just asking everyone to do better and to sell more. Now the company had over twenty salespeople and would bring more on over the year. They had a proven playbook for their implementation. But their key metrics had to change: to be a mature company looking for an IPO in a few years, they now had to focus on predictability.

The old way of doing things was to have the reps have as many meetings as they could. Some did better and some did worse, and the ones who overachieved carried the rest. That formula was not going to work anymore, Alex and I agreed. Predictability had to come from the shared performance of the team. Alex worked on the math and got a surprising insight: "If each sales rep has only four solid meetings per month, that should yield one opportunity per month. If each then closes one opportunity per quarter, we will make our number." So the key metric in sales changed: it was now the number of meetings per month.

The key metrics for you will be different if you are a SAAS company, an e-commerce company, a hardware company, or a marketplace. And the key metrics will change as your business evolves. But in every case, your dashboard should show the status on the most important things, marked green, yellow, or red. Green means that everything is on track. Yellow means that the project is off-track, but there's a viable plan to get it back on track. Red means it's off-track, and there's no plan for how to get it back on track. The dashboard shows where the problems are and lets the team examine them every week or so, so that problems become clear and the team can work together to troubleshoot.

BRIAN BERGER
Founder and CEO of Mack Weldon

When we think about our business you can say, "All right, I spent ten bucks to get a cohort of customers that generated twenty bucks." And let's just say all my costs to get that customer were 50%, gross margin was 50%, then I'm net neutral. I spent $10 to get $20, but I have to subtract out the $10 of other costs, so I'm at zero. But if that customer shops again, then I don't have to spend anything to get that customer. Then whatever they spend, minus the cost of sale, is profit. We also know that the type of product they buy on their first order determines how quickly they become profitable and how frequently they reorder. So, isolating those things and thinking about that, tuning our marketing to those things that will not treat all customers as equal will help create an additional advantage for us in terms of our profitability and growth.

Also, the highest probability you will have to get a customer to repeat or demonstrate loyalty is in the first thirty days. Because customers will say, "Oh, let me try this." And if it works well, then they'll say, "Oh, I love this, I've got to buy more of it."

So we know that if we generate repeat purchases in those first thirty days it has a disproportionately higher impact on growth.

So that first month repeat rate is something we want to drive as a business. If we tune our efforts to that, we can say, "Okay, our thirty-day repeat rate is 30%. If we can nudge that up by 5%, this is the impact it has on the business."

For our employees, we have to spend some time thinking about how to explain it to them so that it feels exciting and tangible and real. And what's cool is that we have a very simple dashboard that tracks how we're progressing against these four or five KPIs. So all the efforts that people are doing, they can map to one of the specific KPIs. And they can see, at the end of the month, we went from X to Y, or we lost ground, or whatever. So it's a digestible way for them to track their own efforts as they relate to the business goals. And to see how the business goals are tracking overall, month by month.

But it's not the kind of thing that you can stand up and say, like, "Forward profitability!" If you say, "We're opening up ten more stores!" they're like, "Sweet! I totally get that!" That is high risk, really expensive, very long term, but people get it. The way we tune the business using metrics, though, is much more esoteric and in the weeds, but if you can impact some of these metrics by a very small amount, across a huge number of customers, it has a very big effect.

Sometimes there's a legitimate reason why a project is red. Maybe someone quit, and there's nothing to be done until a new person is hired. Maybe someone outside the company is not providing necessary materials. During the pandemic, at times it was hard to get the materials needed because the supply chain has been disrupted by the virus-related shutdowns. But at least you and the team know where the problem is and can readjust and possibly put more focus and resources toward the project to change it from red to yellow.

One fintech company I worked with, for instance, really needed a dashboard. They were building a financial services company—whenever you deal with a regulated industry it adds a layer of complexity to your start-up. They were supposed to get a pilot version of their new product up and running in April. That first launch date moved to June, which then moved to August. What was going on?

I helped the team surface the issues by asking them to build a dashboard of key metrics for the company. In this case the key metrics were: release of the new product: red; number of users: red (with no updated product, they were lagging on new users); months left of cash: red.

This was not exactly a surprise to the team, but seeing it all in one place gave everyone a shared sense of reality (in this case a real wake-up call) and a context and sense of urgency to troubleshoot. What were the problems? The general counsel told the team that his contact at the agency they needed sign-off from had been sick. Each week they told him she'd be back next week. He agreed to push for another person. The VP of engineering was waiting for more explicit directions from the product team. The product team had thought that engineering had everything they needed. They made a separate plan to increase the number of users for their existing product. And the CEO secured a line of credit in case they needed it. Once the team as a group saw the specific bottlenecks and roadblocks, they could plan a course of action to fix them.

Take Stock of Your People

Looking at the dashboard leads you back to people. The metrics tell you which people need more attention, and your knowledge of that person and your sensitivity to the whole situation tell you how to approach them. If it's a junior person, maybe they need more guidance or training. Or maybe a team is understaffed, and you think about hiring. It's not about blame; it's about understanding.

No matter what color a project has, you should be curious about why your people have decided that something is green, yellow, or red. Ask them, in a nonthreatening way, what their evidence is that a project is green—how do they know it's on track? People often have a hard time being rigorous in these judgments, for a variety of reasons. When this discussion goes wrong, it can easily turn into an exercise in finger-pointing, so you have to provide the right cultural frame for it. This is a moment where a culture of curiosity versus a culture of blame makes a tangible difference. If your people are open to being reflective and feel safe to own up to their mistakes, you'll get to the truth faster and be able to course-correct together. If instead there is an air of fear, the executives will defend and protect themselves and their people, and it will take you a lot longer to figure out what the problems are and fix them.

Debrief regularly and emphasize that these "retrospectives" (or "retros" as they are often called) are not about proving who's wrong, they're just about clarifying where things stand and how to move them forward. Reinforce an attitude of how to help each other win, not where you want to assign blame. If that attitude of shared work is baked into the culture from the beginning, people won't take a retro as punitive, it will be part of their job and their working life. If you instill the attitude that questions are asked in the spirit of just gathering information about their work, they'll know they should be ready to answer questions and will feel comfortable to do so honestly.

Goals Are Rocket Fuel

The dashboard also provides clear goals. People are motivated by understanding what they are shooting for, and it's so much easier for you to have the right conversations with people if both of you understand what the expectations are.

A very common tool to track goals is called OKRs, which stands for "objectives and key results." Literally, entire books have been written about OKRs, but in short the objective is the clear goal and the key results are the specific measures to track that goal. For example, the fintech company I mentioned earlier might have had as an objective: "To successfully launch the new product by the end of September." The key results might be: (1) product goes live, (2) initial week of launch 50,000 new users sign up, (3) reported bugs are less than fifty in the first month.

OKRs are extremely helpful to keep track of the most important initiatives of the company and also when talking about performance with your people. Susan, the founder and CEO of a community-building platform targeted to companies, had concerns with her VP of marketing, Jacob. He was always busy and always enthusiastic, but she wasn't so sure about the results he and his team were getting. That's the problem—she wasn't sure. She was reluctant to give him honest feedback because she couldn't quite articulate what was wrong and because she felt bad when he was obviously working so hard.

I asked her what his goals were, and after we talked it through, she realized that they didn't have clear goals in place. I showed her OKRs, and we created some for Jacob. His objective was to "Attract new leads." The OKRs could be: (1) updating the website to increase engagement and (2) create a weekly newsletter to send out to people who sign up. There might have been a third, but two were good for now. "It was a revelation," she told me after we worked that through.

"The thought of having everyone do OKRs was a relief. Now we would all be on the same page and know what the goals were."

Two more things I'd like to add about this. First of all, you may think this sounds basic, and yet I see all the time in quite large companies the lack of real clarity on goals. It's actually hard to quantify things that aren't numerically obvious, like sales. As the CEO of a start-up you have a lot clawing at your attention, and sometimes, especially when things are going well, you don't think to put those structures in place. That's OK, but there is no time like the present.

The second thing to note is Jacob's reaction when Susan had this discussion with him. We had to role-play the discussion because she was sure he would be defensive. To her shock, he was relieved. "It turned out that he knew he was underperforming but didn't know what to do about it," she told me. "I thought he didn't want to be pinned down, but he was also relieved to have a concrete goal to shoot for." Right. This happens more often than you think. People wake up every day hoping to do a good job! You may be uncomfortable with these discussions, but believe me, you are not helping them when you let them stay confused and don't help them clarify their targets.

I asked her what she took away from this situation. "It sounds so obvious," she told me. "When you have goals for the business, everything is better. When we don't have clear goals, we let things slide. I can't talk to people about performance, because I don't have any way to measure it."

Right. We talked about accountability in Chapter 6. OKRs or some other system for goals is the centerpiece of accountability. They give your employees something to shoot for and something solid to address with your team if you sense issues. OKRs or something like them also lead you to a comprehensive company plan that shows everyone what the overall objectives are and what their role is in it. Moving fast is rarely about asking people to work harder. Moving fast arises when your employees have clarity about the plan, work the plan, and debrief and course-correct when something isn't working according to plan. Metrics give you the guide for that and targets to shoot for and celebrate when you make them.

Your Systems Set You Free

As you build your metrics, inevitably you begin to see that you need systems, tools, and processes to work efficiently and keep track. This is going to cause groaning for the early-stage folks who like the lack of structure, who like solving one-off problems, and like going directly to a person rather than filling out a form. You implement one standardized process, and all of a sudden people moan about "big company stuff" even when your start-up is a hundred people.

But when your start-up starts to grow up, you'll need this kind of structure. The point of having systems, processes, and tools in place is to create predictable outcomes. Once you have the thing that you're making, you've got to know how to make a whole lot of the thing, or the thing for a whole lot of people, different people, not all of whom want the same thing from the thing. If you're lucky and good, you'll have to make the thing at scale, for maybe millions of customers.

Some of the processes are digital. You'll need technology to communicate internally, like Slack or something like it. You'll need a customer management system, such as HubSpot or Salesforce, since you need to know in a centralized way who your customers are and what contacts you've already had with them. You can't do this when each of your sales reps is keeping track on their own spreadsheets. You'll need a project management system, like Asana, so that everyone can see the bigger projects and their status. At some point you'll probably want a system to track OKRs and other internal company processes. There are likely to be other software systems that are specific to your company. Do some research with people who know the parts of your field where you are not knowledgeable.

Then there are the human systems, the guidebooks to how we do things around here. John Wooden, the famously successful coach of the UCLA basketball team in the 1950s and 60s, insisted that his players follow his five steps in putting on their socks. It seems incredibly niggling and mundane, micromanagement of the first order, but what's a big problem for a basketball player? Blisters. When you put on your socks and sneakers the wrong way you might get blisters. When you do it John Wooden's way you won't. "I think it's the little things that count," he said, "the little details that make the big things come about."[1]

I am not suggesting that you police your employees' way of dressing (although from me to you: everyone should wear sunscreen), but the point is that it is worth the time to pay attention to details that matter. And when you hire your key people, make sure they have the right level of attention to detail too.

THE GREAT RACI

One very helpful human system is a RACI matrix—a responsibility assignment matrix. It tells everyone who needs to do what to accomplish a project, and sometimes it is a magical tool to the start-up CEOs I work with. (I felt that way too when I saw it for the first time.) RACI (pronounced race-y) is a very simple chart that lists who is responsible for doing the work (R), who is accountable for making sure that all the goals and parameters have been met (A), who will be consulted on the project (C), and who will be informed of the outcome, but not necessarily involved in the project (I). In its basic version, it is a chart with team members listed across the top, and tasks, milestones, decisions, and any other key steps listed down the side. Each item on the side is assigned to one or more team members. Usually only one team member is the accountable person, but multiple people may need to be consulted or notified. That's because if more than one person is accountable, then nobody is accountable, so make sure you have only one person in that box. But consulting, as in getting input? Often plenty of people. And informing? Sometimes the whole company needs to know.

The RACI matrix is useful for deciding who will decide. It also clarifies who is accountable for certain things and lets people know whether or not they will be consulted, which avoids the... how shall I say, pettiness and FOMO that happen when people expect to be consulted but aren't.

For example, let's say you have customer service in one location and sales in another location, but then you grow and need to decide about where to open up a full customer service office. Who makes that decision? Sales? Marketing?

Or maybe you're making decisions about which features to cut. The product team decides which features can go, but you haven't consulted with engineering to know what's hard to eliminate and what's not. And you haven't consulted with sales even though they're out there selling the product with all the features.

FIGURE 7.1   RACI Matrix

	CEO	CFO	Project Manager	VP Marketing	VP Sales	Engineer
Project Planning	C	C	A	C	C	C
Project Initiation			R			C
Budgeting		R	A			
Design			A			R
Testing			A			R
Launch	C	I	R	I	I	A

Legend: R = Responsible   A = Accountable   C = Consulted   I = Informed

SOURCE Jon Hugo Ungar (2021), jhungar.com

Maybe that's happened more than once, and now sales doesn't trust engineering and the customers don't trust their salespeople.

To keep things on the rails your people need to make those difficult decisions and have those conversations about trade-offs. If you haven't clearly laid out that they need to be consulted, then they get missed and everyone gets annoyed at each other. Keep this up enough, and then you call me to lead an off-site to work on "relationships" or "trust." Listen, I'm happy to help and I like the job security, but sometimes a RACI chart is all you need to make sure everyone is clear, informed, and more or less happy.

Process is meant to speed you up, to provide a structure, and to point people in the right direction. That's how you make sure that the steps are being applied and are being successful. Or if they're not successful, you look at how to change them to make them more successful.

Remember that fintech company I told you about? They didn't have the metrics to measure progress, but neither did they have a process to set off the alarm bells. The CEO told me initially, "You have to have patience. It's running late, but it's a complicated problem." (This is the first time any CEO ever told *me* that *I* had to have patience! That's usually my line to them.)

No amount of patience is going to get a stuck project back on track. And you, the CEO, orchestrating a lot of things, can't always see that a key project is stuck or why it's stuck. A process of looking at a weekly dashboard gives you the frame to notice that something is stuck and to unpack it with your team. When they finally did that work, they figured out the issues and could then correct them as a team.

As the CEO, you need to manage how these systems and processes land on your team and, as you get bigger, to make sure someone else (not you!) is managing this. Process gets a bad name because it's too heavy for the situation and slows things down or because it makes no sense (like why do six people have to sign off on this one decision?). But the flipside is people like guidance. Having a playbook provides consistency, equality, and persistence of quality as the staff changes and grows. If you think about this early, the systems and processes get grooved into your culture in a holistic way, and people won't feel like they're being put in a straitjacket.

Throughout the course of your company's growth, there will be experiments, changes, detours, and roadblocks. You're hiring people and winning a lot, but then you'll lose people, and you'll lose customers, and issues will come up that you haven't anticipated. You solve some problems, and then that brings up other problems. That's the messy middle, as Scott Belsky, founder of Behance (sold to Adobe) and author of *The Messy Middle*, calls it.[2] You're growing fast and dealing with issues that you can anticipate, as well as the ones that take you by surprise, day by day, year by year, all the way to the end.

As Belsky points out, there is a lot of excitement about the end and the beginning, but no one glorifies the day-to-day grind of the middle, and that's where leadership really comes into play. You're a direct-to-consumer company, and, what seems like suddenly, your site can't handle all the traffic. Should you rebuild the site or use a service like Shopify? You're a B2B company, selling your solution to large enterprises. It's going great, but suddenly your rather makeshift customer team is not organized enough to handle all the service issues. How should you reorganize them and who should lead that team? And are some of those customer service issues actually consulting opportunities in disguise? Are you leaving money on the table? Then a pandemic hits.

The right metrics show you the goalposts, and the right processes give you structure in hitting them. But the secret sauce that keeps you aligned is the lowly meeting.

The Magic of Meetings

Unlike most of you, I have a passion for meetings. Give me a good meeting every day to get everyone on the same page and to build connection. Many of you may fall into the opposite category, as in "I can't get anything done because I'm in meetings all day." Let's see if I can help you think differently about meetings.

A little-known fact about meetings is that the preparation for a meeting is more important than the meeting itself. People don't prepare for the meeting because, they say, they don't have time, but then they have bad meetings that are a massive waste of time and in some cases take more time away from them later.

Great Meetings Start with Why

The preparation for a meeting starts with why. Why are we having this meeting? And here's the good news: if you do some prep in advance you may find that you don't need to meet! For example, a typical coaching conversation about this might start, "What are you trying to get done in this meeting?" The CEO might say, "I want to make a decision about which features we are going to include in this release and which we're going to defer."

"Terrific! Who's the decision-maker?"

"Well, obviously it's the VP of product."

"Awesome!"

"But I want to make sure she gets input from everyone."

"Totally agree! Does she just need to get a few emails or have a few quick calls with the other executives to get on the same page, or does she need a longer discussion?"

"A few quick calls or emails would be great."

"And do you need to weigh in personally?"

"No, at this point I am the least informed. I just want her to coordinate with everyone and let me know what she decides."

"Can you let her know that and give her a time frame?"

"Sure."

"So do you guys need to meet?"

"No, I guess not!" Boom—how much time did we just get back with that five minutes of prep?

Think about that for yourself. Do you need more than one person to make the decision? If no, then don't meet. Do you need to have a discussion about it or is it something that has already been documented? If it's been documented in processes, then don't meet—just go check the documentation. (Don't know where the documentation is? You might need to make sure your process includes a consistent way of storing important documents. See how I did that?) Could the goal be accomplished with an email? If so, then don't meet. You get the idea. When you start with why and get really specific you may surprise yourself with when you need to meet and when you don't.

Even when it's a meeting you have every week with a predetermined focus, it's good to remind yourself what the purpose of the meeting is and why you have it every week. Why are we having an executive meeting? The answer is not "because that's what we do every Monday morning." A good answer is "to sync everybody up." Starting with why ensures two things: people will prepare better, engage more, and have deeper conversations when they know why they are meeting. And it prevents the meeting from being a check-the-box activity.

When you do decide to meet, and you've thought about the purpose of the meeting and the goal of the meeting, communicate those to everyone. You may want to send out some prework—some questions to get them thinking, a request to prepare some data, or an article or memo to read that someone has prepared. This gets people in the right mindset and gives them time to prepare their thoughts.

A Crash Course in Meeting Planning

You should also plan how you will accomplish the goal of the meeting. This all sounds simple, but when you go to do it, it can be surprisingly slippery. I regularly ask the CEOs I work with what the goal of a meeting is, and in response they tell me the agenda rather than the goal: "First we're going to talk about the sales numbers; then we're going to discuss the roadmap for next quarter." Examples of good goals are: "to sync everyone up," "to communicate the status of everyone's projects," and "to decide on a certain strategic course."

OK, you've given some thought to the goal of the meeting (the why) and the agenda (the how). Let's figure out the right people to be there (the who).

When a start-up is a baby you tend to have all eight of you meeting together and making decisions together fluidly, as needed. Practically speaking, you all can also fit into the same conference room. Then you're fifteen and it's a squeeze. Then suddenly there are thirty of you. One of my clients once told me, "When we reached thirty employees we mostly still all met together. We just found a bigger conference room." Right. That's why everyone complains that they're in so many meetings they can't get work done. I don't have to tell you that companies of 500 or 5,000 people don't all meet together, but when do you start going from everyone to only some?

Let's assume that day is right now. Let's figure out who needs to be in the room. Obviously, you need the most knowledgeable people on the topic there. You may also need the cross-functional peers. For example, if you're making some decisions about what features you're going to leave out of the product release, you need the salespeople to tell you what their customers are expecting, and the tech people to tell you what's harder and what's easier to drop out. If you're making a decision about strategy, you need the HR folks to think about how the staffing plan will be affected by the change.

Finally, do the people attending the meeting know what they need to know to have an informed discussion? Amazon is famous for its six-page memo that provides the background, the context, the necessary data, and a recommendation for what should happen. You may not want a six-page memo for every meeting, but figuring out how you'll get everyone up to speed either by prework or something you read together is worthwhile.

The next question is, who's in charge here? You have to decide how you're going to decide and how the decision will be made. Are you looking for consensus? Are you looking for input to help you make the decision yourself? Are you all there together to resolve some conflict and then one person will make the decision? Facilitative leaders think that they always need to get input from all their people and use those points to guide the decision itself. Sometimes that's the right idea, but it's worth asking, "Are these the right people to ask?" and "Who is the right person to decide?" Figuring that out and having a philosophy about that is important.

I'm giving you permission to sometimes make the decision yourself. As the founder and CEO, you may have the best feel and the best line of sight for key topics. Sometimes the data is too murky, or half of your team wants one thing and the other half wants something else. One very experienced CEO I coached a few years back once said, "Sometimes it's 49% one way and 51% the other. You just have to decide." If that's the case, make sure to tell them clearly that you want to hear what they think, but that you will make the decision.

Finally, the thing to remember about any meeting is that it's part of a process. There's the preparation for the meeting, there's the meeting, and then there are the actions that flow from the meeting. My secret to ensure meeting effectiveness is to ask three questions: (1) What did we decide here? (2) Who's going to do what by when? and (3) Who needs to know?

The Art of Running a Great Meeting

When the meeting starts, the first thing to do is have a little chit-chat. I know you hate small talk, I know you want to get down to business, and I know you don't like to waste time. But a little bit of small talk before meetings builds community generally and actually makes the meeting more effective specifically.

A personal opener warms up the room and gives everyone a personal connection before you dive into business topics, some of which may be controversial or possibly cause some tension. Emotions can run high in the intense world of start-ups! The small talk helps ease the way and gives everyone a moment of connection. An advanced move to foment connection is to do a mini-check-in at the beginning, which could be a simple question such as, "How are you feeling today?" or "What's a highlight of your week so far?" One of the CEOs I work with started asking his team silly check-in questions at the beginning of meetings, like "What's your spirit vegetable?" or "If you were a toy, what toy would you be?" It started as a joke, but he found it really opened people up. They spontaneously explained why they answered the question that way, and they learned about each other in a lighthearted way. It doesn't take that long, and the socialization value you get far outweighs the time it takes.

This is especially important when you are working remotely or semi-remotely (that is, when some people are in the office and some people beam in using video). There's a lot less opportunity for informal socializing when you and your employees interact remotely rather than in person in the office. You most often don't get to the room early and have some informal conversation in advance. If people do show up early on video, they often tend to finish one or two more emails rather than talk to the other people who show up a bit early. There are not the same side conversations, and certainly there is not a lot of lingering or walking to grab a coffee or lunch together afterwards.

If you have a longer meeting and a little more time, you can do something more involved, like an exercise called "rose, thorn, and bud." A rose is a small win, a positive thing; the thorn is a challenge you experienced, some difficulty; and a bud is something you're looking forward to or a new idea. Everyone could do that at the beginning. One of the CEOs I coach told me that he interviewed a junior HR person who asked him if he wanted to end the meeting with a rose, a thorn, and a bud. They did. It took about five minutes. "I feel more connected to her than members of the team I've known for years," he told me.

Meetings can provide that kind of unquantifiable benefit. A meeting helps people understand how everyone else thinks. Meetings build relationships, because you spend time together and have some laughs. Having good relationships helps you get work done, helps you deal with conflict and resolve it. Relationships give you access to information. Good relationships help you feel like a team so you move forward together even when you lose on a certain decision; they help you feel engaged about work even when things aren't going well.

Meetings also build a shared reality. Harry, the CEO of a robotics company I work with, tends to think as he talks, which means things can slide a little bit. He might talk about the product with his head of product, and they come to an agreement about a nuance of the roadmap. He then talks to his CTO separately and finds out that the nuance is a problem for the engineering team. Then he finds out from his VP of sales that the customers are clamoring for something different.

Now obviously these decisions shouldn't be made in separate conversations, and those functions need to work together. But the CEO is human, and things happen fast in a start-up. It's natural to have side conversations with various people who make the plan, and your expectations change slightly and over time that drift builds up. So a regular executive team meeting gets everyone on the same page.

The Meetings You Need to Have as a Leader

The most important meeting you'll have is the one you have with yourself, every day. What you want to get done, what your priorities are, who needs more attention from you, and even who you want to be. That last one may sound surprising, but as we saw in Chapter 2, a morning ritual was a great help to start your day off right. You might need a certain frame for who you want to be, for example you might remind yourself that you need to be patient, or celebrate wins, or give more positive feedback. Either way the meeting with yourself, whenever you have it, is a good way to make sure that you keep the most important thing as the most important thing.

YOUR MEETINGS

- Yourself—every day

- Your cofounder—once a week

- Your executive team—once a week

- Off-site executive team strategy meeting—four times a year

- All-hands meeting—variable, but once a quarter at the beginning

---

If you have cofounders, you should absolutely have a cofounder meeting once a week or so, to sync up and stay aligned on the relationship, and also to keep each other up to date with how things are changing as you're growing and the culture you want to build. This is also a good time to go over any issues you might have—even practice having conflict so that you can be comfortable when you actually do have conflicts. (I will get into this in more detail in Chapter 9.)

Make sure you have a leadership team meeting once a week, and start doing that as soon as possible. Typically, the road to good leadership meetings is paved with bad leadership meetings. You need to become a team so that you can work together effectively, and that takes a little time and work. There will be problems, people will make mistakes, and there will be unforeseen external shocks. You as founder/CEO have to manage those bumps in the road, but your best strategy is to be able to rely on a strong leadership team whose members know and trust each other.

Come up with a leadership team meeting structure that works for you. This is the time for each executive to take off their functional hats (marketing or sales or product) and put on their company hat. (One CEO I worked with got actual baseball caps for his team, and they all wore them during the leadership meeting. Corny? Maybe. But it worked as a ritual to remind everyone they were thinking about the company over their own teams.) The leaders are the stewards of the business, and everybody in the meeting should know the business overall, not just their area. Make sure everybody knows the goals, both short-term and long-term. This is where the dashboard of the company's three or five most important goals comes in handy, so everyone can see what's going well and what needs people's attention.

The executive team meeting is also where the cascading of information up and down happens. I described cascading in Chapter 6, but to recap, the team needs to know what they should tell their people, and they need to know that they have to tell their people. They should bring back to the meeting the reactions they're seeing and hearing from their people. For example, you may decide in the leadership team meeting to standardize on one consistent way for people to report on goals. The executives should go back to their teams and tell them about it, teach them, handle concerns. They can tell their functional teams in their own regular team meetings or in small groups—whatever makes sense for them.

As they socialize this with their teams, they may hear feedback like, "We don't get a heads-up from product early enough," or it may bring up other topics like, "We don't know where we stand and want more sense of a career path." Then at the next leadership meeting, the executive reports, "My folks are saying they aren't getting information soon enough—can we talk about that process?" or "My team want more of a sense of their career path; did anyone else hear that?" Now you can discuss that as a leadership team and make some informed decisions about how to deal with that based on insight from the employees themselves.

Finally, the executive meeting is a great place to celebrate successes, big or small. That will reinvigorate everybody so that they can pump up their people.

Preparation is the most important part of the meeting. Ask your people to be prepared when they come to the meeting to talk about their top projects, their status, and their plans. They should come with a finger on the pulse of their people and report on how their people responded to the message from last week. This is a good time to bring up any issues they're seeing in the culture. Use this time to get everyone to ask questions of other people about what they're doing and where it fits in the bigger picture. If there's a question of shuffling resources, they should be prepared to negotiate them.

There may be disagreements—and there *should be!* It's a great opportunity for everyone to build the skills and habits for learning to negotiate and reaching a compromise. That comes back to culture. The key to all this is that everyone feels they can be honest without getting blamed, that everything is done in service of making the company better, and that debriefing, gathering information, and exploring options are tools you do that with. Use words that reinforce that: "We're exploring," "We're experimenting," "We're all doing our best." Listen to people and make listening part of the culture, a culture where people can say what they have to say without being attacked or dismissed.

Naturally, you'll have one-on-one meetings with your executives, and you should insist that they have regular one-on-one and group meetings with their people. One-on-ones have the same rules: prepare properly, know what you've decided, and know who will do what by when. One-on-ones have a few additional principles that make them unique. When you meet with your folks like this you may want to get their status updates, but even more importantly, have a personal check-in with them. This is the time to see how they're really doing, to see if anything is blocking them or upsetting them. About once a quarter, ask them about their career aspirations and discuss ways you can help by giving them opportunities or training. It's also a time to praise them for their contributions, remind them how their work fits into the bigger goal, and help them get remotivated by having a good conversation. People stay at companies, they do extra work without complaining, and they are more willing to accept constructive criticism when they feel their manager cares about them and is looking out for them. Give your executives a structure for their expectations and your own about the way they conduct one-on-ones.

(I give you a script for this in the Sample Scripts at the end of the book.)

You should have an off-site strategy meeting for your leaders four times a year. You'll probably miss one, but it's OK to do it three times a year. When your executives have some time to step back and reflect together, they are more likely to step out of the weeds and work together more creatively and at a higher level. They also get to know each other better and learn to appreciate and trust each other, which is one of the best outcomes of great meetings.

All-hands meetings are necessary, and the frequency depends on your size. One company I work with does a business strategy all-hands and a demo all-hands. Dennis Crowley at Foursquare says that he ran the all-hands meetings as if they were a class in how to create a start-up company, and the only company they would study was Foursquare. Every week he'd have a "guest speaker," and the guest was just the head of product or the head of marketing. That person would describe what they were doing, what they wanted to do, and what they needed to do it.

People groan about going to the all-hands meeting, but they groan worse when they don't know what's going on. Pick your poison. It's helpful to have everyone feel they know what's going on with the business and to see themselves as part of the business. You can ask them questions about what they want to know and how they should get it. And when someone inevitably says, "I don't know what's going on around here," you can point out that you're having the all-hands meeting and you can challenge them back. Ask them what they need to know and how you can tell them. Make them a part of the solution.

Every once in a while, you might need to pull the "let's stop" card. I was facilitating an off-site with Greg, the CEO of a marketplace company in Houston. We were going around in circles on a session he was leading on values. He finally said, "Let's stop. We're not getting anything accomplished here. We didn't prepare adequately and so this is not productive. I'm sure it's my fault because I didn't give you enough background or time to prepare." Everyone looked at me: What's the coach going to do? I put my hands together and applauded. I am a lover of truth. That right there was truth. Let's call it and move on with our lives rather than torture ourselves. Don't be afraid to stop a meeting which is going nowhere. You don't have to be frustrated, you don't have to blame anyone, and you can feel free to blame yourself. Remember the mantras I gave you before: "Everyone is doing the best they can" and "We're all learning." Use those words and more importantly that tone, and you'll show people that it's OK to make mistakes and that you recognize everyone's time is precious.

By the way, if it is someone else's fault, like maybe your head of product didn't ask people for the right information in advance and now everyone is confused, you can calmly help her stop the meeting too. You can say "Linda, I have the impression that folks are a bit confused. Do you think it's a good idea to stop the meeting for now, let everyone know what you need, and then we can meet again later this week or next week?" Hey, it happens! Normalize it for your people, and you'll find that you have more good meetings and that people feel more permission to end meetings that just aren't working.

GOOD MEETINGS BRING

- Shared reality

- Better relationships

- Decisions

- Clarity

- Next steps

- Messaging to the team

- A sense of accomplishment

These three things—metrics, systems, and meetings—are the tent poles that help you build out your company. All of that structure is there to create a space for winning. Clear goalposts, a blame-free zone, discussions that focus on data not personality, and an environment where people feel safe are the elements that point toward success. Mistakes get made. When you create an environment of course-correction and learning from those mistakes, you won't get bogged down in blame and defensiveness, and you will be able to mine for the truth.

Nothing about the growing pains of a company is easy, but having systems and processes can help you and your people stay together and stay focused. That's the overall goal of all these aspects of operation. Used with judgment and a strong sense of the big picture, metrics, processes, and meetings build teamwork and alignment, sharpen the vision of the goal, and help you reorient when problems arise.

TAKEAWAYS

- Metrics, meetings, systems, and processes give your people structure and clarity about goals and how you're going to achieve them.

- Create clear goals and a dashboard so that everyone in your company can see the most important projects.

- If you're not that interested in systems and processes, hire someone who is and then support them.

- Productive meetings start with preparation.

- Make sure you know what you decided and who needs to know after key meetings.

REFLECTIVE QUESTIONS

- How do you know if a project is going off track?

- Do your people know what is the most important thing they should be doing?

- How do you set and keep track of goals?

- How do you prepare to have productive meetings?

Endnotes

[1] Gordon, D (1999) John Wooden: first, how to put on your socks. John Wooden as told to Devin Gordon, *Newsweek*, October 24, www.newsweek.com/john-wooden-first-how-put-your-socks-167942 (archived at https://perma.cc/7ZDL-48JJ)

[2] Belsky, S (2018) *The Messy Middle*, Portfolio, New York

08

Managing the Board

Reflective Question: How well do you know your board members?

Up to this point we've been talking about you as the boss. Now it's time to meet your boss: your Board of Directors.

There are two kinds of founders: those that have had issues with their board and those that will have issues with their board. It's just inevitable that you will have some rocky moments when money, pressure, and certain personalities all collide.

By the way, that's not fatal! Many of these disagreements—once you get through them—make the relationship stronger. When you use bumps in the road to understand people better, to clarify your role and their role, then that's part of healthy growth.

But, sorry to say, I have seen the opposite as well. I've seen highly dysfunctional boards, highly disruptive directors, and dramatic political scheming on a par with *Game of Thrones*, minus the flying dragons.

However, here is the truth: if you're building a start-up, and especially if you raise money, you can't wiggle your way out of having a board. So in this chapter we'll talk about this necessary relationship. I'll help you identify the kind of board directors you have and how to raise the level of functionality to the point where you see them as a net gain.

A Field Guide to Board Members

Charlie, the CEO of an education start-up in San Francisco, called me one day after another CEO had referred him to me. We had a good chat, and even though he decided he didn't want to work with a coach, we agreed to keep in touch. A year almost to the day later he called me back and said, "I need you now" and launched into the situation he was facing with his board director, Jesse.

The gist of it was this: the company was not meeting its numbers. Charlie understood the issues and was working with his head of sales and planning to bring in an executive to work with him who had experience selling to colleges. Jesse, however, was insisting that Charlie bring in a new CEO. And when I say insisting, I mean that Jesse said straight up that his firm would not reinvest in the company and that Jesse would give up his board seat if Charlie remained CEO.

Dramatic, right? At a moment like this, I urge clients to work immediately on two things in parallel: emotional self-control (calm down) and a step-by-step analysis (what's going on around here?).

Charlie was understandably in a state, so we handled that first. Did Jesse have the power to fire Charlie himself? No. Did Jesse have enough influence over the rest of the board to get them collectively to fire him? Well, he had some influence, but not that much. Did Charlie need the money from Jesse's firm? Yes. Did he need Jesse on the board? No. In some ways it would be better if Jesse wasn't on the board—he was smart, but he dominated board meetings and slammed everything to a halt when he disagreed. (More below about the characters on your board.)

As Charlie remembered that he had incredible support from the other board members and that Jesse actually couldn't fire him alone, he calmed down. That let us move on to what he should do, which was...

Don't you want to know what happened? We'll get there, but let me point out that this was a sudden crisis, and when that happens, it's too late to prepare. I hope this kind of surprise won't happen to you, but just in case it does, I want you to know how to think about your board and board dynamics and to be familiar with some tools you'll need to manage your board. The one thing you know for sure with a start-up is that things will go wrong—sometimes horribly so—and you will want the board on your side.

Let's start by acknowledging that you will certainly come across terrific board members! My client Matt had one. Her name was Jacquelyn. Jacquelyn was a venture capitalist, so, yes, she measured herself on good outcomes of the companies she invested in. But her role as a board member was important to her and she wanted to be a great one. She worked to build relationships with her CEOs and her fellow board directors. She gave wise advice and helped pull board meetings up to a strategic level of dialogue. She opened doors for her founders. She solicited feedback a few times a year from the CEOs and the other board members she served with. She prided herself on being the first person a founder would text in a time of crisis. If you have a Jacquelyn on your board, congratulations! Enjoy her, savor her, leverage her.

There are other types of directors that you may find more challenging to handle, however. Here are some:

- The alpha director: Look, I have to speak the truth and acknowledge that this is usually a male. He dominates the discussion, has outbursts, and makes declarations rather than engaging in discussion or debate. The other board members may roll their eyes, but he's hard to deal with and mostly causes others to shut down.

- The checked-out director: She flies in just for meetings and flies out immediately, often leaving early, or decides to dial in at the last minute. She is on her phone during meetings and is very hard to get ahold of between board meetings.

- The detailed director: Details are actually good, but this board member wants to immediately drill into topics that are not that important or relevant to the discussion that you as CEO want to have. Your meetings go way over, and you can't finish the discussions you wanted the board's input on.

- The micromanager board director: This board member loves to give you advice and is overly prescriptive in telling you what you should do. She may ask you to do a lot of homework, like gathering analytics that aren't that meaningful, that takes up a lot of time. She gives you very specific operational advice and expects you to do it. But since she doesn't really have line of sight into the operations of your company, her view lacks nuance, and her advice is often too narrow and incomplete.

- The general-fighting-the-last-battle director: This director starts making strong recommendations about strategy and tactics that seem to be slightly out of step for your company, like a specific vertical you should go after or a way to reorganize the sales team. If you probe enough, you'll find that it's a strategy that one of the other companies he's on the board of either used or should have used.

- The inexperienced board director: This one panics at the first sign of trouble. He doesn't understand your market or your product and asks questions which are basic and often not relevant to the stage of your company.

That's not a complete list, but it gives you a sense of who you might encounter on your board. When you don't understand the personalities and dynamics of that board, you can get blown pretty far off course.

Margot, for example, was the founder of a gaming company. One of her board members was a general fighting the last battle. He had seen issues when CEOs didn't build their networks and brands externally, so he encouraged her to be an outward-facing CEO, which meant she should focus on talking to large customers, talking to the media, and speaking at conferences. He minimized her role as manager inside of the company, declaring that was "moving the deck chairs on the Titanic." (Why he wanted to compare the company to a doomed ship I do not know, but that's what he said.)

Margot was naturally oriented to those activities anyway, so she felt very empowered to step away from her day-to-day management and dive into the external world. Chaos ensued. While Margot was following the advice of the general fighting the last battle, the release of the latest product was delayed by nine months, a key employee resigned, and the company got bad Glassdoor ratings related to lack of direction and managers doing power grabs. Margot had to return her attention to her company with urgency.

Or take Brad, the young founder of an e-commerce company. He was full of creative ideas, but he definitely needed and wanted a lot of mentoring. His board director, Steven, spent plenty of time with Brad and gave him a lot of advice. Steven definitely meant well, but as a director, he was pretty inexperienced himself, as well as being a micromanager (sometimes these characteristics play in tandem). Steven tended to send Brad on a bunch of data-hunting trips that required a lot of work and didn't yield all that much insight. Steven insisted that Brad hire an expensive COO. By the time I showed up, Brad was barely speaking to the COO, who was almost fully checked out. The company had lost direction, and Brad himself was worn out. We reinvigorated the company finally, and Brad fired the COO, but a year had been lost.

Take Charge of Your Board

Now that you're forewarned about board personalities and dynamics, what should you do? Each board is a complex stew of its own dynamics, but your job is to figure out what that is, shape it as much as you can, and get your board to work for you.

That's right. What many founders, especially first-timers, don't get is that their role is to guide the board even when the board doesn't act like it wants to be guided. I know: you thought *you* were supposed to get guidance from *them*—after all they've done this before and you haven't. But you are the leader of the entire company. Your board will have many opinions—some of them very strong—and they will give you good (and sometimes bad) advice and strong (and sometimes zero) support. Even though they may be experienced board members and investors, they may not be experts on your business or even in running a business. So you can never forget that you are the leader of your whole company. That includes the board.

One way to think about your board is as another direct report. (Strange, right, since they're the ones who can fire you?) What that means is that you have to think about their unique personalities and manage them to get the most out of them, just like you manage your executives to get the most out of them. The way to do that is to build your relationships with them one by one and as a group, build a healthy board culture, take charge of board meetings, and handle difficult personalities.

Boards Are People Too

CEOs have a lot to do and a lot of people to do it with. You can be forgiven for thinking that you don't need to nourish your relationships with your board. After all, your board directors have a lot going on themselves, they are adults and don't need coddling, and your board schedule is pretty well set for the year.

ALEXA VON TOBEL

Founder and CEO of LearnVest and Founder and Managing Partner of Inspired Capital

I was very honest with the board. I told them, "I have never managed a board. Please let me know if there's anything that you expect." And then I asked two people who had had boards what their advice was. I said, "Hey, how do you relate to your board? What do your board meetings look like?" And I tried to assess from other people what should that look like. I was fortunate to get a lot of advice up front. I have always felt business relationships are not business relationships. They're genuine friendships. You can go farther, you can do more, when people really enjoy the work and working with you. I'm really fortunate that a lot of my board are still some of my closest business relationships and friendships. That's been wonderful. So I just think taking the time to build genuine relationships goes miles. I had board members that, I don't know, I had some of my most fun meals in my life with, and who were really, really wonderful. And by the way, that was really important because when we did have hard calls, I always knew how much they cared about me. It never felt personal. It truly was about the business. We made big decisions together.

But failing to build your relationships with your directors is a mistake. You need to create a reservoir of goodwill with your board directors individually and as a group so that you can have honest conversations when you need to and so that they understand where you're coming from and forgive you your inevitable mistakes. Yes, you probably had some good interactions with them as you were getting to know them through the funding process. But then they were selling. Now you're the one selling.

First of all, meet each board director one-on-one as soon as you can. This may have to be over video, but if it's possible to meet them in person try to do that, especially over a meal or some other informal activity. I know a founder who does a day-long hike every quarter with one of his board members and another who meets with one of her board members over dinner at new restaurants since they are both foodies.

Obviously this is the time to build personal rapport. Being genuinely interested will help you find out more about your director's personality, home life, drivers, and interests. This hopefully sounds familiar to you from earlier chapters. When you work with your executives, you want to find out who they are and what makes them tick. The same is true for your board directors.

You should also start finding out how they tend to operate on a board. In one of your initial one-on-ones with them, ask them questions to help both of you get aligned. For example:

- What excites you most about being on this board?
- Where do you tend to focus your energy and attention when you're on boards?
- How can you and I best communicate? (This is a good place to share your personal operating manual from Chapter 5, at least informally, and ask them about theirs.)

The Basics of Your Board Meetings

As you may recall from Chapter 7, I just love meetings! Or, more accurately, I love the *potential* of meetings. Sadly, most meetings don't live up to their potential, and that certainly goes double for board meetings. This is too bad because there is simply so much talent, brains, and experience in the room!

This book is not about how to hold great board meetings, but I want to make sure I give you the foundational elements. Part of your role as CEO, a part of your managing the board, manifests itself in those meetings.

As always, the secret to a great meeting lies in the preparation. In the case of board meetings, you can have a rhythm in place so that even though it's time-consuming you can fit it into the schedule without making it such a scramble.

You tend to set your board meetings in advance for the whole year, so once those are in the calendar count six weeks back and use that as the start of your board process. At that six-week mark, talk to your executives about the strategic topics the company is facing. Use that input to sketch out an agenda to include the key topics you'll plan to bring up to your board. Then do a pre-meeting call with each of your board members. These calls are a great way to build rapport with each director, hear what's on their minds, and walk them through what they can expect at the board meeting. If they have concerns they want to address, they can tell you now. This discussion also prepares their mind for the upcoming board meeting, which is now in about four weeks. As you're preparing people, have another meeting with the executives who will attend the board meeting. It's good for them to get to know the board, and it's good for the board to get to know them, so make sure they are prepared and ready to be at their best.

Use all of this to prepare a board deck which contains, of course, the financials and key updates as well as brief sections which lay out the two or three strategic issues that you will cover in this meeting.

Everyone already knows that you should send out your board materials in advance, but here's a pro tip: send them out at least three days in advance, and put the strategic items first, not the financials. Most boards are used to getting their materials late, either two days or one day or four hours before the board meeting. Show your board you're engaged, and encourage them to be engaged by giving them enough time to read the material and prepare. When you flip the order by putting the strategic items first, you instantly engage the directors' minds by tantalizing them with interesting problems to solve.

When you run the meeting, set ground rules. It may feel weird, but ask everyone to turn off their devices. Everyone. All of the devices. People may want to take notes on their iPad or laptop. Ask them to use pen and paper. Their notes are not as important as their presence. If you need to keep track of action items, either stop regularly to capture them on the whiteboard to take a picture of later, or see if your assistant or someone else can be the one person in the room with a laptop open. If someone only has a small role in the meeting, ask them to wait until that part comes or sit in the room and listen and don't multitask. If they beam themselves in by phone or by video, put them on the honor system to turn off their devices and focus fully on this meeting. Trust me, it really works better. The most well-intentioned people in the world cannot help but check email and texts, check the market, check Twitter. We just don't live in a world where you can count on people stopping themselves. Help them help themselves by keeping devices out of the meeting.

Start out meetings with some sort of personal question—it could be "How are you feeling?" or it could be "Tell us a bright spot in your life since we were last together." Having an opening like that relaxes the room and centers everyone on their humanity. Then when you move through the agenda be clear about how much time you want to spend on it, what you want from the board, and that you want to hear from everyone (which lays the table for insisting that a quiet person speak up and that a loud person shut up).

Finally, include informal time. Ask people to fly in the night before or earlier in the day for lunch; have cocktails and dinner after. Having meals together and finding ways to socialize together is a critical part of fostering strong relationships among your board directors. If your board meetings are remote, find ways to foster informal ties, like virtual drinks or another activity you can do together remotely. Their great relationships with each other are important since everything in the life of your company is routine… until it's not. Your board may need to pull together very quickly to help you deal with fallout from a crisis or negative press or to help you make a quick decision. Foster a collegial board culture so they are in good shape to work as a team during moments of critical decisions.

How to Manage a Prickly Board Director

As I mentioned earlier in the chapter, most boards have a few—shall we say—challenging personalities on them. That's normal, and all the preparation you've done will help you handle them. When you foster a healthy board culture and set clear ground rules for behavior, people tend to fall into line. If they don't, the good relationships and open dialogue you've worked to build on your board will allow you to give direct feedback.

For example, if a board director is checked out, find a way to address it with them. You can be calm and pleasant. Start by simply making observations: "I notice that you tend to leave meetings quite early and that it's a bit hard for us to connect between board meetings. I'm sure you're busy and have other commitments. I'm wondering if we can discuss how we can better engage together." Or if a board member is overbearing, you can ask for a private chat and say, "I appreciate your enthusiasm and intellect, and I know your heart is in the right place. There are times when your voice tends to be the dominant voice in the room. I'm hoping to create a culture on the board where everyone speaks up, and I need your help. I need to ask you to please notice when you're speaking up a lot and ask others to weigh in."

If you're not sure that will work or if you can't quite bring yourself to do it, a friendly word from another board member might help. That's another benefit of having invested in strong one-on-one relationships with all the board members. It allows you to approach another member and ask for her advice or even her help in having delicate conversations with the director who needs some self-awareness. Peer pressure helps.

This does not mean you can solve all board problems. You can't give ten years of experience to a brand-new board member, and you can't give the alpha board member a pill to stop domineering. In that case, remember the wisdom of the serenity prayer: to accept the things I cannot change, courage to change the things I can, and the wisdom to know the difference. Sometimes this is your best strategy.

Laura had a regular complaint about her board member Gil. He was several bad board personalities rolled into one: he was out of step with the strategy, disruptive, *and* checked out. Plus, he was simply an unpleasant person. We spent more hours than I care to think about strategizing about how to handle him. One day she called me to tell me about Gil, her voice gleeful. "What happened?" I asked. "Their firm took the buy-out offer from another investor. They're out of the company and Gil is off the board." Sometimes you get lucky.

The Work Is in You. Again

A founder once stormed into a coaching session with me, pretty spun up about a board meeting he had just had. The company was behind on its numbers, and the board asked to review his updated plan in two weeks. I waited to hear what horrible thing they had said to upset him so much, but there was nothing. That was the whole story. The board was simply doing its job, and that had set him off. We talked it through and realized that the scenario was triggering his feelings of shame for falling short on his commitments. He saw that we could deal with that separately and also take action to solve the problems of the business, in concert with his board.

This really goes all the way back to Chapter 1. *The work is in you.* As a founder, you tend to be independent and self-motivated. You may not like disappointing people, and you sure don't like to lose. So sometimes interactions with the board set you off for your own internal reasons. That's normal, but part of growing up is to come to terms with your triggers. Maybe you feel insecure because of your imposter syndrome, and so you shy away from engaging with the board and don't do the work to build your relationships with the board. You can force yourself to do it by simply putting a regular call on the calendar. Maybe you tend to get overly emotional when you're under stress. Your board will forgive you for one outburst, but you will need to develop your personal tools to handle your temper and stay on an emotional even keel. A steady diet of too much sensitivity, temper, or defensiveness is going to make them question your judgment.

Now let's finish that story that we started at the beginning of the chapter. Remember Charlie, whose board member Jesse told him that he needed to replace himself as CEO? Since Charlie was so upset, we worked on his triggers first. Yes, this was really frustrating, but what was Jesse tapping into inside of Charlie? Charlie told me about his difficult relationship with his domineering father. He had started his own company in part because he never wanted to be under anyone else's control ever again. Jesse's behavior was ruffling every nerve Charlie had.

When Charlie saw that, he could calm down and see Jesse as just another issue to be resolved. Charlie was a chess player and a great problem-solver. This was in his sweet spot.

We sketched out a plan. Charlie was very personable and open, and he had taken the time to get to know the other board members. He thought he had great support from his other board members, so his mandate was now to go confirm that support with the most important ones and confide in them the issues he was having with Jesse. When he talked with them some of his investors agreed that they would put more money into the company, and he had some creative conversations with a few about how he would be able to fill the hole if Jesse's firm really dropped out.

Armed with the confidence that came from this, we were able to strategize for his meeting with Jesse. We agreed that since Jesse was an alpha it would be best to fly out to see him in San Francisco. He should lead with vulnerability to try to reestablish the rapport in the relationship and be clear with what he wanted: the firm to reinvest. Charlie would stay on as CEO, but he wanted to hear candidly all the concerns that Jesse had so he could fix them with his coach and create a new relationship with Jesse or ask for a different board member from his firm.

None of this was easy, and I reminded Charlie that when Jesse got heated and tried to goad him (as he certainly would), Charlie should not take the bait. "Focus on the goal" we kept repeating as we role-played the meeting. (Role-playing emotional board members is my specialty.)

Charlie called Jesse and set up a time for the meeting. Charlie was able to steer Jesse into a constructive conversation that gave Charlie insight into why Jesse wanted to replace him. Charlie really swallowed his pride and asked Jesse to personally mentor him, and to his surprise Jesse agreed. After six months their relationship was far from perfect, but Charlie had made some good progress and brought in a few strong executives to help him fill in his gaps. Jesse remained supportive and—very unpredictably—was his ally in helping him negotiate terms when they went to sell the company.

When I coach start-up CEOs and speak at seminars, managing the board is one of the topics that is sure to come up. You may be surprised that this is one of the unnatural acts of leadership. But it is. Embrace it from the start so that you can use these important people as the allies they are meant to be.

TAKEAWAYS

- Build your relationships with each of your board members.
- Foster good relationships among them (have informal meals, encourage them to talk to each other).
- Take control of board meetings.
- Handle difficult personalities.
- Clarify your own triggers that your board brings out in you.

REFLECTIVE QUESTIONS

- How are you building relationships with your board?

- Who is your best board director and who is your worst?

- How are you using the board to help you?

- Do you need to tighten up your board meeting process, and if so, how?

- What do you think your board members would say about how you show up as the leader of the board?

09

Cofounder Care and Feeding

Reflective Question: What do you do to stay aligned with your cofounder?

When you have a cofounder, you have a marriage. It may be a good marriage or a bad marriage. It may be a marriage filled with great communication and talking about feelings, or it may be a marriage with underlying resentment and hurt. You may have known your cofounder since third grade, or you may have met them as you looked around for a cofounder. If you cofound with your spouse or romantic partner, the marriage within the marriage is a whole other thing entirely. By the way, I will focus on cofounder scenarios of just two people for simplicity, but all of this applies to three and more cofounders as well.

In the high-stress environment of a start-up, this relationship can often get gummed up. Tension, conflict, intrigue, and full-on fights are very common. I'll give you some tools to try to reduce the frustration that comes along with this and help you use conflict to improve your relationship. Sometimes—not all the time, but sometimes—founders part ways, and I'll show you that's not always a bad thing.

I'll also help you start off on the right track with your cofounder (or restart if that's where you are) and work with you to answer the question: "Can this marriage be saved?"

The Flavors of Cofounder Conflict

The first time I met with Sherry, the CEO of an online professional networking start-up that focused on healthcare professionals, she brought me into a bright, spacious conference room with a lot of plants. Sherry had been a nurse, and she was warm, intelligent, thoughtful, and articulate. We talked about strategy, culture, communication—all the right things that you're supposed to talk about with your coach. But something felt off, like she was just going through the motions. Question, answer. Question, answer. I was beginning to wonder what she actually wanted coaching on, and then I asked her about her cofounder, Jennifer. Whoa! If I wanted to be dramatic, I could say that fire came from her eyes. Things were about to get interesting.

Sherry proceeded to tell me a whole lot about Jennifer. Jennifer didn't work as hard as Sherry. Jennifer only did what she wanted to do. Jennifer played favorites on her team. Jennifer didn't challenge herself intellectually. The recitation of Jennifer's sins took about ten minutes. Sherry also wanted me to know that, contrary to what had been reported in the press, the company was *her* idea, and she had asked Jennifer to cofound with her. It was not an equal split of intellectual property, effort, or equity.

Well, OK then! I saw we had hit on a good topic for coaching: how should Sherry navigate this dance she was having with Jennifer—and, by the way, stop the rage she was feeling from getting in the way of the company's success and her personal happiness?

Let's take a quick intermission here to remind you that healthy cofounder relationships can be as rewarding as Sherry and Jennifer's was toxic. When the relationship works, you have someone on your side who cares as much as you do. Your cofounder can comfort you when you're feeling down, commiserate with you when bad things happen, and cover for you when you need to be somewhere else.

I worked with two cofounders, Jason and Jason (yes—people referred to them by their last names to tell them apart) who had this kind of partnership. They had met in college and were good friends by the time they started their digital security company. They had plenty of ups and downs, including a massive hack that cost them eight months of work, plus their largest customer. But I marveled at the way they interacted through it all. They had regular disagreements, certainly their share of spats, but you could tell they were always on the same team. I asked them how they thought of their partnership, and Jason the CEO said, "I think we both put the relationship before the business. That may seem counterintuitive, but if we're good, the business will be good."

They had come to that naturally. You may be having a different experience with your cofounder, and if you are, you are hardly alone. Dealing with other people is hard; dealing with your partner when you're not on the same page is infuriating. There's nobody like your cofounder—the person you think you can rely on—to push your buttons.

In my experience, there are a few common sources of cofounder conflict.

When your cofounder isn't growing fast enough. Most often the CEO is forced to learn and grow rapidly, so staying stagnant is not an option for her. But it's incredibly frustrating when your cofounder is not keeping up, especially when she isn't showing the drive to accelerate her learning or doesn't have the self-awareness that she's not cutting it. Since this is a hard topic to bring up to your cofounder, you may not be talking about it. But it's there, all right. That tightness in your chest is undigested fury.

When the cofounders haven't clarified who decides what. In the early days of starting your company there's just the two of you. You talk everything out and make decisions together. Then you get a few employees, then a few more. You may feel self-conscious to have a formal meeting with your cofounder to figure out who should decide what. But if you haven't laid out your separate roles, things will slow down as people wait for you both to weigh in. Or one of you will simply decide on something, and the other will be offended. If you haven't really worked out who and how you will decide things, this conflict will keep coming up and continue to erode your relationship.

When cofounders have different points of view on direction. I once asked two cofounders how they knew they were aligned on direction.

One cofounder turned to the other and said, "Hey, should we sell the company?" and the other one immediately said "No, never." The first one turned to me and said, "We're aligned." We all laughed, but—even as a party trick—it was a good demonstration of alignment. But that's not always the case. Cofounders all too often don't talk enough about the kind of business they want to build—how big they want it to be or what the ultimate goal is. When that happens, rifts develop as the company grows. Or the cofounders may have very different ideas about direction, which leaves employees feeling like there are two companies, one for each cofounder. The result is that when employees have a question, they decide which cofounder to ask based on the answer they want.

When one cofounder doesn't get enough recognition or feels ignored. When your company is doing well, the CEO will often be the one asked to talk to the media, speak at conferences, appear on the cover of *Fast Company*, and look like the hero. That can be very isolating for the other cofounder, who likely feels that she is working just as hard and is just as responsible for the company's success as her more visible partner.

When the cofounders let conflict get personal (and end up hating each other). Starting and building a start-up is incredibly intense and high pressure. Nobody takes the brunt of this like you. You work long hours. You have to make decisions in uncertain environments. You have to navigate a lot of high drama. In the best cases, cofounders support each other through this. But if you get offside with each other, you start attributing bad intent to your partner and then misinterpret everything she says and does. Unchecked, these little problems can build a massive wall between you.

When Cofounders Are Actually Spouses

I've said that your relationship with your cofounder is like a marriage. When you're really married to your cofounder (or are a sibling or a parent or a child) the relationship is the same, just more extreme. The highs are higher and the lows are lower. When you're cofounding with a family member whom you trust, there is no founder relationship more solid and comforting. When it's absent, the feeling of betrayal by a cofounder *and* sibling can be excruciating. There are certainly plenty of examples of bad blood between cofounders who are also family members.

Things can get even more complex when your business partner is your romantic partner. I once coached the husband-and-wife cofounders of an Austin, Texas, lifestyle brand company that made trendy jewelry, clothing, and home goods. The cofounders also had four kids (they joked that their company was their fifth kid, but that unlike their actual children they could predict what the start-up would do).

On the whole they had a good relationship and a clear working rhythm. They talked through issues, and for the most part had their lines of responsibility mapped out. But one day the wife confided in me that when things were going badly, she couldn't go to her husband for comfort. He was very high strung and would get anxious when things weren't going well for the business, and when he was anxious, he was not an effective leader. Since she didn't want to upset him and she needed him working at full capacity, she kept her concerns to herself. As she told me: "Some people can confide in their cofounders. Some people can confide in their spouse. But I can't confide in either."

The tools and tactics that we'll talk about below are even more important when you're working with a family member. Even if they make you uncomfortable, use them!

The "Cofounder Prenup"

The best way to ensure that you and your cofounder have a happy, healthy life together is to consciously get on the same page initially. If cofounders are like spouses, a healthy relationship may not need a ring, but it does need a prenup.

There are two kinds of prenups: a legal agreement and an emotional agreement. I'm a coach, not a lawyer, so as you can imagine I focus with my clients on the emotional agreement and let the lawyers handle the operating agreements. Those discussions should include division of equity, percentage of ownership, what happens if a cofounder leaves, and other legal topics.

But a discussion of values, directions, and working styles is at least as important because it forces cofounders to talk about squishy or uncomfortable topics. It allows you to set expectations and ground rules. It also creates a baseline and precedent for future discussions. You will almost certainly need to reset expectations and ground rules more than once as your company grows. If you have seriously discussed them at the inception of your start-up, each subsequent conversation will be more comfortable.

So what should you talk about? I have a list of questions (see the following box) that I give cofounders to structure needed conversations. You should talk about your goals in starting this company, your values, and your working style. It's helpful for each of you to articulate why the other is a good partner for you. You absolutely want to address how you will handle normal conflict and decision rights. Do not shy away from tough topics like what you'll do if one cofounder isn't scaling or wants to leave.

I know that you think that won't happen to you if you're already good friends, but neither did Sean and Connor, the cofounders of an energy start-up based in the UK. The two had met when they served together in the Royal Air Force. They had gone through boot camp together and become very good friends. They had already reached 150 employees, on their way to 200 by the end of the year. Sean, the CEO, wanted me to coach Connor, the CTO. (It's common—but not a good sign—for one cofounder to address conflict by asking me to coach the *other* cofounder.) Sean grudgingly agreed to a few joint sessions so we could get a handle on their overall relationship. They were both imposing figures, even over video, and I wondered what it was like when they butted heads. It didn't take long to find out. Just a few minutes in, our initial session erupted in anger, and it took quite a while to restore rational conversation. Starting a company together, it would seem, can be more stressful than an RAF boot camp.

PRENUP CHECKLIST QUESTIONS

Each cofounder reflects on the questions personally, and then cofounders share their answers together.

- Why do you want to create this start-up?

- What are your most important values?

- Why is your cofounder the right partner for you? What do they bring to the table?

- What are three words that describe the culture you want to build?

- How will you divide up roles and make decisions?

- How will you decide important company topics when you strongly disagree?

- What will you do if something your cofounder is doing really bugs you?

- What if one of you isn't scaling? How will you know and what will you do about it?

- What will happen if you get into a massive disagreement that you can't resolve?

- What does success look like and how will you know?

If you have just started your company together, you can use the cofounder questions immediately. If you've been together five years, you can use these questions immediately. If you get into a conflict or issue you didn't expect, you can pull out these questions to help you address it. Feel free to pull them out once or twice a year and review them together anyway. There's never a bad time to revisit this list and never a bad time to talk about your relationship. These questions can provide structure and space to do that.

Trust Is the Foundation

This is maybe more of a concept than a tool, but it grounds all the other tools. Trust is built over time, and your job as a cofounder is to do your work to build trust, maintain trust, and restore trust when it inevitably gets broken (we're human, after all).

How do you do this? Start with the intention. Then do things that build trust. Talk about the cofounder questions I suggest and others that occur to you—real talk builds trust. Do things together like having dinner once a week or another regular ritual that is relaxing, comforting, and allows for open-ended time together. One set of cofounders I work with in Santa Monica have a sacred "taco Tuesday" dinner together where they also have fun one-upping each other by finding the best taco place in Los Angeles. Two cofounders I work with love theater and make sure to go to shows together at least once a month (during the pandemic they turned this into watch parties of shows online). And two other founders who live in different places frequently travel to see each other. Rather than stay in hotels they stay in each other's cramped apartments. "Not comfortable," one of them told me, "but worth it."

You can think about the way to do this that will work for you and your cofounder, but make sure you do it. Founding a start-up guarantees you two things: you will feel pressure and you will be starved for time. For both of these reasons, make sure you don't neglect scheduling time with your cofounder. Having informal time together will build and maintain the trust you need to navigate the tough times.

Talk About Goals and Values. Repeatedly

I always think it's interesting how many assumptions we make about what other people think. You assume your partner has the same work ethic you do and will be working around the clock, just like you. You think your cofounder's goal is to build a big business just like yours is. You even think that your styles for handling conflicts and making decisions are the same. They're not.

The result, all too often, is that cofounders hold massively different views on pretty important topics. I'm not saying that cofounders can't have different values and different work styles. That's actually a good thing! Why do you need a cofounder if they're pretty much a carbon copy of you? The problem shows up when you don't discuss these things. When you don't surface your differences and work them out in advance, they will tend to bubble up under pressure, and that's where it gets ugly.

I saw this with cofounders Jocelyn and Raj, who were building an online marketplace. Jocelyn was the CEO and ran the tech team while Raj handled operations. They had known each other a bit in college but not that well. They met by chance again when they both ended up in Salt Lake City, and they found that they both had the same idea. Things happened very fast: they formed the company, raised about $10 million, and got office space. They quickly hired eighteen people and gained some early traction with initial customers. Things seemed to be going great.

But there was a big problem, Jocelyn told me in frustration. She could never find Raj when she needed him. She was in the office every day at 7 a.m. and left—on a good day—at 8 p.m. Raj would roll in at 10 and head out to dinner with his wife at 6. He worked from home, he said, but Jocelyn couldn't see any signs of that.

We spent a month or two untangling the issue. It was hard because both of them shied away from conflict or even straight talk. In both of their families there was an unspoken rule that nobody talked about difficult stuff. They brushed over conflict and kept everything under the surface. (By the way, it's an interesting question to ask yourself: How is your dynamic with your cofounder like the dynamic of the family you grew up in? We tend to unconsciously gravitate toward the people who help us play out our family drama.) We finally got to the underlying issue, which was: Raj had a lot of other things he wanted to do with his life, and he expected his work—even in a start-up—to fit into that. He wanted to build a lifestyle business and thought this marketplace could be that. Jocelyn, on the other hand, wanted to disrupt an industry and build a big business. They had assumed the other wanted the same thing they did and hadn't compared notes about any of these topics before they jumped into starting the company, and their first year was so heady they never paused to reflect.

I got them to talk through their goals and values. After a number of difficult conversations—and some tears—they got to a solid place. Jocelyn would remain CEO, and they would hire a new COO. Raj would stay in the business at a very reduced role (with reduced salary and equity) because he still had a lot of interest and plenty to offer. The tension dissipated once they reset their expectations of each other, and they could then be productive cofounders. When Jocelyn didn't expect Raj to put in as much time as she did, she could appreciate his great ideas and perspective as well as his innate optimism. Raj for his part was perfectly happy to cede control to the immensely capable Jocelyn and was inspired to give more discretionary effort now that he didn't have to feel like a schoolboy who was always in trouble. Talking out shared expectations and differences in goals and styles will bring you a much better understanding. And better understanding always leads you to a more productive and harmonious relationship. (There's a script for a cofounder alignment discussion in the Sample Scripts at the end of the book.)

MICHELE ROMANOW
Cofounder and President of Clearco (formerly Clearbanc)

We took a pretty high-risk move because we really didn't overthink this. We were dating for a year at the time, and we decided that we were going to start this thing together. The positive is you get to know this person better than anyone else on the planet, and you get to know what they're really good at and who they are. There are so many things we don't really know about our partners. We know that they have a job, but we don't know what they're really amazing at, and I think it builds a whole different depth and level of respect when you see someone kill it at work, because work is such a big part of our identity. So that was probably the part that is the best part of this—that level of respect. The worst part of this is that you just have to actually learn to spend time apart because by default you would spend every day together and you would just talk about work. That inevitably means you're spending most nights talking about something that isn't going right, but when we go on vacation we don't really talk about work unless it's a huge problem. And so I think that was also another really important thing that we figured out in our relationship quite early on.

Before this I had previous cofounders, so I understood what the "regular cofounder fights" looked like! Cofounders (including Andrew and me) fight about how to price the product. We fight about how fast to grow versus how well to maintain unit economics. Cofounders are *supposed* to be fighting about things like that, that's very normal. We put that in the bucket of these are the things we're supposed to be talking about. They're not a fight, as a couple fighting, it's just, "This is just a part of a discussion we want to be having."

We didn't talk about values and vision formally. But you naturally do that a lot through your relationship. You really know what kind of person you're going into business with because you've just seen them in such a personal way and seen their relationships with their families and their relationships with their friends. We talked a lot about the type of company we wanted to build, things like, how do we use technology to scale so we have fewer people doing things? We've always both been very mission-driven people. We really deeply care about founders and how the world is really stacked to be unfair to founders.

Here's what I've learned about cofounders. You can actually have different motivations. One person could be in it for the money. One person might care more about the credibility. You just need to both equally care about the mission that you're doing. I think people sometimes focus on "We have to have the exact same reasons for doing things." Very rarely in a human will you get a match like that, but if you want the same outcome, it all works out OK.

Decide Who Does What

Not having clearly delineated roles is a surprisingly common problem in start-ups. It just feels weird to have a formal conversation about decision rights even if you've gone to the trouble of carving out your own titles and roles. (Don't get me started on the complexity that comes with co-CEOs—that deserves its own chapter!)

There are a lot of ways to make decisions when you disagree. You can talk it out to see if you can come to agreement. You can carve out clear swim lanes and consult with each other when necessary. Or you can use decision rules like the person who cares the most decides. No matter what you decide, if you pick one and stick with it you'll at least have some ground rules to use to help you handle it when you disagree.

Decision-making is one thing, but control is another. In the case of Sean and Connor, the root of their conflict was power. Connor was a well-known expert in his field. He was used to being catered to, and he felt that Sean was trying to dominate him. Sean was shocked to hear this—wasn't his job as CEO to be a strong leader and make decisions? Once I helped them restore a baseline of trust together, they could talk through their expectations of each other. Connor stopped taking things so personally, and Sean adjusted his style to be more deferential to his cofounder. Once those issues were raised and resolved, they could move on with the thing they both wanted: to build their disruptive business.

Talk Straight to Each Other

The cancer that eats away at the cofounder relationship is not the conflict itself. It's the tension that comes from unresolved conflict. At first you have the exciting honeymoon period, and you agree on everything. Just like with new love, there is so much euphoria that little issues are like a speck of dust.

Then, just like with love, the honeymoon ends—sometimes with a crash. That's why you need to get into the habit early of bringing up issues even if they seem small. The accumulation of small things over time adds up to big things. Small problems raised early are like training wheels for bigger issues that come up later. Since they are small, you can raise them without getting heated. You come across as rational and accessible. Your cofounder can hear you, can respond comfortably, and the two of you can probably resolve the problem easily. You then groove the habit of being able to deal with things you disagree on. Another way to build your ability to talk about difficult things is to first talk about anxiety and concerns about people in the company. Name names.

Two cofounders I coach actually set up a "conflict night" once a month specifically to explore areas of tension or misalignment. This forced them to think about where they might be out of sync with each other. Other cofounders I know put something like "tough topics" on their weekly agenda to make sure they have a prompt to cover them.

It's easy to gloss over things that are hard to raise. We all do that. But when you chicken out, the cost is high. You plant the seeds of little issues that blossom into big ones, and you rob yourself of the opportunity to build your skills. Lean in and gain the skills to cofound harmoniously.

What to Do When Your Cofounder Can't Keep Up

I was working with two cofounders of a consumer app company based in Miami: Jessie, the cofounder and chief product officer, and David, the CEO. Jessie was both literally and figuratively a craftsperson—her hobbies were knitting and sewing, and she would make handmade gifts for all the employees at Christmas and when they had babies—one of the many reasons that all the employees loved her. She was in her element reading about design and endlessly fine-tuning the product to delight their customers. The problem was that as the company grew, her job was to hire more senior people and manage them, conceive of and integrate new products, and operate strategically with her fellow executives. She resisted that role and took out her resentment on her cofounder, David. I would observe their interactions as David patiently and quite reasonably asked her to operate at a higher level, tried to coach her to give her day-to-day tasks to one of her capable people, and work with him to set a longer-term vision. She just didn't want to and would get angry in every discussion they had.

I finally pulled her aside to try to get a handle on what was going on. After she vented for a while, I asked her to tune into what was really going on inside of her. "I can understand that this is hard and there are times you are frustrated. But you seem really angry. What's going on beneath the surface?" I asked her. There was silence for a long time as she really thought about it. Then she said "You know, I almost feel like I'm in mourning. I loved our little company. I loved knowing everyone's name, and I loved tinkering with the product. I don't like trying to cajole the others on the executive team and to be really honest, I love coaching, but I hate managing." Another long silence. Then, "I'm not sure if I want to keep doing this." Finally, the truth was talking.

We worked to get her to a place where she could tell that to David, and for David to be able to hear it. It was hard for her to admit it, and David, in turn, was upset initially at the idea of losing Jessie, a long-time friend, as partner. Eventually, though, they parted ways amicably, with Jessie staying on the board and offering David advice and a shoulder to cry on while he found more seasoned executives to help him continue building a massive business.

There was a satisfying resolution here, but not all stories are so neat. If you want to have any chance in teasing out issues like this, you have to maintain a safe space for each other and learn to talk about hard things in a compassionate and honest way.

This is all very well and good, but what about the really uncom-fortable topics? What if your cofounder is really not keeping up—maybe not even showing up—and refuses to discuss it? How about the cofounder who is blatantly playing favorites, overindulging at the bar, or taking up romantically with an employee? Or how about if you are concerned your cofounder might be playing a bit too loose with her expenses or have a drug problem?

I wouldn't be mentioning this if I hadn't seen it. This is the time that you need strong communication skills, delicate interpersonal style, and a whole lot of fortitude. Founders will say to me all the time, "If it were an employee, I'd just fire her. But this is my partner!"

Luckily, unlike many issues in your start-up, this situation is an "if" and not a "when." Most likely this won't happen to you. But if it does, let me give you two thoughts about how to handle it.

First, you have to address the behavior. That may sound obvious, but I know a CEO who put off talking to her cofounder about his drug problem until he was doing cocaine in the conference room with the team. Repeatedly. One of the CEOs I worked with confided in me that his married cofounder had been having an affair with one of the employees for six months. This is not easy stuff, and it can be all too tempting to ignore the issue, hoping it blows over by itself.

All delicate situations vary, and you probably want to get some advice from a trusted coach, mentor, or maybe a board member. (If this behavior brings risk to the company, you do have to tell the board.) But at some point you'll need to pull your cofounder into a room and talk about it. Be as even-keeled as you can be, bring curiosity and compassion to the conversation, and see if you can get your cofounder to open up. He's still your partner, and even if he is the problem and you're the wronged party, you still have to work this out together. You will get better results if you can create safe space for a real conversation, even if you're furious.

Once you have the right mindset, a good way into the conversation might be: "I've heard a few things (or I've observed a few things) that are pretty serious. We need to talk about them, and I want to hear your experience of what's going on." And then lay it all out compassionately but directly. Depending on how the conversation goes, there is a multitude of outcomes, but you have to keep in mind the health and survival of the business.

The second thought is much more emotional. You may likely feel all sorts of upset. A sense of betrayal that your cofounder did this to you. Anger that she put your business at risk. Self-blame that you didn't see it coming or address it earlier. Isolation and a sense of burden that you have to keep this to yourself. And, possibly, grief at the dissolution of the partnership.

I get it. Your feelings are normal. Accept them and forgive yourself. Really. You are doing the best you can. Seek out a trusted therapist, coach, mentor, or at least a good friend and talk things through. And remember that you will get through this. Companies—and founders—survive all sorts of surprising things. This is a rough one, but in perspective it's another crazy twist on your road to success.

Your cofounder is one of the most important relationships in your work and even in your life. In your start-up you'll probably spend more time with your cofounder than anyone else, including your spouse. So be deliberate in how you structure and nourish that relationship. When you take care of this relationship you will reap a lot of benefit from it as your start-up—and the pressure—grows.

TAKEAWAYS

- Your cofounder relationship is like a marriage.
- Getting on the same page—repeatedly—will help you maintain a good relationship.
- Talk about your vision and your values.
- Figure out clear roles and ways to decide when you disagree.
- Practice having conflict.

REFLECTIVE QUESTIONS

- Have you and your cofounder talked through vision, values, and culture?
- How do you regularly invest in the relationship?
- What are you holding back from your cofounder that you need to talk about?

10

Your New Workplace

Reflective Question: Have you made sure your systems are optimized for a virtual workplace?

Cameron, the CEO of a tools and workflow company, was telling me about one of those email blunders that happen when everyone is moving too fast. There was a group email conversation involving several people, and it started getting heated. (Why do people keep emailing each other when their blood pressure goes up? Pick up the phone and talk it out.) Ellie wrote a few things she shouldn't have, and Julia got angry in return, all in the public space of a "reply all" email chain.

It happens. But Cameron told me it was becoming a real issue. The two of them were both angry with each other and couldn't resolve it. "If we were still in the office together, they'd talk it out and it would be over. But since we're remote it's so much more complicated."

Darn that pandemic! The thing is, though, I don't have to tell you we are in the middle of an evolution of where and how we work. The pandemic made us all go home, but there was a movement toward remote work already. Plenty of companies are remote-first anyway, and the pandemic accelerated the trend toward working from home. This is the new world of work. From remote workers to gig workers, there will be all kinds of different work relationships that you will have to learn to navigate.

Everything we've talked about still applies. I want to touch on some important elements that need additional attention in the new world of work. So let's talk about relationships and culture, communication, hiring, onboarding, managing, and processes.

How to Get the Faces on Zoom to Trust Each Other

That little email problem spinning out of control is one tiny marker of what happens every hour every day when employees work remotely. They communicate by email/Slack/text. There is no opportunity to go out to coffee/lunch/drinks. Video is not the same as hanging out in the office together or sliding your chair over to someone's desk. And people don't organically run into people in their group or out of their group. So the whole process that we've relied on to naturally build relationships in the workplace—the in-person workplace—is simply absent.

The problem with this is that the relationships people have at work make people feel happy and give them a sense of belonging. Tangibly, people get things done through their relationships. When they don't see each other except on video, they can easily misunderstand each other and then it's hard to get back on the same page. Employees miss the rich insights they get from being in person—body language, micro-expressions, empathy. They also don't get the signals and background noise—overhearing people on the phone, walking in on some side chats in the snack room—that tell them what's going on. On any level, it's lonely. At its worst, that isolation can make people uncertain, suspicious, or paranoid. So when you're remote—either temporarily or permanently, either because you chose it or external factors chose it for you—you have to be really intentional about helping employees bond.

Help Your People Get Personal, Remotely

In the office, you see pictures of family or vacation, ornaments, pictures, and decorations. (I came across a massive rubber chicken once at one employee's workspace. Let your flag fly!) It's fun, and it's humanizing. It gives people a context to say, "Who's that in the picture?" or "What's with the rubber chicken?" That helps people get to know each other.

You can also create a ritual for teams to spend some time in meetings now and again sharing mini-collages of "this is me in my natural habitat." People will groan about it, but I promise you it will be a net gain. Double down on starting meetings with chit-chat or with some of the rituals we talked about in Chapters 4 and 7 to foster connection.

Take time and ask questions to get to know people in the same informal way that you would if you ran into them in the office or if you were going out for a coffee or lunch. Encourage others to do the same. Challenge yourself to figure out how to create situations that would have happened naturally in regular office life.

Find ways to do social activities remotely. One of the companies I work with held team trivia sessions and took a remote guided tour of Prague by video. Another company did virtual scavenger hunts. Many companies use an app or other system to randomly assign people to have one-on-one or small-group virtual coffees or lunches. Yes, it takes time. But it's worth it for everyone to find ways to invest in building relationships with both their colleagues and people they don't work with that often.

In addition to building relationships, in a remote environment you have to step back and think about your culture. People regularly conflate feeling connected at work and liking each other with culture. Feeling a sense of belonging is a part of culture, but that's not the only thing. Your culture is distinctive. Is being proactive one of your values? How can you continue to reinforce that when people are remote? How about creativity? Talk in your all-hands and other meetings about how people are showcasing the traits that are important to you inside of your culture. Encourage and reinforce these traits, and challenge people to maintain the elements of your culture remotely. Go out of your way to encourage the unique elements of your culture above and beyond caring about each other.

Help Your Team Stay Mentally Fit

Mental health challenges got brought to light during the pandemic. Even during unrestricted times, you need to support people who work from home. We already talked about the importance of psychological safety. People also need help structuring their time and workplace when they work from home. Get your leaders to help everyone establish a time and a place for their work, and separate that time and place from the rest of their life at home. Encourage people to get outside and get some kind of regular exercise, getting together virtually with their colleagues. Find ways to help them get their personal structure right.

However, some people may be affected more deeply than others by the isolation of working at home. There are real instances of depression and crippling anxiety and not only during the pandemic. You need to let your people know that you are aware that the danger is there and that you care about their mental and physical health. Be on the lookout for people who aren't responding well. Have heart-to-hearts with your people, and make sure your leaders are doing that too. Share resources that can help them if they think they have a problem, and encourage them to take advantage of them. When people think they have an understanding workplace they are more likely to thrive inside of it even if it's remote.

Keep Communication Flowing

The biggest change and the biggest risk for conflict in remote work is in communication. Since nobody gets information organically by walking around, people get misaligned. Since people don't see each other casually they don't get to know each other organically, which means they know fewer people, information doesn't get transferred as fluidly, and they tend to have more conflict because of misinterpreting each other. Your employees don't see each other's body language and are not careful with how they phrase their emails, so it's easy to get offended (like with Ellie and Julia above—and they actually knew each other and were friendly).

The fix for all this is overcommunication, which is easy to say but hard to do. You as the leader have to be very disciplined about setting the tone for this by sharing what you're thinking and working on in regular emails, all-hands, one-on-ones, and other group meetings. You have to be pristine at digital body language, as Erica Dhawan calls it in her book *Digital Body Language.*[1] There is an art to writing emails and Slacks that signals good intent (pleasantries), giving context (preamble), and tone (emojis, explanation marks, and other markers of upbeat communication).

Your natural style may be different. You may be annoyed by too much small talk in an email or cascades of exclamation points and emojis. You know, it's not about you. It's about trying to determine how the reader (whom you know a little or a lot about) will receive your email. If you keep the focus on that, you'll write better emails, which may seem trivial, but it's not when email is one of the only ways people get to know you.

Speaking of email, let's talk about the tools. People use all the tools indiscriminately. They use Slack when they feel like it, they text when they feel like it, they send email when they feel like it—with no rhyme or reason about why they chose the medium they did. So channels get crossed. I'm looking in my email, but he sent a text. Or I sent him a text, but he answered me a Slack. He sent me a Slack, but then he sent an email to a lot of people who had never seen the Slack that provides the context that makes the email make sense.

So this may sound like a bean counter here, but you will save massive amounts of time and aggravation if you create an agreed-on logic to why your people communicate through a certain channel. Like use Slack for internal communication, use text for quick questions, use email for longer threads or external communication. Naturally, there will be times when a discussion needs to jump from one channel to another as your people realize they need input on a question from another team or another department. In that case, the person who's making the shift needs to provide the background and context for the question. And she needs to include everyone who was in on the previous channel. You need to keep the thread of context in a certain location that someone else can access. Otherwise everybody is looking for background information and trying to figure out what people want. This wastes time and, more importantly, energy, especially when you can't just roll your chair over and ask someone. Come up with a good standard that works for your company and then stick to it.

AN EMAIL COMMUNICATION CHECKLIST

- Did you open with a pleasantry?
- Did you set context?
- Did you read your email through to make sure that it's clear and the tone won't be misread?
- Did you keep it focused on the subject?
- Did you keep it to one or two or at most three topics?

I work with a mobile training platform start-up based in Tel Aviv, Israel. You'd think because they were mobile they would be adept at remote work! Nope. They were as surprised as anyone by having to start working from home during the pandemic.

During one of our meetings, one of the leaders I was coaching confided in me that since they were remote, she couldn't tell what people were working on. "I know this is crazy. It's just that when I don't see them I worry they're not working."

It *is* crazy but it's also normal. The overcommunication necessary on this is simply ground rules and goals. Ground rules relate to your expectations for people. Do you think they should be more or less immediately available to get back to you on Slack, or is that not important to you as long as you know when you'll talk to them again? Are there certain expectations you have for specific office hours and meeting times? Would it help everyone stay in sync if everyone sent weekly status updates—or "snippets" as one of the companies I work with calls them—to each other? Talk to your team about what you'd like to see as team ground rules and have them give input as well. Then model the way by sticking to them and reminding everyone that you all agreed to them.

The second part is goals. It's more important than ever to define clear goals so that people know what they're working on when you're not there. By the way, that's also the way *you* know what they're working on when they're not there. You can chart if someone is getting their work done by seeing their milestones toward their goals and the work product of their goals. Someone may be able to hide a bit when they work remotely (although I hope you didn't hire hiders!) but not forever if their goals aren't being met.

Yes, You Can Have Real Talk over Video. In Fact, You Must

One of my clients once said he didn't feel comfortable giving his team feedback over video. I can understand that. Some conversations may be best done in person. But that's not the world we live in, and that was true before the pandemic as well. Even if you start with a team right in your office, eventually you are going to have multiple sites, maybe in multiple time zones and countries. You can't put off difficult conversations forever. You have to develop the capability to have serious conversations, emotional conversations, intimate conversations over video.

When you're talking to someone on video, you don't get all the social cues that you do in person, or at least you don't get them as quickly or fully. You can't feel all the feelings, you can't see their head movements, their nods, their blinks, their fidgets. So it's harder to read people and relate to them the way you would in person.

Sometimes I say to my leaders, "You have to sit down next to them and show them what you have in mind, or help them do it." In the office I mean literally and over video I mean metaphorically. What that means is that you need to create space, safety, and intimacy. Over video that means you have to go out of your way to signal good intent when you're about to give some tough feedback. You have to go slower, overexplain, be ready with examples, and be especially sensitive to body language and tone.

How to Hire (Remotely) Right

When you work remotely, you'll be hiring people remotely, and it's a different experience. Even when we are no longer forced to work from home as we were during the pandemic, it's likely that remote work will be much more common and that you may have people spread out all over the world. This means that much more hiring will take place much more remotely. You'll have to learn how to do it, which means there will be a learning curve. Which means there will be mistakes. Forgive yourself, and use the opportunity to learn.

If you absolutely cannot meet your candidates in person, plan to spend more time talking and more time thinking about what to ask them. You'll find that even in a video call, you're missing a lot of nonverbal cues that we all depend on in forming impressions of people. Maybe have a formal interview and a less formal one. When you interview key people in person you typically spend time with them, have meals with them, and get casual time with them as well as formal interview time. Find ways to replicate this over video if you can.

You should be more diligent in your research about this person and talk to references in detail. Make sure you hear stories about specific actions and reactions. If someone becomes a very serious candidate, try to meet them in person at least once. Most likely both of you will be more comfortable about moving forward.

Making New Hires Stick, Remotely

One of my clients told me during the pandemic that her husband was starting a new job. He hadn't heard from anyone by the Friday before his start date. He was getting uneasy. Where should he go—virtually—on his first day of work? That kind of uncertainty does not make anyone feel excited about joining the company.

New hires need to feel that they have a home, that somebody knows they exist even before they start. I work with a consumer app company in Chicago that moved to remote work at the beginning of the pandemic, and it was not an easy transition. At the same time, since the company was now remote they could search for executives outside of their geography. After a lot of digging, they found the new VP of product they had been looking for in San Francisco. Finally!

But sometimes in the start-up world everything goes wrong. The CEO was in the middle of fundraising and the Head of People was focused on hiring in other areas of the company, so nobody fully took responsibility for onboarding the new executive, whose name was Wei. The company just didn't have a process in place for getting equipment to Wei, so he used his personal computer for about a week and couldn't get on the company intranet.

Because the company was remote Wei had a lot of trouble figuring out who was who and whom he should meet. The CEO and Head of People answered questions when asked, but they didn't sit down with him to give him a comprehensive overview.

Wei, for his part, didn't recognize that he should proactively meet with all his employees, and so he met haphazardly with some and not others. He criticized much of the work they had already done and didn't share any kind of road map for how he would run the department or his plan for the product. Worst of all he committed the mortal new-guy sin of saying, "At my last company we did it this way," about 100 times in the first two weeks. Sooner than that his team decided they hated him and put up Slack channels to discuss his blunders in detail. When the CEO announced that the company was parting ways with Wei after two months, the Slack channels were populated with celebration gifs and champagne emojis.

In retrospect it's sort of obvious what went wrong (and Wei was probably a bad hire). But I want to share the cautionary tale with you because this was and is a terrific company! This kind of thing can happen when someone in your company is not on top of the onboarding process, especially when it's remote.

So have a plan to embrace a new hire before she starts. If there are a few weeks between hiring and actually starting, make sure you welcome her. People should start to feel that they are part of the company even before day one. Call (preferably) or email to tell them that you're excited that they're coming, and you're looking forward to making them part of the company world. Ask her for her operating manual and give her yours. An operating manual, especially one keyed to remote work, can save everyone a rocky start.

Then let them know what's going to happen when. Let them know soon after they are hired what they can expect over the weeks until day one. Tell her when her computer is coming. People like to have structure. Set up a schedule for the first day, and schedule things for the first week so that she knows there's a structure and that the rest of the company is aware of her. I'm a big fan of sending physical objects. Send them swag from the company. So send them a hoodie, preferably with their name on it. Or send a pie or bagels or cupcakes.

Then say that Sally from HR will call to give the new hire a walkthrough of the company systems, such as Asana, Slack, etc. "She'll set you up with a username and password. We'll send you these supplies in a care package. Anything else you can expense like this." Have Jim, your IT person, set up their computer so that they can log in and feel like they are part of the ecosystem. You'll give them some pointers about who to talk to and what to talk about.

Of course someone should actually call on day one. Normally you would take them out to lunch, but since you're remote, send them a lunch voucher or ask someone to have a virtual lunch with them. For the end of the week, have someone send them a pie, or they can have a virtual pizza lunch at their local time.

Even after that start, the social aspect of onboarding is complicated with remote work. People feel they're missing out on the chemistry, and they have trouble bonding. You can't walk her around to the offices of the leadership team, but you can have them be in touch with her one way or another. Find ways to have a personal conversation, and bond like you would if you were having dinner together. Find online social experiences—a virtual lunch, a team meeting of some sort, show pictures, share songs.

You can't do those social meetings that you might do in the office, but you can have a virtual cocktail party, and on Friday send her a pie or whatever she likes (because you've already found out what she likes because you asked her in an earlier call).

The foundation of successful onboarding is focus and constant communication—you with the new hire, other people with the new hire, the new hire with all of you. Remember that your job as the CEO is to hire the right people and—equally importantly—to set them up for success. Ensuring that they have a strong onboarding plan and way to connect into the company helps give them the right structure to create quick wins so they can have a strong start and a good chance of success.

Structure Is Still Sexy

One day Sidney, the COO of an energy tech start-up in Houston, told me, "I just spent hours trying to find out why the salespeople are selling something that the product team have discontinued." That was a pretty unusual mistake for this company to make. What happened? "We moved to remote work really quickly," he told me, "and our tools really didn't keep up. Everyone kept their records on their own spreadsheet. We used to rely on just telling each other, but I can see that's not working now."

There are whole bunches of obvious issues around people keeping their own spreadsheets and especially when you're working remotely because you can't just turn to the person down the hall and ask for it. If you need the information and they're not sharing it, you're going on old information. If you need the information and it's in some system somewhere, then you have to do what Nick Sonnenberg, the founder of Leverage, calls the "scavenger hunt" to find it, and not the fun kind.[2]

One of the issues that infuriated Wei whom I described above is that it took him so much time and energy to find things. "I keep asking people for things and they keep pointing me in different directions," he told me before they parted ways. "I can't find the spreadsheet of customers. I can't find the dashboard for the company's major projects."

Your systems that maybe used to work in the office don't support remote work. There has to be a place for things, and they have to always be in that place and everybody needs to know what that place is. You have to be more pristine about it.

You also need to reconfirm and clarify how people are making decisions. If roles and responsibilities haven't been defined clearly, people make decisions without knowing what their decisions are going to affect. They don't tell the people who need to know about that decision. People get mad or feel left out, and in any case, work is slowed or disrupted and the company suffers.

All of these things are very solvable, and there is tons of information and tools out there to use to fix them. Your biggest role as the CEO in all this is to recognize that remote work is different from work in the office in obvious and not so obvious ways. Pay attention and engage your team to ensure smooth operations no matter where you are.

TAKEAWAYS

- Communication is both more difficult and more important in remote environments. Make sure everyone adjusts their style, including you.

- Make sure your leaders are giving coaching and feedback to their people, even when everyone is remote.

- Your systems and processes have to be more thought through to support remote work.

- Make sure your leaders are giving coaching and feedback to their people.

- Do extra research and due diligence in hiring for the new workplace.

- Pay extra attention to onboarding new hires.

- When you're remote, you need to double down on systems and processes.

REFLECTIVE QUESTIONS

- How have you changed your processes and systems to enable remote work more easily?

- How are you onboarding new employees remotely?

- Do you have a communication protocol everyone knows about and follows?

- Are all your important documents and tools in a central place so everyone can find them?

Endnotes

1 Dhawan, E (2021) *Digital Body Language: How to build trust and connection no matter the distance*, HarperCollins, London

2 The Draw Shop (2020) Work smarter, not harder with Nick Sonnenberg– Backstage business #26, The Draw Shop, May 26, https://thedrawshop.com/work-smarter-not-harder-with-nick-sonnenberg-backstage-business-26/ (archived at https://perma.cc/UG6J-FMZM)

CONCLUSION

I'll end where I began: leadership is an unnatural act. But as I hope you've seen in this book, you can learn it. And if you want to grow from the entrepreneur who founds a company to the CEO who leads a large enterprise, you're going to have to. After all, the work is in you.

The many founders and CEOs I've been honored to work with over the years have found it comforting to realize a few things. They are not alone in their feelings of loneliness. There is a confounding mismatch between rational thought and tough emotions. There is hardly ever perfect information or a playbook for what you should do right now. People are hard to figure out and even harder to manage. Working with a cofounder is both comforting and maddening. Founding a start-up is the hardest thing they've ever done, and they didn't always know what they were getting themselves into when they started.

At the same time, there are well-trodden paths and tools to help them—and you—on the journey. It's not supposed to be easy. The founders I've worked with have learned to embrace the struggle and find their way through it. They've mastered the techniques and ideas that I've shared in this book. They've grown tremendously. They've become amazing leaders. They've built successful companies. They've made the world a better place. And my fervent hope is that you will too.

For more tools, worksheets and strategies to help implement
the practices provided throughout the book, go to
AlisaCohn.com/book

SAMPLE SCRIPTS FOR DELICATE SITUATIONS

There are always times when you know that a conversation will be difficult, or you have to deliver bad news, or you have to point someone's attention in a particular direction. Sometimes you need to focus your intention to have this kind of conversation, sometimes you just need a structure, and sometimes you just need to get your mouth around the words. These scripts will give you the framework you need to do those things, help you do them yourself, and help you teach other people how to do them. The scripts are for:

- One-on-one meeting
- Career development conversation
- Difficult feedback or when someone is underperforming
- When someone wants a promotion that they're not ready for
- Hiring your friend
- Firing your friend
- Firing an executive
- Telling an executive they are no longer on the executive team
- Conversation about layering a good employee under a new manager
- Cofounder alignment discussion
- Delivering bad news at an all-hands meeting
- Layoffs announcement
- Follow-up to 360-feedback

One-on-One Meeting

One-on-ones are best used to create connection and psychological safety between the manager and the employee. Status updates you often can do by email or a quick meeting. Let the employee know about the one-on-one ahead of time so that they can think about what they want to bring up.

Script

After small talk: As always, I want to cover things that are important to you. Is there anything you want to make sure we talk about here? (Pause to listen for an answer. If there is, make sure to cover that.)
Topics to cover:

- How are you doing? (rapport building)
- What was a highlight of the past week? What was a lowlight?
- Anything else particularly exciting you? Anything particularly upsetting you?
- What are your top goals or milestones you're working toward? (Make sure you are both on the same page.)
- How is your work going and are there any blockers you're coming up against?
- Are there any concerns you have about the team, the company, or the environment that you want to share?
- Do you have a suggestion for me to be a better manager for you or for the team? (If you are genuinely looking for feedback—which I encourage—you can probe a bit by saying, "I know I tend to do this or this" or "Someone recently told me I do this." Give your employee an opening and make it safe.)
- Is there anything you'd like to change in the way we do our one-on-ones?

Career Development Conversation

Managers shy away from career development conversations for several reasons: they are afraid they don't know how to help their employees, they don't know that career development is on the minds of their employees, or they don't realize it's part of their job as managers.

And yet, at some point in the life of your start-up, your employees are going to care about their career development. Get in front of it and empower your managers with a script to help them.

The manager's job is to ask good questions, listen, and think through career development plans with their employees, not necessarily solve their problems or do the work for them. The manager should also support career development efforts like training and creating a coaching culture inside of the company.

Script

I think it's a good idea to sit down regularly and talk about your career development. Let's do that a few times a year so I know what you want to do and can help you achieve those goals.

Questions to ask:

- What parts of your job right now do you like the most and what parts do you like the least?

- Do you have a sense of where you'd like to go in your career and the next few steps? It's OK if you don't, but it's also a good idea for you to be thinking about it.

- Has anything about your career aspirations or goals changed since the last time we spoke?

- What are you doing now that points you in the direction of what you think you'd like to do?

- What kinds of training or experiences do you need to get there? If you don't know, how will you find out? (You as the manager should help, of course. If you have advice and suggestions, share them. But you should not do all the work for your employee. Help the employee see their own role in their career development.)

- How can I help you get this training?

- Is there anyone in the company you think you could learn a lot from and want to spend more time with? If so, do you need help from me?
- What would you specifically like to commit to starting on before the next time we chat about your career growth?

I'm here to help you with your career growth and of course to help you do a great job. I am happy to initiate these conversations, but if you ever want to discuss these topics with me, just come to me. You don't have to wait until I initiate them. If you ever think we are off track on these topics, please proactively tell me.

Difficult Feedback or When Someone Is Underperforming

When things are going great, when your employees are overachieving, managing them is easy! And then you have the tough moments: when someone is underperforming and not hitting their goals, when one of your employees keeps doing the same thing even after you've asked them to stop, when someone is chronically negative or has stopped communicating with the people they need to be communicating with.

There are many flavors of giving difficult feedback. Here is advice, structure, then a script. The script is one-sided, but obviously you should find space for your employee to weigh in with her point of view.

Two Pieces of Advice

1 It's hard to have a conversation with someone about hitting their goals when you haven't clearly defined what their goals are. Before you have the conversation make sure their goals are clear to them.

2 Show your appreciation for them, that you value them, and that you're on their side before you give tough feedback. This is important even if you're frustrated and not really feeling it. Dig

deep. That will tell your employee that you want them to succeed, and they will be less likely to be defensive. When you appreciate your employees, you earn the right to tell them hard truths.

Structure

1 Make a deposit into their emotional bank account—people hear you better when they see that you come in peace. Start by telling them something positive.

2 Tell them what you need to say. Directly. And kindly. You can be candid and still compassionate.

3 Give them hope for the future—share that you see a way out, that there are solutions, that you have faith in them.

4 Get a clear commitment from them about what will change.

5 Arrange a time for a follow-up discussion.

Script

I wanted to talk to you today because I've noticed a few things that I think we should address. First of all, I appreciate everything you do—I know you are one of the hardest workers here, and your sense of humor brings everyone up. That's great.

That said, I want to make sure you're getting great results with all your work. What I often see from you is a number of projects, a lot of activity, but I often see that projects are delayed and remain unfinished. Also you don't let others know about the delays, so they come as a surprise. That's a problem for your coworkers, who are counting on you to do what you say you will do. Then other things get delayed waiting on you.

I'm sure you have your reasons—things are not perfect here. Maybe you're waiting on other people. But I expect you, as a leader here, to work constructively with your peers, to fix process problems if they come up, and to raise flags early if things will be late. I also expect you to make sure you are communicating regularly with your peers on all the things you guys are working on jointly.

I know you are super-talented and have so much to contribute to our company! I want your efforts to have the right impact, and I want you to be able to move forward in your career. That's why I'm raising this with you.

We can discuss some of this right now. And I'd love you to think about this and come back to me in three or four days with what you see as the problems and how you propose to fix them. What day should we plan to sync up again so you can share your plan with me and let me know what help you need from me?

When Someone Wants a Promotion That They're Not Ready For

When you're building a start-up, you'll probably get a bit behind on the HR processes like building a career ladder for people. That's understandable, but most often that comes up as an issue before you've put a mechanism in place to address it. One way you see this is when your people start asking to get promoted. Often people ask for a promotion based on how long they've been at your company or when they see others—it doesn't matter who—get promoted. You probably haven't thought much about what you are looking for when you promote people, so you don't quite know how to say no, but you do have a strong inkling that you don't want to promote this person.

This is a good early warning system that you need to start thinking about creating career ladders (see Chapter 6). It's also a great prompt for you to start thinking right now about the qualities you'd like to see in your managers and leaders and start to articulate those qualities. Here's a script to tide you over. You can give this to your leaders to help them have this conversation too.

Script

First of all, I want you to know I really value you and think you're terrific. I probably don't say that often enough. Secondly I can see we need to do a better job giving people a career road map so they see there's a path to promotion. That's on me. I'm going to work with the team to fix it.

Let me tell you how I think about promotions, let me give you feedback about how I see you, and let's put a plan together to help you get where you want to go.

Promotions are not about longevity; they are about job function. You've been doing a terrific job here doing the work you've been assigned—and I especially appreciate these qualities about you, A and B.

For me to see you at the next level I'd like to see you (here are some examples):

- For a manager: start to informally lead people and coach them, give them feedback without getting everyone upset, enable the people around you to be at their best rather than doing everything yourself.

- For a director: manage your team more independently, lead people to solutions rather than fix their problems, manage priorities and make trade-offs with your peers without having to escalate.

- For a vice president: independently bring forward new ideas, keep in mind the business needs over the needs of your own team, become an excellent coach, develop your strategic thinking, communicate more regularly about what you and your team are doing in light of the bigger picture.

If those are some things you'd like to shoot for, then I would love to help you. I'd love you to go think about this and come back to me (or to your manager) with some thoughts and a plan of action about how you will develop those skills. Then we can talk about what support you need.

Hiring Your Friend

Founders often hire their friends, for many reasons. Your friend may well be completely professional with you in the office and may grow into her executive role just like you grow into the CEO role. In fact you may grow even closer because you are so in sync from working together. If so, that's great! You will never have to have a difficult conversation with her about shifting her role or having her report to someone else. But have this conversation in advance to lay the groundwork for what might happen in the future.

Script

I am so excited that you are going to join the company!

I wanted to have a frank conversation with you so we get on the same page about a few things. It might be a bit awkward to discuss these, but it seems like it would be even more awkward in the future to come up against some problems and not have talked about it.

A few things: I know you can do this job and that's why I'm so excited to bring you on! You are so strong at X and Y, and I've always loved your work ethic and your attitude.

I love hanging out with you! I just have to be honest with you and myself that we have to be careful about how we talk to each other at work or hang out after work. I don't want people to feel like they can't disagree with you or that I'm always going to take your side because we're friends, so we need to be professional about being together after work and how we act together in the office.

At some point I'm sure that I'm going to have to give you feedback and ask you to change some things, or the person who is managing you will. It's weird because we're friends, but when I'm your manager that's what I'll have to do.

Also at some point we're likely going to disagree about something. Obviously I want to listen to your opinion like I want to listen to all employees, and I hope I'm going to be a good manager and leader to all my employees. But I just want us to agree that I'm not going to give you special treatment because we're friends.

Hopefully, the company will get bigger and more successful. When that happens, I'm going to probably bring in more senior people who have done this work before. At that point I may ask you to do a different job, and you may end up reporting to that new person. I hope you will see that as I do, as an opportunity to learn. To be honest with you, I hope that happens! I know I have a lot to learn as CEO, too.

Firing Your Friend

Any founder who hires friends is, at some point, going to have to fire one or more of them. Make peace with that. Here's a script to help you get into the discussion, which is the hard part. Plan out the details of what you want to say after that, and maybe even bounce them off of someone to get your mouth around the words. This is an important conversation for you and for your friend, so it's worth the time to prepare.

Script

There is no pleasant way to say this. It's time for us to part ways. I appreciate you and all the things you've brought to the company. I value your friendship, and I love you personally. But I think we have to be honest and see that it's just not working. I can't keep you on the team with the issues we've been having. I hope we can maintain our friendship. Let's talk about the transition plan or the best way to move forward.

Firing an Executive

Firing an executive is made more complicated if you have not set crystal-clear goals for the executive, or if you didn't have a good process integrating the executive, or if you haven't given him as much clear feedback as you wish you had. You may also feel particularly self-critical or unsure: Did I hire the wrong person? Am I a terrible manager? Did I not give them what they need to be successful? I'm sympathetic. It's probably murky, and I'm positive you made some mistakes either in hiring, onboarding, or communication. Forgive yourself, you are learning.

At the same time, there's a cliché that turns out to be true: by the time you are 100% sure you should fire someone it's too late—you should have fired him a year ago. So here's how to do it even if you've made your own share of mistakes, which I'm sure you have.

Some quick principles to lead to success: Prepare what you're going to say. In all of your communications, do not disparage the executive. Do not show the months of frustration you have been feeling. All of your communication is part of showcasing to others that you have the situation in hand and that the company will move on.

The Order of Communication

1 Tell your board. Let them know your reasoning, the soul-searching you've done to fix the issue that might be in the hiring or onboarding process, and your time frame and transition plan.

2 Tell your HR executive and work with him on the process and transition plan.

3 You may want to give your marketing executive a heads-up to get help with communications to the company and externally.

4 Tell the executive you are firing.

5 Tell her direct reports.

6 Tell your other direct reports. Prep them with the communication plan and have them ready to discuss this if necessary with their teams.

7 Tell the rest of the company. Depending on the scenario, you might email the rest of the company or you might hold a quick impromptu all-hands. One of the CEOs I worked with once called it an "emergency all-hands." Do not say this. You can call the meeting "quick sync" or something else. This is not an emergency.

Script

I've decided that we need to part ways. We can go over the details if you like, but the main issue is (insert your issue here; for example: You have been here six months and not achieved any of your goals, or you were brought in to scale the team and not only have you not hired anyone, but the existing team is confused about what you want them to do).

I know this is not the outcome any of us were hoping for. Again, we can talk it through if you like. But what I want to focus on is the transition plan and how we work together to move this forward professionally and also communicate this to the company.

Telling an Executive They Are No Longer on the Executive Team

This is a hard conversation that many CEOs and executives have to have in a growing company. Here's what happens: You hire an employee in the early days. He's great—gets involved in everything, great attitude, scrappy. You put him in charge of various groups, and before you know it he's an executive on your still-new executive team. Over the years you hire more seasoned executives, and so your team "grows up." But still you have this person sitting in the executive team meetings, maybe reporting to someone else on the team, but definitely not participating at the same level. It's time for him to be gently moved off the executive team.

Script

You're such a valuable part of our company, and you add a ton of value. I need to let you know that I have decided to move you off the executive team. Let me tell you why.

(If this is true.) Every other member of the executive team is a direct report to me or to the COO, and it's time for us to formalize that.

You're great at X and Y, but I don't see your strategic thinking at the level we need to move us forward. As the CEO, my job is to give us the best opportunity to succeed. That's why I've been consciously working to bring in the right talent, people whose experience will take us to the next level. I think we all have a lot to learn from them.

I also think you will be in the best position to be successful by using your time and energy to focus on your job of X. You are very talented at that, and I think if you focus there you will be able to have more impact.

I know this may be upsetting to you, and you may need time to digest it. Also, we can work together to communicate this to others in a way that will work for you. Ultimately this is a move I'm making to streamline the executive team and help us make better decisions faster.

Conversation About Layering a Good Employee Under a New Manager

At some point your start-up will grow up and you will earn the right to hire seasoned, talented executives to help you scale. This is exciting and a key marker of success!

The only problem is breaking it to your long-term employees that they will now be reporting to a new leader, and it may mean that they are no longer reporting to you, the CEO. Many people see this as unfair since they've been there so long and also a demotion since there is a new layer between them and the CEO. You have to help them understand this move and see how it benefits the company and them long-term.

Script

I'm making some changes, and I want to discuss them with you. You've done a fantastic job bringing your department to where it is now. What you've accomplished has been amazing, and we literally could not have gotten where we are without you. Because of your hard work and everybody else's hard work, we are hitting our milestones and doing great and are on the right path to success. To help us get where we need to go, I'm going to bring in seasoned leaders. The people I will be looking for are ones who have scaled companies like ours before, so they have the experience and the contacts to bring us to the next level.

What that means is that I'll be bringing in an executive to run your department, and you will report to him or her. I want you to know that I will certainly find the right leader who will also mentor you and help you build your skills and your career so that you continue to grow. If this is a surprise for you or if you want to talk this out, I'm happy to discuss it, but I want you to know this is what I'm doing.

Cofounder Alignment Discussion

There is no one-size-fits-all cofounder discussion. You and your cofounder(s) should have multiple discussions at the outset and throughout the life of your company. Also, you need to have legal agreements and especially an operating agreement. These discussion points below are not a substitute for that.

These questions are prompts for you to start having the real conversations you need to build a smooth partnership. Truly, there are no wrong answers. Start-ups are stressful! Have these discussions before you get hijacked by tough times.

Preamble

As we embark on this journey together, I think it would be a good idea to talk through some of the issues I'm sure we'll come up against, and to discuss where we are aligned and not aligned.

(Following are categories to discuss and questions to ask. Each cofounder should respond to these questions from her own point of view.)

VALUES AND DIRECTION

- What are the things I hold most dear and am willing to make trade-offs against?
- What are elements of company culture which are important to me?
- Would I rather be rich or famous?

HOW WE MAKE DECISIONS

- What are the core things we always have to agree on?
- What decisions can each of make autonomously?
- How do we handle it when one of us strongly disagrees with a decision the other has made?
- When there are opportunities for publicity or press, how will we decide who will be in the public eye?

HOW WE HANDLE CONFLICT

- Every family has their way of handling conflict. How did my family handle conflict when I was growing up?
- How would my close friends or significant other say I react when there is conflict?
- Do I tend to avoid conflict or do I tend to seek it out? Does my cofounder avoid conflict or seek it out?
- Am I a peacemaker who tries to smooth things over or am I a provocateur who likes to catalyze debate and discussion, even if it's controversial? How about my cofounder?

HOW WE SEE THE END GAME

- What size business do we want to build?
- How do we see the end game of the business?
- If our company gets bigger and I realize that I'm out of my depth, do I want to work hard to (painfully) learn what I don't know or would I prefer to hire someone who's done it before?

IF WE DECIDE TO PART WAYS

- What's our plan if one of us decides to leave?
- How will we handle it if one of us thinks the other should leave?
- Do we have an operating agreement in place?

Delivering Bad News at an All-Hands Meeting

When you have bad news, you might be tempted to cancel the all-hands. Do not do this. Your employees know that something is going on, and if you don't address it they will make up their own explanations, which will be much worse. You also have the opportunity to use bad news to build trust and bring the team together. Here's a script to help you do that.

Script

I have always committed to sharing with you what's going on so we are always on the same page. That means good news, but of course it also means bad news. It's obvious that we didn't meet our sales targets this quarter, and that's in itself a generous observation. The truth is we were 50% below our target.

As much as I hate telling you this, I know that Henry, our CRO, feels even worse about it. I'm going to let him share his point of view, but I just want to say that it always sucks to lose. However, we can and do always learn from our missteps. We have taken a lot of time to dissect what went wrong this quarter, and we are going to put into place changes to help us both forecast and execute better. I believe that we are going to emerge even stronger from this.

I also think that our future is brighter than ever and here's why. (Share market conditions, share product updates, share customer letters.)

There are always ups and downs on the way to success. Setbacks make us stronger, and we're looking forward to a stronger set of numbers to celebrate next quarter and even more importantly for the rest of this year.

Layoffs Announcement

Layoffs suck. But they do happen at start-ups. It's common to hire the wrong people, to overhire, and to need a change of direction that forces a change to the makeup of your workforce. Here is a script you can use when you announce layoffs to the employees who are remaining. You can't change the facts, you can't (and shouldn't) pretend that it's good news, but you can handle it gracefully.

Remember that your remaining employees are losing friends and coworkers. They are also concerned about their own jobs. Your messaging needs to address these concerns.

Have your executives and manager meet with their teams either in a group or in one-on-ones right after to check in, express empathy, and see how they are feeling.

Always consult with your attorney before you do things like this to make sure you are covered legally.

Script

This is not easy news to share, but I need to let you know that we parted ways with X number of coworkers today.

Here's the background: In order to be financially responsible, we had to take a look at our expenses. Because of the uncertainty ahead of us, we needed to make the difficult decision to lay these people off. I want to stress a few things:

We are done with layoffs so don't worry about your own jobs.

I have thanked every single one of them for their work with us— they have helped us get where we are today.

They did nothing wrong, and we are parting ways because we feel we need to do a reduction in force in these areas.

We have mechanisms in place to help them find new jobs, and we will do everything we can to help them. I am personally putting them in touch with my network and am reaching out to friends for them.

Please feel comfortable getting in touch with them and offer to help them. They are part of our extended family and you don't have to feel weird about being in touch.

(If appropriate) We are reducing emphasis in this area, but, as we talked about in our company strategy meeting, we are increasing our focus in a different area. So it may sound strange, but I want to be up front with you that we may hire people with different skills. I don't want anyone to be surprised by this.

As the CEO, it pains me immensely to do this. It just sucks. I would not do this unless I was 100% certain that it was necessary for us to achieve what we hope to accomplish. So I didn't want to leave this meeting without sharing what I see in store for us and why, even despite this difficult moment, I am so positive about the future. (Share some thoughts about the strategy, the vision, the plan, why you see a bright future.)

If you have any questions about this, talk to your manager, or I'm always available to talk to.

Follow-up to 360-Feedback

Getting 360-feedback isn't just about the feedback you get. It's also about letting the stakeholders know that you are taking the process seriously and working to be a better leader. Your goals are: to follow up; to signal change; to drive deeper, more authentic conversations; to improve relationships; to normalize "taboo" topics; to set the table for better conversations in the future; and to thank stakeholders. They often want to interrupt you and talk, including talk about themselves. Let them talk any time they want to. You can always come back to your agenda. Note one of your goals to drive deeper conversations.

Your tone should be honest, humble, and natural—no guilt! We are all humans with our own beautiful gifts and troubling blind spots! You are, I am, they are.

Script

I wanted to follow up with you about the 360-feedback process I went through and that you participated in. First of all, I want to thank you for talking to the coach. We are all busy, and I appreciate you taking the time for my development.

This has been a very valuable process for me. I wanted to tell you what I found out and then what I plan to do about it. I found out some good things—people think I am X, Y, and Z. I certainly hope to come across that way, and it was validating to hear that.

I found out some difficult things—people think that I am A, B, and C. Honestly, that was hard to hear, but I own it. I'm sure that I did some of that to you, and I do want to apologize—I'm sorry.

So given all that, I plan to do this (crisp explanation) and this (crisp explanation).

Do you have any additional suggestions for me at the moment?

I'd love to be able to come back to you and see if you have noticed these actions I am taking and if they are bearing fruit. I'd also like to come back to you now and again to see if you have any additional ideas or suggestions for me. Would that be OK? And please feel free to point out if you see me doing any of this stuff I said I wouldn't— I'm only human, and I'm sure I'll make mistakes—and give me additional suggestions if you think they will be helpful.

ABOUT THE AUTHOR

Named the number one start-up coach in the world by the iconic CEO whisperer Marshall Goldsmith at the Thinkers50 Global Coaches Awards, Alisa Cohn has been helping start-up founders mature into world-class CEOs for nearly 20 years. A former start-up CFO and strategy consultant, Alisa has coached scores of young companies. Among them are several that have gone on to become household names, including DraftKings, Etsy, Foursquare, Venmo, InVision, Tory Burch, Mack Weldon, and Wirecutter. She was also named the number one global guru for start-ups by the Global Guru research organization.

As a speaker, Alisa has appeared at high-profile events including the IBM Digital Summit, KPMG Leadership Summit, the Inc. Women's Summit, OpenView CEO Summit, and the Naval War College Accelerated Leadership Forum. Inc.com named Alisa one of the top 100 leadership speakers. Alisa's style is distinctive for its humor, energy, optimism, and straight talk. In naming her one of its Top 10 Executive Coaches, *Women's Business* described her as "a superhero" and "absolutely brilliant, laugh-out-loud hilarious."

Alisa's coaching is not limited to start-ups. Her enterprise-coaching clients include Dell, Sony, IBM, Google, Microsoft, Bloomberg, *The New York Times*, and Calvin Klein. She is the executive coach for Runway—the incubator at Cornell NYC Tech that helps post-docs commercialize their technology and build companies. She serves on the Entrepreneurship at Cornell Advisory Council and the President's Council of Cornell Women. She lectures at Harvard, Cornell, and Henley Business School.

Her articles have appeared in *Harvard Business Review*, *Inc.com*, *Forbes.com*, and *People & Strategy*, among other publications. A recovering CPA, she is also a Broadway investor—her shows have been awarded two Tony Awards (and counting). She is prone to burst into song at the slightest provocation. Hum a few bars from any popular Broadway song and stand back. Or check out her rap video "The Work Is in You," the only rap song about executive coaching (yes, you read that right) on YouTube. You can find Alisa at www.AlisaCohn.com.

ACKNOWLEDGMENTS

I have so much gratitude for the people who have been so supportive and helped me make this book happen.

Thank you Kathe Sweeney at Kogan Page for believing in me and for encouraging me to write this book. Thank you to the entire team at Kogan Page who helped me bring it to life. Thank you Walter Bode for your incredible collaboration, consistent cheerfulness, encouragement, and your ability to get me to tell my stories. Thank you Randy Komisar for our fun coffee chats and for your wonderful opening words to set the tone for this book.

I am grateful to my mentor and friend Marshall Goldsmith who has always been my muse and pushes me to be more and do more than I think I can. Thank you, Marshall, for walking me around the pond that day I came to see you in April 2006. You have made my life so much better.

Much gratitude to my "thirty-year-old mentor," business partner, collaborator, coconspirator, and amazing friend, Dorie Clark, who has helped and supported me in ways I truly cannot count, including the introduction to Kathe. I am grateful most of all for your friendship!

Thank you to the people who helped me on this path at critical moments: Erica Keswin, Erica Dhawan, Michael Bungay Stanier, Mark Reiter, and Tahl Raz. Thank you Ginny Byron who was the first person who told me I had a book in me. Thank you to all my friends in the Marshall Goldsmith 100 Coaches family—your support and generosity mean everything to me.

Special thanks to the entrepreneurs who generously shared their wisdom with me so I could augment my stories with their own words: Alexi Robichaux, Alli Webb, Suzy Batiz, Jon Stein, Dennis Crowley, Chip Conley, Maxine Clark, Jerry Colonna, Scott Harrison, Michele Romanow, Alexa von Tobel, and Brian Berger.

To all the founders, CEOs, and other leaders I have been privileged to coach—thank you. I hope you've learned from me and I know I've learned from you.

To Eric—you are my rock and my hero. Thank you ever so much for your love and support on this journey.

To you the reader: thank you for reading! Thank you for reading the acknowledgments too! I would love to hear what you took away from this book and what you did with it—please reach out to me and let me know at Alisa@AlisaCohn.com.

INDEX